Digital Democracy

Digital Democracy

issues of theory and practice

edited by

Kenneth L. Hacker & Jan van Dijk

SAGE Publications
London • Thousand Oaks • New Delhi

First published 2000

SAGE Publications Ltd
6 Bonhill Street
London EC2A 4PU

SAGE Publications Inc
2455 Teller Road
Thousand Oaks, California 91320

SAGE Publications India Pvt Ltd
32, M-Block Market
Greater Kailash - I
New Delhi 110 048

British Library Cataloguing in Publication data

A catalogue record for this book is available from the British
Library

ISBN 0 7619 6217 4
ISBN 0 7619 6218 2 (pbk)

Library of Congress catalog record available

Typeset by Siva Math Setters, Chennai, India
Printed and bound in Great Britain by Athenaeum Press, Gateshead

Contents

List of Contributors

Michel Catinat is adviser to the Director General for Industry of the European Commission and Professor at the College of Europe in Brugge.

William H. Dutton, Professor at the Annenberg School for Communication at the University of Southern California, was National Director of the UK's Programme on Information and Communication Technologies. He is the author of *Society on the Line: Information Politics in the Digital Age* (1999). He is involved in research on technological and institutional change in higher education and the 'news industry', as well as in government and politics.

Anita Elberse is a PhD candidate at the London Business School, where she is working within the Future Media Research Programme. Her research focuses on the implications of technology developments for the media industry. One of her research projects, 'News is a Digital Age', focuses on the news media industry.

Kenneth L. Hacker is Associate Professor of Communication Studies at New Mexico State University, USA. His two main areas of research and teaching are communication technologies and political communication. He is editor of the book *Candidate Images in Presidential Elections* (1995). He has served as Secretary of the Political Communication division of the International Communication Association. He has written numerous Political Communication articles and is presently writing a book chapter about President Clinton's political image management strategies.

Martin Hagen has been a full-time researcher for Applied Computer Science at the University of Bremen in Germany since 1997. He is currently working on his doctoral thesis, a comparative study on the role of political programmes and ICT use in German and US public administration reforms. Among his publications are *Elektronische Demokratie* (1997), an analysis of concepts of digital democracy and their roots in American political thought (with Prof Dr Hans Kleinsteuber), and *One-Stop-Government in Europe* (forthcoming), edited with Herbert Kubicek, which gathers the current status and challenges of integrated service delivery in 11 European Nations.

Matthew L. Hale is a PhD candidate in the School of Policy, Planning and Development at the University of Southern California. His research interests include technology and media effects on the political and governance processes. His current activities include a content analysis of local television news coverage of the 2000 elections and a study of how community and neighbourhood organizations are adopting and using the World Wide Web. His teaching focuses on public policy analysis.

Nicholas Jankowski is Associate Professor at the Department of Communication, University of Nijmegen in the Netherlands. He has published on small-scale electronic media, interactive cable systems, multimedia developments and various Internet applications. He is co-editor of *New Media and Society* and Associate Editor of *Communications: The European Journal of Communication Research*. Jankowski co-edited a handbook on qualitative research methodologies and is currently writing a textbook about new media research methods with Martine van Selm.

John Keane is Director of the Centre for the Study of Democracy and Professor of Politics at the University of Westminster. Among his many books are *Democracy and Civil Society* (1998), *The Media and Democracy* (1991), the prize-winning *Tom Paine: A Political Life* (1995), *Reflections on Violence* (1996) and *Václav Havel: A Political Tragedy in Six Acts* (1999). *The Times* has ranked him as one of Britain's leading political thinkers, whose work is of 'world-wide importance'.

Sheena Malhotra has a background in the television and film industry in India, earned her PhD at the University of New Mexico and presently teaches communication at Regis University.

Everett M. Rogers is Professor at the Department of Communication and Journalism, University of New Mexico. Rogers is widely known for his book, *Diffusion of Innovations*, published in its fourth edition in 1995. He has published many journal articles and books concerning communication theory, communication technologies and mass media.

Sinikka Sassi studied human communication at the University of Helsinki and has since 1985 worked as a researcher and lecturer at the Department of Communication. Before 1985 she worked at the University of Technology, administrating and studying one of the first computer conference systems, the PortaCom. Her research interests include the social impacts of new communication technology, the issues of democracy and public sphere, and the cultural study of the West-African media, both old and new.

Jan van Dijk is Professor of Communication Science at Twente University (formerly Utrecht University). He teaches and develops the sociology of the information society, in particular the social-cultural, political and organizational aspects. He is author of *The Network Society* (1999). Finally, he is adviser of the European Commission in the Information Society Forum.

Martine van Selm earner her PhD at the Department of Psychogerontology of the University of Nijmegen, the Netherlands. At present she is Associate Professor at the Department of Communication at the same university. The focus of her research in the area of new media is on the (older) users of information and communication technologies in organizational and other settings.

Thierry Vedel is Senior Researcher with the National Centre for Scientific Research in Paris.

Acknowledgements

The conceptualization of this book was initiated at the 9th annual European Institute of Communication and Culture's colloquium on digital democracy held in Piran, Slovenia, 10–14 April 1996. At that conference, scholars from numerous nations discussed the theory and application dimensions of CMC and democracy. Despite the fact that this book concept was inspired by the colloquium, it is important to note that it is no way a proceedings book. About half of the contributions are from outside the colloquium. In fact, this is a whole new project which only benefits from some conclusions of the colloquium, but mainly builds from subsequent research done for this book. While the authors may agree on what issues are emerging, there are points of difference in what recommendations fit those issues. This should make for lively reading and intellectual stimulation. We regret to say that one of our initial contributors, a wonderful person and scholar, Ian Connell, passed away during the writing of this book. He will be missed.

Colin Sparks, Slavko Splichal and other organizers of the 1996 Piran conference are to be thanked for hours of useful discussion about many issues regarding digital democracy.

We are grateful to numerous people for making this book possible, helping the project, conceived of quite a few years ago, to come to fruition. First, we are grateful to all of the contributors of their professionalism, hard work and steadfastness in answering editor criticisms and meeting various deadlines. The quality of this book directly reflects the stature of our contributors. We also need to express hearty thanks to Julia Hall of Sage, who saw the potential of the book and helped us make it all come together. Everett Rogers is thanked for being supportive of this entire project.

Kenneth L. Hacker and Jan van Dijk

PART I

INTRODUCTION AND HISTORY

1

What is Digital Democracy?

Kenneth L. Hacker and Jan van Dijk

The objective of this book is to address how the Internet, World Wide Web and computer-mediated political communication are affecting democracy. It focuses on the various theoretical and practical (application) issues involved with digital democracy.

Digital democracy is the use of information and communication technology (ICT) and computer-mediated communication (CMC) in all kinds of media (e.g. the Internet, interactive broadcasting and digital telephony) for purposes of enhancing political democracy or the participation of citizens in democratic communication. Comparable terms like 'virtual democracy', 'teledemocracy', 'electronic democracy' and 'cyberdemocracy' are frequently used in other places. Much of the talk about electronic democracy is loose and atheoretical. This book is different. In these pages, you will not encounter yet another book about the virtuality of new media with superficial treatment of the critical concept of democracy. Instead, you will find that this book brings together the scholarship of numerous communication scientists who concentrate directly on the issues of digital democracy theory and practice, and the relationship of CMC/ICT to democracy.

We prefer the term 'digital democracy' to similar sounding terms because it is clearly related to the use of ICT and CMC in all kinds of practices that are presumed to be democratic. We define digital democracy as *a collection of attempts to practise democracy without the limits of time, space and other physical conditions, using ICT or CMC instead, as an addition, not a replacement for traditional 'analogue' political practices.*

The concept of digital democracy gives us the kind of specificity that allows us to abandon the similar sounding terms mentioned above. The term 'virtual democracy' suggests that political CMC is an altogether different type of democracy breaking with the traditional ones grounded in particular times, places and conditions. In contrast, the authors of chapters in this book demonstrate that most fruitful practices of digital democracy are the ones which combine virtual and organic reality, connecting ICT or CMC with other media, and most of all with the conditions of face-to-face communication. The term 'teledemocracy' has become overly associated with direct democracy of the type advocated by Ross Perot, Alvin Toffler and others. We do not share their faith in direct democracy as the most important type of democracy. In this book, you are likely to see indications of a move toward possible combinations of direct and representative democracy.

The term 'electronic democracy' is too general as the old media of broadcasting and telephony were electronic as well. We are trying to show what the use of CMC or ICT might mean to democracy. Finally, 'cyberdemocracy' is the most loose and vague of all terms used, sometimes suggesting the Internet is the only relevant new medium. Because this book is intended to be scientific, our authors attempt to debunk the morass of wild expectations that some observers have connected to the advent and increasing adoption of digital media.

Of course, wild expectations and claims about new media are certainly not new. In 1922, Thomas Edison said that motion pictures would replace textbooks in school classrooms (Oppenheimer, 1997). Predictions like this abound in the history of communication technologies. Samuel Morse, inventor of the telegraph, made the prediction that world peace would result from his invention and the completion of the trans-Atlantic cable (Steffen, 1994). J. Licklider, key ARPAnet designer, foresaw that what became the Internet could also be used as a tool of world peace, albeit in a more reserved manner than Morse. Some observers claimed that radio would be a 'university without walls'. Cable TV companies promised a revolution in education with their systems in the 1970s and 1980s. Such replacement rhetoric ignores the fact that new technologies of communication more often displace existing means of communication than totally replace them, given that the older means have continued utility.

Scholars and social commentators are making grandiose assertions regarding digital democracy. Many of these claims are hyperbolic, gamelike or unrealistic, including those about 'third waves', new forms of Greek agora, 'virtual communities', 'teledemocracy' and a new age of citizen participation. While portions of these claims are supported by some data, most suffer from oversimplistic assumptions about human communication and about democratic political systems. In contrast, the authors in this book forcefully debunk numerous fallacies about digital democracy. Still, as communication scientists, most of us perceive our role as advocating neither a Utopian nor a Dystopian view about political communication using digital media. Instead, we discuss the possible illusions and even harms to democracies that may follow efforts to enhance democracy without serious work in relating digital democracies to what we call organic democracies. However, we also identify and specify as clearly as possible where ICT and CMC can help promote democracy and what forms and processes may be part of what is genuinely digital democracy. For example, John Keane argues that micro-level democratic communication can have positive effects on a democratic political system.

Teresa Harrison, Timothy Stephen and Lisa Falvey (1999) have made some interesting observations about how communication scientists have treated the relationship of new communication technologies and democracy. They argue that there are more claims about democracy and communication than there is research concerning the same. They also argue that scholarly assessment of digital democracy requires that theorists specify what designs and processes of ICT contribute to democracy as well as show how democratic goals are facilitated by particular communication practices. The authors in this book share this concern for moving beyond the glory days rhetoric about new golden ages of democracy as well as the hell-in-a-handbasket predictions of contemporary Luddites.

Richard Davis and Diana Owen (1998) observe that the political effects of new media and ICT are mixed in terms of possible benefits and possible drawbacks. Users of ICT can gather documents about politics and government more easily than ever before. They can also find and join political discussion groups and work with others to organize certain political activities. Citizens can follow legislation with their access to committee transcripts. Research on voting records, campaign contributions and policy positions is easier than ever for those who navigate through the World Wide Web. They say that all of this is good, but there has not been a great deal of movement toward direct democracy with CMC and the Internet. Perhaps there should not be such a simple straightforward movement towards direct democracy and perhaps what is occurring with digital democracy involves a subtle and complex fusing of elements of direct democracy and new ways of representation. Davis and Owen (1998: 127) fear the advocacy of 'teledemocracy' stating that, 'at the touch of a few keystrokes, opinions can be expressed and communicated far and wide. Yet such rapid reaction should not be the lodestone of public policy resolution.' While some of this view is shared by our authors, there is also divergence in how democracies are conceptualized.

Once beyond the dichotomies of the past regarding either good or bad effects, we can face the useful issues such as how, in what ways and with what variations, ICT and CMC affect democracies. We can ask important questions such as does increasing public access to government documents increase citizen empowerment and if so, how does this occur? We have to specify how new forms of communication may contribute to democratization, as well as how we know this to be the case. It is arguable that if the Internet simply becomes another channel for those who already are high in political sophistication, then it does little to enhance democratization and a great deal to enhance the status quo of existing democratic or non-democratic systems.

Increasing attention is being given to the political uses of new communication technologies such as the Internet and the World Wide Web. Whether one sees the new technologies as serving or working against democracy, most scholars agree that communication and political communication are changing in relation to the newly emerging forms of communication. Some observers believe that the new types of communication are revitalizing democracy and others perceive dangers to democracy. From a variety of perspectives, this book examines the concept of digital democracy as discussed in theory (Part II) and in descriptions of applications (Part III). Topics addressed in this book include concepts of democratization in general, propositions of democratization in a digital environment, the emergence of new forms of political communication and public spheres, the perspectives of televoting, the potential enhancement of political participation through computer-mediated communication, communication of citizens with the government through computer networks and the various links of digital democracies to organic democracies.

There are countless claims today about the democratizing effects of the Internet in general and with more localized forms of computer-mediated communication (CMC) such as community networks, international discussion groups and the use of electronic mail in organizations. As noted earlier, throughout academia, and in the mass media as well, there are numerous rhetorical *claims* made about the effects on democracy created by political ICT and CMC. These include the following:

1 ICT increases the scale and speed of providing information. This helps create more informed citizens;
2 Political participation is made easier and certain obstacles like apathy, shyness, disabilities, time, etc. can be lessened;
3 CMC creates new ways of organizing with subject-specific groups for discussion, cheap distribution costs, etc.;
4 The Net allows new political communities to arise free from state intervention;
5 A hierarchical political system becomes more horizontal by increasing political CMC;
6 Citizens will have more voice in creating agendas for government;
7 CMC will help remove distorting mediators like journalists, representatives and parties;
8 Politics will be able to respond more directly to citizen concerns as ICT and CMC enable a kind of political marketing research; and
9 ICT and CMC will help resolve the problems of representative democracy such as territorial bases of constituencies, etc.

This book is grounded in the assumption that there are two important sets of issues for the study of digital democracy; one is theoretical and the other concerns practices. The theoretical issues centre around concepts of democracy in general, ideas and definitions for electronic democratization, the role of the Internet, ICT and CMC in the political system, the influences of existing political cultures, comparisons of America and Europe in the development of digital democracy, structural transformations of public spheres and new concepts of public opinion.

Practice (applications) issues concern policies for constructing applications, policies in the design of interaction, content policies, the relationship of CMC to other existing media as channels of communication, the gap between communication rich and communication poor, qualities of virtual political debates, and means of managing social interaction to maintain democratic access and participation. More specifically, political communication scientists are addressing the following kinds of questions:

1   Which theoretical models of digital democracy are most desirable and why?
2   What happens when anti-state or anti-government opinion is combined with liberal policies on expanding voting and individual access to the political system?
3   Does this result in an emphasis on direct democracy as opposed to representative democracy?
4   Could a system of direct democracy with the use of ICT be envisaged and be made to work anyway?
5   Is political community formation equal to the creation of democracy?
6   Are all types of political communication with CMC to be considered democratic?
7   How does the pursuit of commercial interests affect attempts to extend democracy in various political systems?
8   Is the current direction of Internet expansion of economic interests and markets along with government distribution of information working for or against democracy and in what ways?
9   How do the structural inequalities of society affect the structural relationships within digital democracy? Are they replicated or ameliorated?
10   Is the Anglo, affluent, male tilt of CMC changing or is this a pattern that requires more efforts from education and government in order to encourage broader participation with more diversity?
11   In what ways do government information superhighway policies influence future perspectives of democracy?
12   How does democracy which often is supposed to be built from the bottom with guidance from the top, get more people involved in the building process?
13   What if they are not interested or motivated at this time?
14   Do people become more or less active in political life as they become more active in virtual communication about politics?
15   How can the concept of political interactivity be refined and related to technical designs for digital democracy systems?
16   Can citizens have confidence in privacy, legitimacy of the counting, and other aspects of digital democracy systems?
17   How do we balance the positive benefits like bringing in individuals not involved before with the negative factors like low general participation and communication stratification?
18   Perhaps most importantly, how do we move from the discursive sphere of digital to the decision-making sphere we call representative government?

Certainly, this is a long list of questions and you will not find answers to all of them in this book. However, you will find ideas and reports about research which shed light on them.

Content of the Book

This book is divided into four sections: introduction and history, theoretical issues, issues regarding practices, and conclusions. In Chapter 2, Everett Rogers and Sheena Malhotra provide a historical description of the emergence of computers and the Internet as a large new system of communication. Here we see early ideas about community formation with computer-mediated communication (CMC). Background on the emergence of the Internet from older networks is provided. The chapter also highlights the visions and accidental discoveries of the people who initiated the Internet. Connections are made between these discoveries and a potential new form of democratic communication. Early Internet visionaries like J. Licklider saw the Internet as functioning to promote communication between leaders of nations in such a way as to facilitate the match between mental models which leaders had for crisis situations. The authors show how this concept and others are part of the history of cyberspace which adds to its ethos as a mechanism for fostering dialogue, debate and sharing of information.

In Chapter 3, Jan van Dijk elaborates on the definition of digital democracy supplied above. The opportunities and limits of digital democracy different people and parties in society perceive appear to depend upon their view or conception of democracy. Van Dijk distinguishes six models of democracy, most of them borrowed from the British political scientist David Held: legalist, competitive, pluralist, plebiscitary, participatory and libertarian democracy. He shows how the supporters of these views emphasize particular pros and cons of the use of new media in politics and choose their own favourite applications. The context of these applications is a political system to be mapped in a (system) dynamic model of politics in advanced Western and Eastern societies. The main actors are the government, the public administration, political parties, (semi) public institutions, civil organizations, private corporations, juridical institutions and international bodies. All lines of communication between these actors will be altered by the use of ICT/CMC.

Subsequently, the patterns of communication in the relationships between the actors mentioned will change with the use of ICT or CMC. Most people think digital democracy means interactive politics. They are right, but what does interactivity in political communication really mean? Van Dijk distinguishes four patterns of communication, all interactive, but with different meanings: allocution (e.g. interactive broadcasting), consultation (e.g. information retrieval), registration (e.g. telepolling or televoting) and conversation (e.g. electronic mail and discussion). What kind of interactivity will prevail in the future, political advertising on interactive television, advanced political information retrieval on the Internet, a system of televoting or public debates on the Internet and other new media?

The chapter by Martin Hagen (Chapter 4) concentrates on the issues of digital democracy from a comparative perspective. It presents an analysis which shows that concepts of digital democracy are heavily influenced by the political culture and institutional settings of the country for which they are intended (or in which they are being constructed). In support of this thesis, a comparison between Germany, the UK and the US is developed. The political cultures and specific institutions of the German, British and American political systems build an important basis for different accents and preferred applications of digital democracy in these countries.

The differences of political cultures and systems require special care in the construction of digital democracy for a particular polity. This is especially true when the attempt is made to adopt American concepts of digital democracy in other countries. One needs a comparative framework taking into account different political cultures and institutional settings. Hagen's chapter elaborates the necessity to carefully analyse democracies in their political and cultural contexts. It points out the clear differences in national approaches and how each nation can learn more about digital democracy with comparative studies.

The chapter by John Keane (Chapter 5) revisits his previous argument that traditional ideas of a unified public sphere are obsolete. Instead, he says, public life today exists in interconnected public spheres, for instance on the Internet. Keane says that a unified public sphere is obsolete because cyberspace communication is not limited to physical territory or nation states. He also sees CMC as part of a new era in which the hegemony of mass media like TV and radio is coming to an end. Within cyberspace, Keane argues there is an emerging and interconnected 'mosaic' of public spheres. The chapter describes three levels of public spheres – micro, meso and macro. Keane describes how the lowest level, the micro-spheres correspond to political communication once done in coffee shops, town meetings and other local spaces. He presents a picture of micro-CMC politics as something which assists in the creation of political consciousness and activity. Keane rejects the importation of ancient Greek assumptions about democracy into contemporary debates about democracy and communication. He explains how all social and political classes attempt to use communication to increase their own power and define their political spaces. Rather than drawing upon first principles of democracy, Keane chooses to build from a non-foundationalist base which assumes that digital democracy will work best when oppositions are allowed and encouraged in digital political communication.

Chapter 6, by Sinikka Sassi, is an excellent follow-up to Keane's discussion of computer-mediated public spheres. Sassi discusses how the concept of public sphere has come onto the scene both with new technologies and more comprehensive discussion of the future of democratic governance and the viability of civil society. Feminist scholars, among others, have paid critical attention to the concept as it implies a division between public and private affairs. They have elaborated it in a radical way but the critical formulation now appears challenged by new communication environments as they are blurring the public–private distinction. The concept is reformulated as consisting of multiple public spheres including a strong notion of and an appreciation of differences within and between these spheres.

There is a growing understanding that the public sphere should be conceived of as plural and decentred, constituted by conflict. On the surface, it looks as though traditional more or less rational political discourse and organized civil society are vanishing. Still, fascinating new perspectives and relations, characterized as undifferentiated, egalitarian, direct, emotional and existential, are unfolding on the network. Sassi addresses the duality and inquires how these two representations of networking, the fade-away of the unitary public sphere and the experience of empowerment and new horizons, are to be adjusted to one another. She attempts to combine the contradictory characteristics and tendencies of the network. The main themes are the dilemma of unity versus fragmentation, the changing boundaries of the private and the public, and their potential impacts upon politics.

Part III of the book begins with a chapter written by Kenneth L. Hacker who views the location of digital democracy in relation to American politics. The Clinton administration consistently made strong claims on this subject matter introducing the 'information superhighway' as part of a way to enhance participatory democracy. Hence, their successes and failures are important matters of inquiry when considering the potentials and risks of digital democracy. In Hacker's chapter, these successes and failures are analysed in light of stated objectives and empirically derived results.

Sociological data about democracy networks, the Internet in general, the World Wide Web, and the White House CMC system are discussed with special attention on trends in the data that have been emerging since 1993. Patterns over time are discussed, particularly in relation to the claims and implications about democratization which were attributed to the Internet, the National Information Infrastructure and the White House CMC system. Hacker's balance sheet keeps a central focus on presenting some defensible generalizations about what role the Clinton White House has had in shaping digital democracy. Hacker concludes the chapter with general propositions about political interactivity between citizens and national-level leaders. This brings together past work on interactivity and current theory regarding reciprocity.

Chapter 8 is written by Anita Elberse, Matthew Hale and William H. Dutton and it examines the early experiences of 'The Democracy Network' (Dnet). This electronic voter guide is used for a case study of how the World Wide Web can be used to overcome barriers to more informative political campaigns, yet still encounter problems. Specific limitations of this type of project are noted in relation to other efforts at digital democracy. The authors demonstrate how technology alone is not enough to assure digital democracy and how there are many questions about effective projects that remain to be answered.

In Chapter 9, Nicholas Jankowski and Martine van Selm examine the quality of information and communication in digital democracy. One condition for a positive contribution of digital democracy to existing political practices, broadly conceived, is the quality of the information and communication content which serve as its main resource. The quality of the information content and the discussions on the Internet, for instance, are questioned by many observers. In this chapter these qualities are evaluated – fully acknowledging the difficulties of operationalizing the concept of quality – in a number of empirically-based evaluation studies of public electronic discussions in the Netherlands using the Internet. This chapter presents general considerations about the interactivity (expanding Rafaeli's conceptualization) and quality of Internet discussions. This chapter's content is related to the history of the Internet, all of the issues discussed in previous chapters, and some of the ideas about political interactivity and reciprocity raised in Hacker's chapter. Strong issues about the nature of political debate or its quality are contrasted with the common confusion that more channels constitute an assurance of more democracy. Generalizations from this chapter provide a good basis for research that can be done regarding extant and future efforts to democratize with CMC.

Next, a chapter by Jan van Dijk (Chapter 10) regarding information gaps in relation to digital democracy. The principal problem for participation in politics, democracy and society generally is the hotly debated 'gap between information rich and poor'. This chapter deals with the question of whether there is such a gap and what the answer means to democracy. Empirically, van Dijk explains, it is apparent that information inequality in the usage of ICT increased in Western countries during the 1990s. This goes for the different categories of income, occupation, age and country or region of origin. The only exception is the gender gap which is narrowing. Theoretically, the concepts of information inequality and a knowledge or information gap are qualified; it is better to talk about a usage gap of the new media; some will use the simple and others the advanced applications. Taking this qualification into account the analysis in this chapter warns for the growth of structural inequalities, the rise of information elites and the exclusion of large parts of the population in Western democracies.

This would mean a threat to democracy in every view. Information inequality has always existed and is likely to remain. However, the scale of it is no matter of natural necessity. Policies to prevent structural information inequalities are possible. They are described along four successive hurdles people have to cross when they want to have access to the information society in general and digital democracy in particular: lacking digital skills, no access to computers and networks, insufficient user-friendliness and the lack of significant usage opportunities of the new media for particular people.

The last chapter in Part III is provided by Michel Catinat and Thierry Vedel. Their chapter informs us about the specific roles of state authorities in the operation of digital democracy. The roles they explain include operators, regulators, sponsors and catalyzers. Catinat and Vedel confront the controversies regarding the commercialization of the Internet, the issues of citizenship versus consumership, how nations like the United States and France differ in their approaches to public policies to assure positive contributions of new communication technologies to democracy.

The book closes with a synthesis and summary (Chapter 12) presented by the editors. We discuss the recurrent issues, propositions, problems and directions for necessary research that have emerged in the theoretical and empirical work of the contributors.

References

Davis, R. and Owen, D. (1998) *New Media and American Politics*. New York: Oxford.

Harrison, T., Stephen, T. and Falvey, L. (1999) 'Democracy and New Communication Technologies'. Paper presented at the conference of The Communication and Technology Division of ICA, San Francisco.

Oppenheimer, T. (1997) 'The computer delusion', *The Atlantic Monthly*, 280: 45–62.

Steffen, J.O. (1994) 'Edenic expectations of new technology: a recurring pattern in American culture', *Phi Kappa Phi Journal*, LLXXIV: 11–15.

2

Computers as Communication: the Rise of Digital Democracy

Everett M. Rogers and Sheena Malhotra

> In a few years, man (*sic*) will be able to communicate more effectively through a machine than face to face.
>
> Licklider and Taylor (1968)

The words of Licklider and Taylor, quoted above, proved to be prophetic in the three decades since their publication, as computers have become an important means of communication for hundreds of millions of people across the world. Individuals are able to exchange information effectively through computer networks like the Internet, connecting with other people at a great distance. Computers were not originally perceived to be communication tools. The early use of computers was limited to number-crunching and other repetitive data-handling tasks. The potential of computers for human communication, and thus for digital democracy, however, has been realized most fully only in the 1990s with the rapid diffusion of use of the Internet.

How did computers change from number-crunching devices to become communication media? This chapter traces a history of how the perception of the computer in the 1960s underwent a crucial transition. Abundant funding, certain key institutions, and several visionary individuals played an important role in this development. One of the most important factors was the vision of computing-as-communication that was held by key individuals like J.C.R. Licklider, who guided computer development in the 1960s. But this dramatic change, from number-crunching devices to communication channels, in how we use computers moved slowly until the 1990s. Then a rapid spread of the Internet occurred.

As interactive forms of electronic communication became widespread, their potential uses for digital democracy evolved through a series of specific applications, such as the Berkeley Community Memory Project, the Public Electronic Network (PEN) in Santa Monica, CA; the Blacksburg Electronic Village (BEV) in Blacksburg, VA; and the La Plaza Telecommunity in Taos, NM. These community-based projects in digital democracy are analysed in this chapter.

However, the potential of the Internet and the World Wide Web for participatory politics has not yet been fully realized.

The Evolution of Computers

Four key visionaries guided the evolution of computers. Computers might have developed in a quite different way had these pioneers not articulated a vision that entailed computers as communication devices. Who were these visionaries? What was their role in the evolution of computers as communication tools?

Vannevar Bush

Bush was an electrical engineer who became one of the dominant influences on science and technology in the twentieth century. In the 1930s Bush, a professor at MIT, designed an early non-electronic computer (called the 'differential analyser'), a room-sized machine of gears and pulleys which could make complex mathematical computations (Zachary, 1997). Bush became the science adviser to President Franklin D. Roosevelt during the Second World War, and the main organizer of the Manhattan Project. After the War, he shaped the conception of the National Science Foundation and the US Department of Defense's Advanced Research Projects Agency, ARPA (Zachary, 1995: 65).

In 1945, Bush wrote an article entitled, 'As we may think', about a desktop computing device called the 'memex' (Bush, 1945). The memex was the conceptual blueprint for a desktop computer. Bush's article provided the path down which future computer designers would tread (Zachary, 1995). It represents one of the first articulated visions of personal computing as we know it today.

Bush's thinking dealt with the symbiosis between humans and computers. His memex machine would access and store vast knowledge for use by human beings in order for them to cope with information overload. The memex was a step away from computers as mere number-crunchers and toward computers as communication devices, although at the time Bush suggested microfilm as the basic technology for the memex. Bush envisioned the important role that information, and the ability to access information, would play in the years to follow.

J.C.R. Licklider

J.C.R. ('Lick') Licklider was an acoustical psychologist at MIT who became one of the main visionaries in the evolution of computers as communication. Licklider had a vision of computing that was revolutionary for his time, a vision that became the dominant paradigm for the computing world, although it initially met with strong opposition from the leaders of the computer industry. They felt that computer technology was too valuable to waste on communication. The computer establishment criticized Lick's ARPA program. Most computer manufacturers and directors of computer centres argued that time-sharing was an inefficient use of machine resources and should not be pursued. But Lick had the courage to persevere (Taylor, 1990).

Licklider was a faculty member at MIT in the 1950s, and then worked at Bolt, Beraneck & Newman (BBN), an architectural and computer consulting company in Cambridge, MA, that was to play an important role in creating networked computing. At BBN, Licklider and his colleagues designed and built one of the first time-sharing systems, based on a DEC PDP-1 minicomputer. In 1962, he moved to the Pentagon to head the research programme at the Advanced Research Projects Agency's Information Processing Techniques Office (ARPA-IPTO).[1] Here, with generous funding from the US Department of Defense, Licklider implemented his vision of computers as communication tools. After the Soviet launch of the *Sputnik* satellite in 1957, President Eisenhower had established a high-technology R and D agency, ARPA, in the Pentagon, in order to ensure that the United States would not again be taken by surprise by a military-related technology (Hafner and Lyon, 1996: 14). The President and Congress recognized that future military superiority would be expressed in technological terms rather than in the number of men under arms.

In 1960, Licklider's influential article entitled 'Man–computer symbiosis' first articulated his vision (Licklider, 1960/1990). He argued that most of human 'thinking time' was used in 'activities that were essentially clerical or mechanical' (Licklider, 1960/1990: 5). The Licklider vision sought increased interaction between humans and computers, so that computers would perform these clerical and mechanical tasks for humans, thereby freeing human time which could be devoted to innovative and creative thinking. He outlined the direction in which computers should evolve, in terms of memory, hardware, organization requirements, languages and input/output equipment. Licklider's passion for computers was based on the general idea that technological progress could save humanity. He saw a future in which computers would help citizens be 'informed about and interested in, and involved in the process of government' (Hafner and Lyon, 1996: 34). Thus, Licklider was one of the first observers to envision digital democracy. Communication was a key element in Licklider's vision of computing and its role in a participatory democracy.

Licklider developed his vision further in 1968, when he (and Robert Taylor) published their important article about the computer as a 'communication device', quoted at the start of this chapter. This vision proved to be prophetic in pointing the directions for the evolution of computer networking as we know it today (Licklider and Taylor, 1968).

Robert W. Taylor

Taylor, also a psychologist, was the key person in implementing Licklider's vision of computing. Taylor started his career as a research manager at NASA in 1962, where he funded research on interactive computing and computer applications related to communication (rather than to data-processing or to arithmetical uses of computers). 'Because that's the thing that interested me most about computing technologies (and still does): Its use as a communication medium' (Taylor, 1993). So to Taylor, the computer's visual display was the most important part of a computer; the function of the rest of the electronic equipment was to deliver what appeared on the computer's screen (Hiltzik, 1999).

What did Licklider and Taylor mean by 'communication' in their statement appearing at the top of this chapter? They meant more than just the transmission of information from one point to another in the form of codes and signals, as in Claude E. Shannon's (1949) Information Theory.[2] Instead, Licklider and Taylor (1968) meant a type of interactive communication in which information is not only exchanged, but in which new ideas emerge in a creative process. Licklider and Taylor (1968) provided an example of communication via computers among a small number of computer scientists meeting at SRI International[3] in Palo Alto, CA, using computers equipped with Douglas C. Engelbart's computer mouse (a user-interface technology whose evolution is traced later in this chapter). The computer scientists were able to engage in collaborative modelling through being interconnected by what today is called 'groupware'. The individual participants together possessed all of the information about the issue being reviewed, but no single participant could remember all that they knew (so they consulted their computer files, and shared them with other participants in the meeting). The work group participants developed a shared written plan.

Next, Licklider and Taylor (1968) participated in establishing ARPANET, which in following years would link computers at ARPA with its geographically dispersed contractors (mainly computer scientists at US universities). ARPANET allowed participants in a communication system to interact across large distances at minimal cost. ARPANET was the prototype for the present-day Internet. Licklider was at BBN in Boston while Taylor was in Washington, DC, when they jointly authored their 1968 paper about computer communication.

By 1965, Taylor became the Associate Director of ARPA-IPTO. He involved outstanding computer researchers in the Licklider/Taylor vision by awarding them IPTO-funded research contracts. They gathered each year for a contractors' conference at an exciting location (such as a ski lodge, a beach resort, etc.). Each contractor gave a presentation on his/her research project to the conference. Taylor encouraged people to argue, debate and to exchange ideas and computer technologies with each other (Taylor, 1993). Mutual stimulation of the principal investigators was of special interest to Taylor. Could this creative exchange occur via communication through a computer network?

The Birth of ARPANET   Taylor conceived of, and initiated, ARPANET. He had observed Licklider start up the early time-sharing computer systems. When he came to ARPA, his office was equipped with teletype machines linking him to three ARPA-IPTO contractors: the Systems Development Corporation (SDC) in Los Angeles; the University of California at Berkeley computer system; and the MIT computer system (Taylor, 1993). Taylor wanted to link the machines: 'If you have got a community growing around any one of these computer systems, why not make it possible for the communities to talk to one another?' (Taylor, 1993). In February 1966, Taylor went to the Director of ARPA, Charles Herzfeld, and in a 20-minute conversation convinced him to approve of the computer network that he envisioned (Hiltzik, 1999). Herzfeld gave Taylor approximately one million dollars to get the network started.

Taylor had the general idea for linking computing systems in a network, but he needed a program manager to implement this project. He identified Lawrence Roberts, then at MIT's Lincoln Labs, where he worked on a research project funded by ARPA. Taylor tried to convince Roberts to join ARPA, but Roberts did not want to become a Washington bureaucrat. After several months, Taylor realized that ARPA funded 51 per cent of the Lincoln Labs budget. So he explained his problem to Charles Herzfeld, who called Lincoln Labs and explained to the director that it would be in Lincoln Lab's best interest if Roberts came to Washington. Roberts accepted the position. By 1967, ARPANET was underway. Taylor stated, 'I blackmailed Larry Roberts into fame' (Taylor, 1993). Larry Roberts is now known as the father of ARPANET. It was Taylor's idea, but Roberts made it work.

The other person who was influential in the planning of ARPANET was Wesley Clark, an ARPA contractor at Washington University in St Louis. During a cab ride from the annual IPTO contractors meeting in Ann Arbor to the Detroit Airport, Taylor got Roberts and Clark talking about how to design a computer network that would link unalike computers. Clark came up with the idea of interconnecting the unalike computers at each ARPANET site with what he called an Interface Message Processor (IMP). Each host computer in the network would have an IMP (a small computer) attached to it so as to provide an interface with the computer network. The network would connect the IMPs. This strategy was effective (Taylor, 1993). By mid-1969, three sites were connected via IMPs. The inspiration for the particular decentralized design of the Internet as we know it today occurred on a taxi ride to Detroit Airport, orchestrated by Taylor.

In 1970, Taylor left ARPA, and joined Xerox PARC in Palo Alto, CA, the newly established research and development centre at which the Camelot of computing would soon occur. At about this time, Douglas Engelbart at SRI took charge of the Network Information Center (NIC), funded by ARPA-IPTO, which was to advance computer communication.

Douglas C. Engelbart

While Licklider was proposing his visionary ideas on man–computer symbiosis, an engineer at the Stanford Research Institute had a similar vision. Dr Douglas C. Engelbart believed that computers should perform as a powerful auxiliary to human communication. His 1962 article entitled, 'Augmenting human intellect: a conceptual framework' (Engelbart, 1962), argued that computers could manipulate human language and that individuals could use computers as communication tools to extend their human abilities. Engelbart saw human intellect as limited by language, a viewpoint influenced by the writings of the linguist Benjamin Lee Whorf (1956). Engelbart cited Whorf and George Herbert Mead, the social interactionist, as two scholars who influenced his thinking about the role of language in communication and intellect. 'But then I began to realize the unusual characteristics that the computer and communication technologies were offering, in just plain speed and quantity. I had done enough work on scaling effects to realize that the whole qualitative nature of some phenomenon can change if you start changing the scale of some part of it. I began to realize in how many ways, and how directly, the computer could interact with the different capabilities that we've already got' (Engelbart, 1992).

Engelbart set about implementing his vision of computer augmentation of human intellect. 'Bootstrapping' was a design principle at SRI, which meant that Engelbart's researchers used the technologies that they created. Thus, the computer user discovered and re-invented the tools that he/she made, in an iterative learning process (Engelbart, 1962). This bootstrapping process allowed the computer researchers at SRI to more fully understand the new technologies they were creating. Furthermore, they communicated their technological innovations to other researchers who were then able to advance them further (Taylor, 1993).

Perhaps the most important new computer interface technology that Engelbart designed was the computer mouse. This device was controlled by one hand in order to enable a user to direct a computer cursor by moving the mouse over a smooth surface. By clicking one of the three buttons on Engelbart's mouse, a user could communicate commands to the computer. The mouse was an important advance in human–computer interaction.[4]

Engelbart's mouse was directly inspired by the planimeter, a device invented by Vannevar Bush to measure distances (Engelbart, 1992). More generally, Engelbart credits Bush's 1945 idea of the memex as his inspiration for thinking of computers as communication devices (Zachary, 1997).

Taylor stated that Engelbart was the only ARPA-IPTO contractor that he had to force to accept funding. Engelbart was using an inadequate computer tool, a CDC 160A, a relatively small computer, with which to implement his vision of human–computer interfacing. Taylor forced several million dollars of ARPA funds on Engelbart, so that he could purchase a large mainframe computer. Engelbart soon began to make technological advances toward his vision (Taylor, 1993). In 1967, Engelbart created the ARPA Network Information Center (NIC), a 'community support center that would really go after the development of collaboration-support tools and methods, and would provide services to encourage the ARPANET R and D folks to evolve their working ways accordingly' (Engelbart, 1988: 226). In 1968, NIC began delivering the ARC oNLine System (NLS) over ARPANET. This online system used a mouse and e-mail, and had a multiple windows interface to connect the various ARPANET research and development workers (at 30 sites in the US). NIC was important in implementing the visions of Licklider, by networking the community of computer scientists through ARPANET. Robert Taylor was the catalyst for this technological innovation, which was a key step in shaping computers into tools for communication.

Xerox PARC

Xerox PARC (Palo Alto Research Centre) was founded in 1970 in the Stanford Industrial Park, located on the Stanford University campus in Palo Alto. Only 5 years later, by 1975, Xerox PARC had developed most of the important personal computing technologies: (a) the world's first personal computer, (b) an improved version of Engelbart's mouse, (c) bit-mapped display, (d) icons and pull-up menus, (e) laser printing, and (f) Ethernet technology (which linked computers into a local area network). The Xerox Corporation, then the world's leading paper copier company, invested $150 million in Xerox PARC during its first 14 years (Uttal, 1983). The company did not expect to obtain marketable technologies from this investment in basic research for about a decade (Pake, 1985). Unfortunately for Xerox, none of the personal computing technologies created at PARC (except for laser printing) were commercialized by the Xerox Corporation into useful products. Instead, most of the personal computing technologies that were invented and developed at Xerox PARC from 1970–1975 were marketed by Apple Computer after 1984 (in the form of the Macintosh computer).

One of the reasons for Xerox PARC's achievements in technological innovation was the peculiar organizational culture of the PARC facility. PARC was 'one of the most unusual corporate research organizations of our time' (Perry and Wallich, 1985: 62). The R and D lab was not tied to any one of the Xerox product lines. Instead it was set up to create 'the office of the future', and given a rather hazy mission to create the 'architecture of information'. PARC was located in California, far from Xerox's headquarters and existing laboratories on the East Coast, because (a) Xerox had just purchased a Californian computer company, and (b) because Xerox did not want the new R and D centre to be limited by existing ideas. This physical and organizational arrangement translated to a high degree of freedom for the PARC researchers to pursue innovative ideas that were not limited by commercial considerations.

Xerox PARC's success in developing innovative computing technologies was also due to the outstanding calibre of the researchers who worked there. Taylor brought together a critical mass of computer scientists at PARC, many of whom had been ARPA-IPTO contractors. PARC researchers like Alan Kay later commented, 'out of the 100 best computer scientists in the country, 76 of them were at PARC!' (Smith and Alexander, 1988: 76). While this statement might have been an exaggeration, Xerox PARC in the early 1970s was 'the best computer science research establishment in the world' (Smith and Alexander, 1988: 76). The climate for innovation at Xerox PARC could be attributed to Taylor's management style, which encouraged the collaborative exchange of technical information among the PARC researchers. The atmosphere at PARC facilitated interaction and creativity. The regular meeting room at PARC was equipped with bean-bag chairs and the walls were made of Chinaboard, so as to provide adequate space for diagramming. Resources were plentiful at PARC. Taylor did not establish a hierarchy within the laboratory, and a great deal of freedom was allowed the PARC researchers in choosing the exact directions of their R and D activities.

The early 1970s were ripe for technological innovation in personal computing. In 1971, Intel Corporation had invented the microprocessor, a crucial component for personal computing (Noyce and Hoff, 1981). The microprocessor made the microcomputer possible, and helped fulfil the earlier vision of a stand-alone personal computer (Bush, 1945), and thus the notion of interactive computing set forth by Licklider and Engelbart.

One of the computer scientists at PARC, Alan Kay, created 'Flex', a programming language, and a miniature personal computer that he had described in his 1969 PhD dissertation at the University of Utah. At Xerox PARC, Flex developed both as a language (Smalltalk) that was accessible to non-experts, as well as a machine (the Dynabook), forerunner to the laptop computer. George Pake, the

Director of PARC, did not support Kay's Dynabook project because he maintained that the requisite miniaturized display technology and lower-cost computer memory would not be available for several years. Nevertheless, Kay convinced two of his PARC colleagues to 'build an interim Dynabook on a skunkworks basis' (Kay, 1992).[5] This interim Dynabook, the Alto computer, did not turn out to be the Dynabook that Kay had envisioned, because the Alto computer was not portable. However, the Alto was the first personal computing system ever built, in that it was a computer designed to be used by a single individual. Until this point, mainframe computers or minicomputers were used by a number of individuals who were linked in time-sharing arrangements. The Alto was originally created for use by the individual computer researchers at PARC.

In 1979, Steven Jobs, the co-founder of Apple Computer, Inc, made a half-day visit to Xerox PARC where he was immensely impressed by the personal computing technologies that he saw demonstrated at PARC. These technologies fit with his vision of a 'friendly', technologically advanced personal computer. Within a few months, Jobs hired several PARC R and D workers who migrated the few miles to Apple Computer in Cupertino, CA. Thus, the computing technologies developed at Xerox PARC became the basis for the widely selling Macintosh microcomputer, announced in 1984.

Growth of Computer Networks

ARPANET, BITNET *and the Internet*

ARPANET, reflecting the computers as communication vision of champions like Licklider and Engelbart, was implemented in 1969. Bob Taylor secured the funding from ARPA, Larry Roberts designed the network, and Wes Clark created with the breakthrough idea of connecting incompatible mainframe computers with IMPs. The ARPA-IPTO funded computer at UCLA became the first ARPANET node, which consisted of their Sigma-7 mainframe computer attached to IMP 1 (Hafner and Lyon, 1996: 154). Soon thereafter, SRI in Palo Alto became the second node in ARPANET. SRI had an SDS-940 mainframe computer and IMP 2. The third ARPANET node was installed at the University of California at Santa Barbara, and the fourth at the University of Utah. These four nodes formed the beginning of ARPANET, and represented the forerunners of the Internet as we know it today. The first cross-country circuit for the ARPA network was installed in March 1970, connecting UCLA to a node in Boston. Thus, the essential elements for computer networking were in place by 1972. However, ARPANET was restricted to the community of ARPA-funded computer scientists who had developed it.

In October 1972, the first International Conference on Computer Communication was held in Washington, DC. Larry Roberts was on the programme committee and arranged for a public demonstration of ARPANET at the Conference. The demonstration imposed a deadline on all those involved with ARPANET to debug the network, and to have the system working flawlessly. The ARPANET demonstration at the Washington conference convinced its several thousand participants of the revolutionary potential of computer networking

(Hafner and Lyons, 1996: 186). 'The importance of its [ARPANET's] role in the history of computer and data communication cannot be underestimated – it epitomized this whole period' (Hellige, 1994: 62).

E-mail on ARPANET   Although ARPANET was not originally intended as a messaging system, that became one of its primary uses between 1972 and the early 1980s (Hafner and Lyons, 1996: 189). This communication function had not been anticipated by ARPANET's designers. 'The way in which the military research network was actually utilized in practice came as a surprise to the ARPANET engineers and operators, because the central service turned out to be the mailbox service, developed by Roberts in 1970 as an additional feature, and not the anticipated wide area sharing of resources and loads' (Hellige, 1994: 63).

The e-mail function of ARPANET was developed when Ray Tomlinson, an engineer at BBN in Boston, wrote a computer program in 1972, called SNDMSG, to send mail messages, and a corresponding READMAIL program to receive computer messages (Hafner and Lyons, 1996: 191–2). Messages could now travel from one host computer to another, so the two software programs, in effect, provided the first electronic mail messaging system. Abhay Bhushan, a programmer at MIT, finalized the protocol for e-mail based on Tomlinson's software, thereby providing the beginnings of a global electronic mail system. Tomlinson chose the '@' sign in the message address, which thereafter became a global icon on the Internet (Hafner and Lyons, 1996: 192).

ARPANET was originally designed to be a resource-sharing system through which the ARPA contractors could exchange computer programs and databases. But as more and more users discovered that they could send personal messages to friends and colleagues, e-mail became one of the most popular features of the network. In 1973, Stephen Lukasik, the Director of ARPA, commissioned a study of ARPANET use. Three-quarters of all traffic was e-mail (Hafner and Lyons, 1996: 194). Many of these e-mail messages were humorous (some were jokes); most were highly personal. Very few messages dealt with military/defence matters. Thus, ARPANET became a publicly available means of electronic communication, provided gratis by the Pentagon.

In June 1975, an ARPA program manager at IPTO, Steve Walker, announced the first electronic discussion group called MsgGroup (Hafner and Lyons, 1996: 200). This discussion group represented one of the first network mail lists. MsgGroup provided for many spirited discussions on ARPANET over the following decades. MsgGroup was, in essence, the first virtual community, which users utilized in order to get acquainted with and to interact by e-mail.

Expansion of Computer Networks

In the early 1970s, several other computer networks were established, using such electronic media as radio waves (on different islands in Hawaii, called ALOHANET) and satellite transmission (SATNET). In 1972, Bob Kahn, who had moved to ARPA from BBN, began thinking about linking all of these different networks into a network of networks. By 1973, the Internetting Project was established at ARPA (Hafner and Lyons, 1996: 222), in which Kahn began to collaborate with Vint Cerf, a computer scientist at UCLA. Cerf and Kahn realized that they needed a routing computer between each of the different networks that would transfer messages from one network to the other. It would function, at a higher level, like the IMP in the early days of the ARPANET. Cerf and Kahn published a paper, 'A protocol for packet network intercommunication', in 1974 in which they described a transmission control protocol (TCP) (Hafner and Lyons, 1996: 226). Messages would be encapsulated and decapsulated in 'datagrams', a kind of message envelope. Gateway computers would only read the envelope, and then route the message toward the appropriate host computer, thereby transmitting messages across networks. While implementation of the TCP design took several more years, the 1974 Cerf and Kahn paper outlined the future path for networking of computer networks.

The computer network expanded consistently over the next 2 years, with an existing computer network added each month. In 1978, Cerf, along with researchers Jon Postel and Danny Cohen, came up with the idea of breaking up the original TCP that dealt with routing packets, and forming a separate Internet Protocol or IP. The resulting protocol, TCP/IP, made it possible to build relatively inexpensive gateways that could read the computer message code, so as to route message packets toward the appropriate destination computer (Hafner and Lyons, 1996: 236–7). TCP/IP became the standard for the Internet, and greatly assisted its expansion.

In 1973, Bob Metcalfe at Xerox PARC invented the Ethernet, a new kind of local area network (LAN) that connected computers in different rooms of a building (Hafner and Lyons, 1996: 239). The system was quickly adopted by companies and by universities, and became another essential building block in the eventual Internet.

In the late 1970s, it became necessary to build a network for computer researchers that would be more accessible than ARPANET, and which could be accessed by any individual involved with the Federal government. The National Science Foundation (NSF) underwrote the development of this new computer network for its first 5 years. Thus, CSNET (Computer Science Research Network) came into being (Hafner and Lyons, 1996: 243). After 5 years, each university using CSNET paid annual dues. CSNET was the forerunner for BITNET, which was launched in 1981.

BITNET stands for 'Because It's Time NETwork' and was started in 1981 by Ira Fuchs at the City University of New York (CUNY) and by Greydon Freeman at Yale University (Rogers, 1995: 315). Both universities had used a LAN system for several years, which proved useful for collaborative academic work by their professors. They decided to lease a telephone line to connect the two university locations, thereby allowing the exchange of messages between anyone at the two universities. BITNET thus was born (Rogers, 1995: 315). Four more East Coast universities joined within the year, each one leasing a telephone line to the nearest university that already belonged to BITNET. In 1982, the University of California at Berkeley leased an expensive long-distance telephone line to join BITNET, and in doing so, made BITNET available for other West Coast universities. Each university that joined helped defray the cost of the transcontinental line. Soon BITNET was adopted by universities at a very rapid rate. Between 1984 and 1985, BITNET doubled in size every 6 months and telephone connections were established to universities in countries outside of the US (Rogers, 1995: 316), forming a massive academic network across the globe.

In 1985, the National Science Foundation (NSF) built a 'backbone network' to connect 5 supercomputer centres that it had funded, each at a different US university. NSF offered to give other computer networks access to this backbone network, which was called NSFNET. Many existing computer networks joined NSFNET and this connection of interconnected TCP/IP networks gradually came to be known as the Internet (Hafner and Lyon, 1996: 245). By late 1989, ARPANET had become obsolete, compared to NSFNET, and was slowly dismantled. Each site on the ARPANET was assigned to a location on the Internet (Hafner and Lyon, 1996: 256). After 20 years, ARPANET had served its purpose, and thus merged into the Internet, for which it had provided the prototype.

How the Internet Works

The Internet is a network linking over 20,000 previous computer networks, including the original ARPANET (Rogers, 1995: 316). During the Cold War era of its creation, ARPANET had been designed to survive a nuclear attack by the Soviet Union. Therefore, no single control point existed for ARPANET. This 'survivable network' had integrated data, text, picture and voice communication (Hellige, 1994: 59). Moreover, because ARPANET was originally built as a defence and as a research network, the US Department of Defense provided ample funds. Resources were not a limiting factor. The Internet, formed out of ARPANET in 1983, continued ARPANET's decentralized network structure, which used a 'many-to-many' communication model. Millions of computers are linked by telephone lines through many millions of different network paths. Any message sent on the Internet moves toward its destination by being passed along from computer to computer. The message may take any one of a multitude of paths. If the computer message encounters a block, it immediately seeks an alternative route.

It is extremely difficult to control the Internet, a decentralized computer network, as it was designed to counter exactly such control. Thus it is difficult to estimate the actual numbers of users of the Internet, or to ensure the accuracy of all messages transmitted via this computer network. For example, the Internet contains numerous messages about cancer cures and AIDS cures, some of which are of a dubious nature. Further, censorship of the Internet is extremely difficult, and most attempts to do so have failed.

The Internet Today

The number of Internet users doubled each year during the 1990s, an extremely rapid rate of adoption, perhaps one of the fastest rates of diffusion for any innovation in the history of humankind. Estimates vary on numbers of Internet users, but it is generally accepted that there are over 150 million users in the world and over 70 million users in the United States (NUA Surveys, 1999; Shapiro, 1999; United Nations Human Development Report, 1999).

The widespread use of the Internet was greatly helped by the creation of the World Wide Web in 1990 by Tim Berners-Lee, a British researcher at CERN (the European Laboratory for particle Physics) in Geneva (Hafner and Lyon, 1996: 257). Gradually, millions of homepages were created on the Web, containing an unmatched information resource that attracted large numbers of people to surf the Net. Increasingly, commercial businesses began to use the Web for marketing and sales purposes, as e-commerce became widely accepted.

In 1993, two computer science students at the University of Illinois invented Mosaic, a graphics program that made the Web much easier to use. Mosaic was the forerunner to Netscape, a commercially available browser that made the Internet more accessible to the user with the point and click of a computer mouse. These two technologies (the Web and Mosaic) were essential in making the Internet more accessible and attractive to users, and helped set off the rapid increase in the rate of adoption of the Internet during the 1990s. Within its first several years of existence, Mosaic was adopted by two million users per year.

The development of these component technologies like the World Wide Web and Mosaic helped the Internet reach critical mass in a very short time. A critical mass occurs at the point when enough individuals have adopted an innovation so that its further rate of adoption becomes self-sustaining (Rogers, 1995: 313). The concept of critical mass implies that an individual's actions are in part dependent on the actions of others (Rogers, 1995: 318). Once critical mass is achieved, an innovation's rate of adoption proceeds rapidly. The ability of the Internet user to communicate with other people increases as the number of Internet users increases. Since the Internet is an interactive communication innovation, it increases in value as it is utilized by a greater number of users. Therefore, once the Internet reached critical mass, due to the increased accessibility and attractiveness provided by the technologies described above, it spread at an ever-increasing pace.

We have reviewed the evolution of computer networking in this chapter, showing how early visions shaped the directions taken by computer technologists (see Table 2.1). By the late 1980s computer systems were in place to allow the creation of virtual communities. How did these social and political systems evolve in certain locations in the United States?

Interactive Communication and Participatory Politics

In this section we analyse and derive lessons learned from four interactive communication systems: the Berkeley Community Memory Project, established in 1978; the Public Electronic Network (PEN) in Santa Monica, CA, which became operational in 1989; the Blacksburg Electronic Village, Inc. (BEV) in Blacksburg, VA, founded in 1993; and La Plaza Telecommunity in Taos, NM, established in 1995. We selected these four projects because of their pioneering nature, and the present authors' personal knowledge and experience with them. Each of these brief case studies identifies the original reasons for founding the community-based system, and describes its applications for democratic politics and for various other uses.

TABLE 2.1   *Time-line of the development of computers as communication devices*

Date	Event
1930	Vannevar Bush designs an early non-electronic computer
1945	Bush writes article on the memex, a prototype desktop computer
1960	J.C.R. Licklider's article 'Man–computer symbiosis' is published
1962	J.C.R. Licklider directs ARPA-IPTO
1965	Robert Taylor joins ARPA-IPTO
1966	ARPANET is envisioned
1969	UCLA becomes the first ARPA node, followed by SRI, the University of California at Santa Barbara, and the University of Utah
1970	First cross-country circuit for the ARPA network links UCLA and BBN in Boston
1972	Development of e-mail on ARPANET
	First demonstration of ARPANET at the International Conference on Computer Communication (Washington, DC)
1972–1980s	E-mail becomes the central service on ARPA
1973	Ethernet is invented at Xerox PARC
1975	First electronic discussion group (MsgGroup)
1981	BITNET is launched (it evolved from CSFNET)
1985	NSF links five supercomputer centres via NSFNET, which comes to be known as the Internet
1990	World Wide Web is invented
1993	Mosaic graphics program is invented
1990s	Use of the Internet spreads exponentially

Berkeley Community Memory Project

The founder of the Berkeley Community Memory Project was Lee Felsenstein, one of the chief designers of the Osborne computer, an early portable microcomputer. Felsenstein lived in a commune in Berkeley, CA, and with his housemates came up with the idea of using a computer to connect everyone in this university city. Public terminals were located in co-operative stores and other convenient public places. Anyone could post a notice, such as 'For Sale: Used VW Bug', 'Wanted: small refrigerator', or 'The Gay Rights Association will meet at the City Library at 7:00 pm next Thursday'. The advantage of the Berkeley Community Memory Project was its capacity; it was the equivalent of a football field on which one could pin hundreds of thousands of 3 by 5 cards.

Felsenstein and his friends wanted to provide computer power to the public, so there was no charge to individuals for using the system. Funding came from Felsenstein's earnings from his stock in the Osborne Computer Company. The Berkeley Community Memory Project continues until the present, although it is presently limited to a dozen or so public terminals. Perhaps its main significance has been through its influence on other community networking projects.

Public Electronic Network (PEN)

The PEN system became available to residents in Santa Monica, CA in February 1989 (Rogers et al., 1994; Schmitz et al., 1995). PEN grew out of an e-mail system linking the city government's departments chiefs and members of the city council. One councilman asked, 'Why can't we link *everyone* in the community to this system?' Thus PEN was born.

Santa Monica is a liberal, politically active community that has a relatively well-educated population of about 90,000, although a large number of homeless people (estimated at from 2000 to 10,000 in 1989) also live in the city. The Hewlett-Packard Company gifted the city of Santa Monica with a minicomputer and other equipment in order to launch PEN. As an afterthought, because of knowing about the Berkeley Community Memory Project, the HP official suggested including a dozen or so public terminals in the $350,000 gift package. The public terminals were placed in City Hall, libraries and in recreation centres. Soon, about one-third of all log-on to the PEN system were made at the public terminals, although approximately a quarter of the city's residents had access to PEN via their own computer equipment.

The first topic discussed on the PEN system was homelessness – many of the entries were negative: 'Why don't these people get jobs? They are so lazy.' Soon, however, homeless people, using the public terminals, responded. They argued that they were *not* lazy; they wanted to work. But they seldom could gain access to job interviewers due to their soiled clothing and body smell. Out of this electronic discussion between the homed and homeless eventually came plans for the SHWASHLOCK Project, in which an empty storefront building in Santa Monica was converted to provide *sh*owers, *wash*ers, and *lock*ers to homeless people. Soon a computerized job listing was provided on the PEN system, along with a training facility to teach computer skills to homeless people. One result was that some hundreds of homeless people secured jobs.

Interaction between the homeless and the homed in Santa Monica, leading to SWASHLOCK, could not have occurred without the electronic communication system. Here we see another dimension of computer networking, its ability to overcome social distance (presumably because of its lack of many types of non-verbal communication, like the communicators' clothing, smell, appearance, etc.), as well as spatial distance. As one homeless man stated on the PEN system: 'No one on PEN knew that I was homeless until I told them. After I told them, I was still treated like a human being.'

PEN rapidly became a regular part of daily life for 3000–4000 Santa Monica residents. They used the system for e-mail about local political news and events, community issues, and other matters, to check on the availability of a book in the city's libraries, or to acquire a building permit from a city government agency. The predominant use of PEN was for e-mail. Early on, PEN faced several important problems, one of which was 'flaming', in which certain individuals used profanity or other types of offensive expression. In the first year of PEN, some young males expressed sexual aggression against female users of PEN, by entering their names in a sexual fantasy game. Women users organized an electronic discussion group, PENFEMME, to counter this problem (Collins-Jarvis, 1993; Rogers et al., 1994). PENFEMME evolved into a female support group.

One of the important uses of PEN, as might be expected in a city actively concerned with local politics, was for the discussion of local political issues. For instance, community opposition to building a new hotel in a beachfront residential area of Santa Monica was organized on PEN. The hotel development plan was subsequently defeated. This political function of the PEN system occurred mainly by means of e-mail and electronic discussion groups.

Blacksburg Electronic Village (BEV)

BEV was initiated by Bell Atlantic, the telephone company serving the small university city of Blacksburg. Early discussions in 1992 led telephone company officials and city leaders to contact officials at Virginia Technological University. The Blacksburg Electronic Village began providing electronic communication services in autumn 1993. By spring 1995, 40 per cent of the town's residents were using the Internet, and 60 per cent were using e-mail on BEV. Use of these two systems expanded jointly in Blacksburg, with the local e-mail system serving community residents. Cost of the BEV was provided by a grant from the National Telecommunications Infrastructure Administration, a grant from the National Science Foundation for educational applications, and by contributions from the three sponsoring organizations (Cohill and Kavanaugh, 1997).

By autumn 1995, critical mass was achieved by the BEV. Numerous training classes, many provided by the city's libraries, were important in diffusing the use of BEV. By 1997, the city's population of 36,000 people sent over 250,000 e-mail messages per day! Many businesses in Blacksburg have Web sites, due to encouragement and funding by the city government. The university provided technical expertise to the BEV, and encouraged students and faculty to use the system. All matter of topics are discussed on the BEV, including local and national politics.

Two other Virginia cities, Abingdon and Radford, have followed Blacksburg's lead in providing an electronic communication system.

La Plaza Telecommunity

Taos County is the poorest county in New Mexico, the state with the lowest per capita income in the United States. La Plaza Telecommunity is a pioneering use of computer networking in a community with very limited resources. The project began in 1993, when community leaders from Taos attended a community telecommunications conference in Telluride, Colorado, where they saw a demonstration of the Infozone, a local computer network project in Telluride (like Taos, a skiing community). La Plaza Telecommunity came online on 7 December 1994, thanks to a grant from the New Mexico State Legislature; a gift of microcomputers from Apple Computer, Inc; and free use of a T-line provided by nearby Los Alamos National Laboratory to connect the local computer network to the Internet. La Plaza won a 3-year grant of $1 million from the Kellogg Foundation in 1996. In 1997, La Plaza Telecommunity began charging users a $6 per hour fee, later changed to $15 per month for unlimited use.

By 1999, La Plaza Telecommunity, through a very active training programme, had over 4000 registered users in the small city of Taos. La Plaza launched outreach efforts in the nearby Taos pueblo, and in the small Hispanic communities of Questa and Penasco. Initial training of potential users was provided in the waiting rooms of local health clinics, both in English and in Spanish. Diabetes is a health problem for 20 per cent of the Hispanic people in Taos, and for 30 per cent of Native Americans in the Northern New Mexican pueblos near Taos. A homepage on diabetes was provided on La Plaza Telecommunity. The health information was obtained from medical journal articles in the computerized National Library of Medicine, which was then organized in narrative form by La Plaza staff, as Taos residents are accustomed to a storytelling tradition. The diabetes homepage became one of the 10 most popular sites on La Plaza by 1999. A number of small businesses arose in Taos to construct homepages; these start-ups grew out of training classes provided by La Plaza staff on how to build homepages.

Conclusions

This chapter has outlined how the perception of computers in the 1960s underwent a crucial transition from data-handling devices to becoming tools for communication. Six factors were important in the development of computers as communication tools.

1 *Visions*   Visions are important in creating the envisioned future. Computers might have completely different uses today, had it not been for the guiding visions of Vannevar Bush, J.C.R. Licklider and Douglas Engelbart. Computers might have been limited to use for scientific purposes. Or computers might have become machines used only to automate and duplicate repetitive work operations. However, the persevering visions of Licklider and Engelbart, especially as implemented by Robert Taylor, led to computers as communication devices today. This communication revolution began occurring globally during the 1990s, and may eventually change the nature of human communication. Visions are road maps for the future, and when stated by credible individuals at an ideal time, they can have great impact.

2 *Adequate resources*   The availability of generous resources contributed to the development of computers as communication tools. The Advanced Research Projects Agency (ARPA) in the US Department of Defense and, later, the Xerox Corporation invested millions of dollars in the development of computer/ communication technologies. Researchers were enabled to utilize the most sophisticated equipment in developing new computer technologies (some researchers, like Douglas Engelbart, at SRI, had the expensive computer tools thrust on them). The availability of government funding also meant that university-based computer scientists were not forced toward commercially viable directions, as otherwise might have been the case. Their imagination in creating the new computer technologies did not have to be justified in the marketplace.

This generous funding led to the emergence of a new academic discipline, computer science. The ARPA-IPTO funds were awarded in the late 1960s and early 1970s to R and D contractors for the development of new computers as communication technologies. Stanford, Carnegie-Mellon, MIT, UCLA and the University of California at Berkeley were IPTO contractors that pioneered establishing graduate programmes in the emerging field of computer science (Taylor, 1993). So one side-effect of the ARPA-IPTO funding was to establish computer science as a new scientific field in universities. The computer scientists thus trained then continued to advance computer software technologies.

3 *Innovation champions* A *champion* is a charismatic individual who serves as an enthusiast for a new idea, thus overcoming indifference or resistance (Rogers, 1995: 398). As Schön (1963) stated, 'the new idea either finds a champion or dies.' Licklider and Engelbart acted as the champions for the vision in which they believed strongly, even when their visions were criticized at the time by the computer establishment. Licklider's and Engelbart's visions led to the development of personal computers, the mouse and computer networks. Without such visions, and the appropriate technological innovations, computers might have remained number-crunching devices.

4 *Key institutions* Throughout the development of computers as communication tools, certain institutions played a key role. ARPO-IPTO acted like a 'venture capital firm', financing researchers in computing technology, playing a key role in encouraging the growth of computer science as a new field, and supporting the technologies needed to advance computers as communication devices. The US Department of Defense was a key institution in the processes described here. MIT was the most important training ground for almost all of the key figures associated with computers as communication tools; examples are Bush, Licklider, Roberts and many others. Bolt, Bernanek & Neuman (BBN) played a crucial role in the development of IMPs and in the spread of computer networking through ARPANET. Xerox PARC served as the R and D institution in which a critical mass of brilliant computer scientists collaborated to develop the crucial technological innovations in personal computing that provided a foundation for computers as communication tools. The crucial innovations occurred in personal computing at Xerox PARC in only a 5-year period, a brief Camelot from 1970 to 1975.

5 *Timing* The popular notions that computers as communication tools magically and instantly burst onto the scene, and that the Internet became popular overnight, are misconceptions. The rapid adoption of the Internet happened in a decade, but after a 20-year wait. The notion of ARPANET as a computer network began in 1966, and by 1969 four nodes were in place, but not until the decades of the 1990s did the Internet diffuse widely among the American public, after the point at which a critical mass of users had adopted.

Why did the spread of computers as communication devices require so long? The prior diffusion of personal computers and modems in the 1980s was necessary before these computers could be interconnected in communication networks; computing as communication had to reach a critical mass before this innovation was adopted rapidly by the general population – that is, the rate of adoption of computers as communication devices had to become self-sustaining; and crucial technologies like Mosaic and the World Wide Web had to be developed before the Internet could be easily accessed by most individuals, and before it would contain information resources widely perceived as valuable.

6 *The role of communication scholars* Vannevar Bush, J.C.R. Licklider and Douglas Engelbart broke the previously existing paradigm of computing. A

paradigm defines problems and guides the theoretical questions to be studied by a particular community of scholars (Kuhn, 1970; Rogers, 1995: 44). None of the key figures involved in the development of computers as communication tools were communication scholars, which is ironic, as computers today are bringing about a communication revolution on a scale that might only be rivalled by the technological revolutions that occurred with the advent of the printing press, radio and television. The perspectives of individuals at the cutting edge of computer research were quite different from the viewpoints of communication scholars. The inventors/developers were mainly electrical engineers, computer scientists and psychologists, although Doug Engelbert was influenced by Benjamin Lee Whorf and by George Herbert Mead, who were important founders of communication study (Rogers, 1994). The disciplinary identification of the visionaries and implementers of computers as communication tools put human communication scholars in the role of investigating the effects of this communication revolution, rather than in the role of revolutionaries.

Bush, Licklider and Engelbert were Americans, and many of the historical events described in this chapter occurred in the United States. This dominant role of American visionaries and institutions, which generally characterizes computers as communication, is not necessarily a quality of many other computer-related technologies, in which Japan, England, Germany or other nations played important roles.

The Potential for Digital Democracy

Four community-level projects were reviewed in this chapter in order to derive lessons learned about the potential of computers as communication for participatory democracy. We note that special resources were necessary for each of these electronic communication systems. These financial inputs came from a computer entrepreneur in Berkeley, from an affluent city government and a computer company (Hewlett-Packard) in Santa Monica, and from government and foundation grants in Blacksburg and Taos. Most American communities do not have a local computer network either because they do not feel a need for a *local* communication system, other than the electronic communication available through the Internet, or because they cannot secure the special resources necessary to create and maintain a local computer network.

To what uses are local communication systems put by community residents? In Berkeley, the first community project reviewed here, the main function of the Community Memory Project is for posting notices and announcements. In Santa Monica and Blacksburg, PEN and BEV are utilized for the exchange of political and other community information, and to organize for certain community actions, such as to oppose the hotel development in Santa Monica. Our research on PEN, however, showed that the most active users of this system were Santa Monicans who were already the most involved in political activity (Rogers et al., 1994). This California city had a high level of political involvement on the part of its citizens, and so when PEN was provided, it was used heavily for political purposes. But PEN did do much to broaden the number of politically active residents.

In Taos, a poor community in New Mexico, La Plaza Telecommunity was used particularly for conveying health-related information, for educational purposes through the schools, and for business creation (the several small companies that make homepages). Thus, each community has particular local needs, and, as might be expected, when a new electronic communication system is established, it is utilized to fulfil these special needs.

To date, a total of only 10,000 or so individuals are actively involved in the 4 community projects in computer networking. So the impact of electronic communication on local political participation has been very small. The potential uses of computers as communication have not yet been fulfilled in local communities. However, there is a good deal of political discourse on the Internet today, although it is more likely to deal with national or international issues than with local politics.

Notes

The authors thank Dr Thierry Bardini of the Department of Communication at the University of Montreal for his help in conducting the personal interviews with Robert Taylor, Douglas C. Engelbart, Alan Kay and other pioneers and visionaries at ARPA and PARC.

1   An important event prior to Licklider's arrival in the Pentagon was the Semi-Automated Ground Environment (SAGE) system, an early warning system for air defence against a Soviet nuclear attack, developed from 1953 to 1963 (Hellige, 1994: 54). SAGE was the largest real-time information system of its time and represented a crucial decision made in the 1940s about developing digital systems (instead of the analogue models of computing that had been dominant).

2   The bit, which is the universal measure of information, originated in Shannon's Information Theory. Shannon conceptualized information as decreased uncertainty, transmitted in the form of codes and signals.

3   At the time, SRI International was known as Stanford Research Institute (SRI).

4   Engelbart also created a key-set for the individual's other hand, which could convey keystrokes representing letters and numbers to a computer, and thus was equivalent to a computer keyboard. Unlike the mouse, Engelbart's key-set was not incorporated into later computer designs.

5   A skunkworks is an R and D unit that has certain privileges including special resources, and which enjoys freedom from many organizational constraints by the quasi-clandestine nature of its operations (Rogers, 1995).

References

Bush, V. (1945) 'As we may think', *The Atlantic Monthly*, 176: 101–8.

Cerf, V.C. and Kahn, R.E. (1974) 'A protocol for packet-network intercommunication', *IEEE Transactions on Communications*, May.

Cohill, A.M. and Kavanaugh, A.L. (1997) *Community Networks: Lessons from Blacksburg, Virginia*. Norwood, VA: Artech House.

Collins-Jarvis, L. (1993) 'Gender representations in an electronic city hall: female adoption of Santa Monica's PEN system', *Journal of Broadcasting and Electronic Media*, 37 (1): 49–65.

Engelbart, D.C. (1962) *Augmenting Human Intellect: A Conceptual Framework*, report to the Director of Information Sciences, US Air Force Office of Scientific Research. Menlo Park, CA: SRI International.

Engelbart, D.C. (1988) 'The augmented knowledge workshop', in A. Goldberg (ed.), *A History of Personal Workstations*. New York: ACM Press. pp. 185–232.

Engelbart, D.C. (1992) Personal interview with E.M. Rogers and T. Bardini, 15 December, Menlo Park, CA.

Hafner, K. and Lyon, M. (1996) *Where Wizards Stay Up Late: The Origins of the Internet.* New York: Simon & Schuster.

Hellige, H.D. (1994) 'From SAGE via ARPANET to Ethernet: stages in computer communications concepts between 1950 and 1980', *History and Technology,* 11: 49–75.

Hiltzik, M. (1999) *Dealers of Lightning: Xerox PARC and the Dawn of the Computer Age.* New York: HarperBusiness.

Kay, A. (1969) 'The reactive engine'. PhD dissertation, University of Utah, Salt Lake City.

Kay, A. (1992) Personal interview with E.M. Rogers and T. Bardini, 17 December, Los Angeles, CA.

Kuhn, T.S. (1970) *The Structure of Scientific Revolutions.* Chicago: University of Chicago Press.

Licklider, J.C.R. (1960/1990) 'Man–computer symbiosis', in R.W. Taylor, *In Memoriam: J.C.R. Licklider, 1915–1990.* Palo Alto, CA: Digital Equipment Corporation, Systems Research Center Report.

Licklider, J.C.R. and Taylor, R.W. (1968) 'The computer as a communication device', *Science & Technology,* April: 21–31.

Noyce, R.N. and Hoff, M.E., Jr. (1981) 'A history of microprocessor development at Intel', *IEEE Micro,* 7(1): 8–21.

Pake, G.E. (1985) 'Research at Xerox PARC: A founder's assessment', *IEEE Spectrum,* October: 54–61.

Perry, T.S. and Wallich, P. (1985) 'Inside the PARC: the information architects', *IEEE Spectrum,* October: 62–75.

Rogers, E.M. (1994) *A History of Communication Study: A Biographical Approach.* New York: Free Press.

Rogers, E.M. (1995) *Diffusion of Innovations* (4th edn). New York: Free Press.

Rogers, E.M., Jarvis-Collins, L. and Schmitz, J. (1994) 'The PEN Project in Santa Monica: interactive communication and political action', *Journal of the American Society for Information Sciences,* 45(6): 1–10.

Schmitz, J., Rogers, E.M., Phillips, K. and Paschal, D. (1995) 'The Public Electronic Network (PEN) and the homeless in Santa Monica', *Journal of Applied Communication Research,* 23: 26–43.

Schön, D.A. (1963) 'Champions for radical new inventions', *Harvard Business Review,* 41: 77–86.

Shannon, C.E. (1949) *The Mathematical Theory of Communication.* Urbana: University of Illinois Press.

Smith, D.K. and Alexander, R.C. (1988) *Fumbling the Future: How Xerox Invented, then Ignored the First Personal Computer.* New York: Quill William Morrow.

Taylor, R.W. (1990) *In Memoriam: J.C.R. Licklider, 1915–1990.* Palo Alto, CA: Digital Equipment Corporation, Systems Research Center Report.

Taylor, R.W. (1993) Personal interview with E.M. Rogers and T. Bardini, 18 March, Palo Alto, CA.

Uttal, B. (1983) 'The lab that ran away from Xerox', *Fortune,* 78: 97–102.

Whorf, B.L. (1956) *Language, Thought and Reality.* Cambridge, MA: MIT Press.

Zachary, G.P. (1995) 'Vannevar Bush on the engineer's role', *IEEE Spectrum,* November: 65–9.

Zachary, G.P. (1997) *Endless Frontier: Vannevar Bush,* New York: Free Press.

PART II

THEORY

3

Models of Democracy and Concepts of Communication

Jan van Dijk

The previous chapter was a description of the historical development of computer technology and networking, the Internet in particular, which gave cause for the notion of digital democracy. Now the stage is open to some theory and conceptual clarification. What is digital democracy? Will it change the current political systems, first of all in the Western democracies? If so, will this change be evolutionary or revolutionary? Is it unidirectional, or can we perceive more potential lines of development? When there are more of them, do these lines perhaps depend upon different views of democracy and communication? For instance, some people are stressing the improvement of information supply and retrieval while others emphasize the new opportunities for interactivity or conversation the new media offer to politics. What is the most likely development of ICT in relation to politics and democracy in the future?

In the introduction to this book, digital democracy was defined as an attempt to practise democracy without limits of time, place and other physical conditions, using ICT or CMC instead. All terms in this definition must be qualified. First of all, digital democracy is still an *attempt* to change traditional age-old ways of operation and habits in politics. It is a matter of exploration and experiment. Some people strongly believe in its potential, while others are extremely sceptical. Most often the case is not a matter of scientific exploration and experiment. Projects and experiments with clearly defined goals and means, so vital for any valid or reliable scientific conclusion, are exceptional. Usually it is a practice of trial and error eagerly endorsed by 'believers' who have convinced some political or public institution trying to find new ways of government and administration or management. The result is that most conclusions after these attempts are contested. The 'believers' just go on, only learning by doing, and the 'sceptics' are not even convinced by highly acclaimed successes.

Secondly, digital democracy announces an altogether new type of *practice* in politics, management and public administration. The extent of change is underestimated most of the time. If digital democracy would become the dominant practice, the basic culture of politics as a set of typical ways of action and communication would change substantially. In spite of the steeply rising importance of the (mass) media for politics and democracy in the twentieth century, almost every political decision is taken in meetings and face-to-face communication only accepting media as means of registration. Politics remains an oral and paper practice to a very large degree. From way back politics is a matter of verbal skills, management capacities and the art of negotiation. It is a collective routine of talkers and organizers. In digital democracy this routine would transform into a practice of people working primarily as individuals at screens and terminals, clicking pages, reading and analysing information and posing or answering questions. It is likely to become a routine of technical and symbolic-intellectual skill instead of a practical-organizational and verbal-intellectual one. This transformation is so radical that it will not happen overnight. Such political changes take time, as they do not simply follow the introduction of a new medium. Moreover, these changes are supported or halted by the interests of social and political groups. Their positions and skills are at stake.

The presumption of a political practice not directly tied to the *limits of physical conditions* departs from the familiar workings and expressions of politics. This has always been a practice strongly tied to place, time and material resources of all kinds. Often it is accused of being too slow in its reaction to current affairs and of being too much committed to local interests and financial conditions. However, it remains to be seen whether the sole introduction of new techniques which enable political practice to cross barriers of place, time and material or organic conditions will reduce or radicalize the importance of these dimensions and conditions (Ferguson, 1990; van Dijk, 1999b). ICT or CMC have accelerated and substantially changed economic and financial processes in business networks and stock markets. Still, ICT (ICT/CMC) has not (yet) produced revolutionary changes in the basic workings of the market economy. In politics ICT is expected to intensify and speed up processes of opinion formation, representation and even decision taking by the directness of the means of transmission. Even so, the political system of representation does not appear to be substantially changing yet. Or does it? Is the political system in the advanced democracies perhaps changing in imperceptible ways by the growing use of ICT in daily practices?

A Network Model of the Political System

To answer these questions we will have to draw a map of the political field first. Figure 3.1 supplies a system-dynamic model of politics as a network of political actors and institutions. In this model the political system is not restricted to government, neither to a combination of government and public administration. Their relationships with other regulating institutions and with organizations of civil society, corporations and individual citizens cover a large part of the model. One can read the most important characteristics of Western constitutions into it: the separation of powers, the distinction between the state and civil society and the levels of (inter)national, regional and local government and public administration. Politics is broadly conceived as *the sum of acts in a community performed with the intention to organize and govern this community.*

The model proposed is a relatively neutral one. It is designed to be descriptive, not explanatory. The only assumption is a relational or network conception of politics and power in general. Politics and power are not viewed as properties of individuals or collectivities as such, but as properties of the dynamic relationships between them. These relationships are made of communicative actions aimed towards the acquisition, allocation and exchange of material and immaterial rules and resources (Giddens, 1984). In this chapter, these relationships are specified as relations of information and communication. Thus, the system-dynamic model presented here is held to be different from static or functionalist models of the political system like the classic one designed by David Easton (1953).

Taking this relational view of democracy as a point of departure one feels tempted to adopt a network theory of society and politics in general. In some of

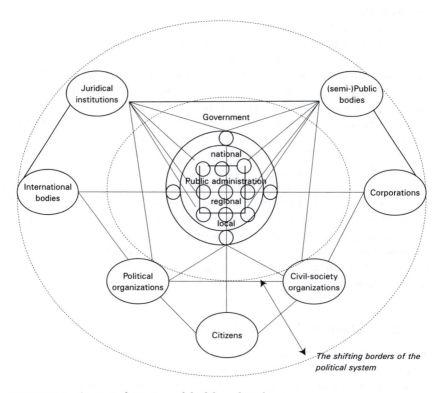

FIGURE 3.1   *A system-dynamic model of the political system*

these theories one can find a lot of explanatory power with regard to modern society (for instance Castells, 1996, 1997, 1998) and politics (Guéhenno, 1995), but one should not reify and exaggerate the increasing importance of networks to society and politics. So, according to Castells (1996: 198) modern economy and society *consist* of networks. They *are* the economy and the society. To our view networks increasingly shape the *organization* and *structure* of modern societies still consisting of individuals, groups and organizations with their agencies, rules, resources and (inter)relationships (van Dijk, 1991/1997, 1999a, 1999b).

On the political field Guéhenno predicts the end of the nation, politics and democracy as we know them, as they are replaced by a relational system of networks without a significant centre. Using social and media networks citizens are able to associate outside the artificial and increasingly irrelevant central institutions of traditional politics, as he calls them. Unfortunately, Guéhenno neglects the fact that networks have a centre and that they can be used by powerful central bureaucracies as well. Articulating and substantiating the formal dimension of networks (the connection), one overlooks their substance (the rules, resources and actions exchanged). And, contrary to McLuhan, the medium (the network) is *not* the message, at least not the whole message. The formal and technological properties of networks are important, but the actions and exchanges of people in these networks finally decide what happens.

The dynamic nature of the model offered here rests upon continuous change of the relationships between the actors and institutions it describes. As it represents a political system, they are relationships of power first of all. The central proposition in this chapter holds that political relationships are increasingly shaped and materialized by means of ICT. *The use of these means changes the relationships between parts or actors in the model.* It is still an open question which direction these changes will take. Two radically opposing tendencies happen to be possible: a centrifugal tendency and a centralizing one.

The Spread and Concentration of Politics

The most conspicuous development of the last three decades of the twentieth century is the decentralization or spread of politics from the modern nation state, with its institutions of the government and public administration, to other actors inside and outside the political system (see Figure 3.2). National institutional politics just can not be called the only political centre in society these days. Politics is spreading into society and beyond. This dispersion is called the *displacement of politics* (Beck, 1992). Other actors in the political system at large with its shifting boundaries – see Figure 3.1 – get involved. The system is getting *polycentric*. All centres are connected by relationships of information and communication supported by social and media networks. We will argue that ICT makes a large contribution to this development.

The first step in the displacement or dispersion of politics is the shift of power from government towards public administrations. The government is still viewed as 'the head' of society, but actually anyone can see that the executive has gained a lot of power in the twentieth century and is going to lead its own life in several respects. The traditional bureaucracy of the public administration has become a powerful technocracy or a so-called *infocracy* (Zuurmond, 1994) using the means of ICT much earlier and much stronger than the government itself, the parliament included. The use of ICT clearly strengthens the independent weight of public administration in relationship to the government it is supposed to serve. The normative power of traditional politics loses and technocracy takes over.

The second step in the displacement of politics is the current policy in Western democracies to make independent, outsource and privatize parts of the public administration. These moves have been made possible by information systems. Using them, the public administration keeps controlling the output of privatized organizations.

Subsequently, these organizations are forced to survive on a competitive market. In this situation market regulation easily overtakes political regulation. With the rise of neo-liberalism in the West the nation states have relinquished

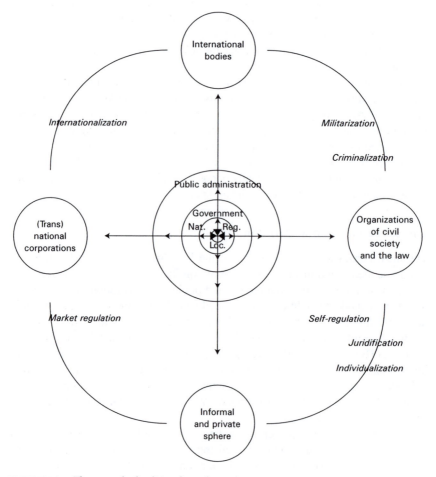

FIGURE 3.2   *The spread of politics from the nation state*

political power to decisions made by the market in general and the (trans)national corporations in particular. The boundless networks of ICT reinforce this development. Using these networks the transnational corporations, first of all, carry away economic decisions with a great political impact. Moreover, political decisions are dispersed and fragmented in this way. Mowshowitz (1992) speaks about *virtual feudalism*, a system clearly bypassing democratic constituencies. In virtual feudalism every transnational corporation forms its own kingdom, a pseudo-political authority that is not based on the control of territory but the control of international production facilities co-ordinated in networks, first of all networks of ICT. The nation state is also losing ground to international bodies giving up parts of its sovereignty and autonomy to them. In the European Union the member states transfer these parts to the Council of Ministers and the European Commission, among others backed by the so-called Schengen Information System. In the world at large we can observe the slowly increasing role of the Security Council of the United Nations, North Atlantic Treaty Organization (NATO), WTO and regional economic block organizations like NAFTA and ASEAN. The clearest case of the impact of ICT to this tendency is the power of the financial administration of the IMF and the World Bank. By means of their advanced information systems they are in a better position to calculate and control the budgets of developing countries than these countries themselves.

Finally, the nation state concedes political, economic and cultural power to regions and city states (Beck et al., 1994; Castells, 1997; Kaplan, 1996, 1998). ICT not only stimulates globalization but also regionalization. It supports scale extensions and scale reductions both being structural reactions to the growing complexity of social systems (van Dijk, 1991/1997, 1999b). Therefore, the locus of democratic control will also shift, in this case from national to international and regional bodies.

The most extreme case of a dispersion or displacement of politics is the break-up of nation states in civil wars. In a number of developing countries (mostly) one observes the rise of narco-states and territories controlled by warlords or ethnic and religious armies. In 1999 examples include Colombia, Somalia, Liberia, Sierra Leone, Congo, Angola, Afghanistan and Yugoslavia/Bosnia. This tendency together with attempts to control it by the NATO or the UN might lead to a militarization of international affairs. At the same time international criminal organizations dealing in drugs, pornography and weapons or engaging in financial fraud, prostitution or terrorism are gaining ground. The 'perverse connections' (Castells, 1998) of these organizations use advanced information technology just as diligently as their opponents: the military, the police and security organizations. The American National Security Agency (NSA), the Central Intelligence Agency (CIA), the Pentagon and others supervise every potential danger in the world with their electronic surveillance by technological superior satellite and terrestrial networks of ICT. Using advanced search engines they are able to spy on every exchange taking place on the Internet (Science and Technology Options Assessment, 1999).

These cases of a spread of politics are valued negatively in every conception of democracy (see below). Power is shifting to non-democratic, less democratic or even anti-democratic unaccountable forces. In this prospect the future of digital democracy looks dark, indeed. It means that digitalization and ICT might just as well bring the opposite of democracy. However, there are also cases of a displacement of politics to be valued positively in particular views of democracy. The first is the rise of oganizations of civil society like social and cultural institutions, semi-public agencies, non-governmental international organizations and all kinds of local pressure and interest groups. Among them one observes a shift from the traditional vested interests of civil society, like mainstream churches and labour movements, to the new identities and organizations of all kinds of localists, ethnic representatives, religious fundamentalists, environmentalists and feminists (Castells, 1997). So, the decline of interest for institutional politics to be observed in some (Western) countries, for instance in lower turnouts at elections, does not mean that the motivation of citizens to participate in political affairs more generally is also decreasing. Perhaps the ways, channels, culture and organization of political participation are 'only' changing. ICT networks certainly offer these new modes of politics all the opportunities and means of transmission required.

In the meantime the use of ICT is strengthening the existing tendencies of individualization, fragmentation and the rise of informal social networking in the Western countries as well. It strongly supports organizations and individuals in the self-regulation of their social and political affairs. In some views of democracy this is the most desirable way to go ahead (see below). Using the direct media of ICT citizens get the chance to address the centres of institutional politics instantly and, if they want so, bypass these centres altogether, perhaps even trying to create their own political system.

The last type of displacement of politics to be mentioned is the juridification of conflict management in general and the workings of the government and the public administration in particular. Both the government and the public administration reveal expanding problems in controlling or managing the rising complexity and diversity of society. This is the main reason why the jurisdiction has to fill the gaps increasingly. One of the effects is the growing importance of jurisprudence, in practice often getting more important than formal legislation. As laws, jurisprudence and regulation in general are summarized and made easily accessible on CD-Roms and information networks and the prospect of a more or less automatic administration of justice is taken seriously by a growing number of people, ICT is reinforcing the tendency of juridification as well.

Now we are able to return to our model of the political system. ICT *does not bring about* the centrifugal tendencies just described. This technology only *enables and reinforces* these tendencies having their own political, economic, social and cultural roots (this is a central thesis in van Dijk, 1999b). In the next section we will argue that they are also supported by a number of views of democracy. The centrifugal tendencies have been noticed by most observers. Less evident and accepted are the opposing tendencies of a concentration of politics in the state, that is the government and the public administration. However, there are at least three tendencies bearing this centralizing movement in the political system and, what is more, they are enabled by the same technology.

The first tendency is the *reaction of the nation state* being under pressure, striking back and using all means to defend its position. According to Held (1995) the autonomy of states is restricted and their sovereignty is affected, but they have not disappeared. States are still the most important *single* actors in the field of global and local relationships. Their share is not diminishing as an increasing number of problems of modern society are shifted on to their back: (the financial effects of) individualization, overpopulation, ageing, migration, criminalization, the constipation of infrastructure, the decay of the natural environment and structural employment. It can be observed that states are confronting these problems in a harder way and, among others, with the means of ICT. The registration systems of the public administration are getting more important for both citizens and the state itself. States are investing considerably more in these systems than in systems of citizen information and means of political participation. One does not have to talk about, or fear a so-called surveillance state (Burnham, 1983; Gandy, 1994; Lyon, 1995) to notice this development.

This development is related to a second one. The state *bureaucracy itself*, as a kind of state within the state, is not helplessly standing by the centrifugal tendencies just described. The bureaucracy modernizes. Most often it is one of the first organizations introducing ICT on a large scale. Traditional bureaucracy transforms into *infocracy*. This is a mode of organization using the networks of ICT for a clever combination of increased central control and decentralization of executive tasks. Apparently this mode makes organizations more 'flat' and actually it removes a lot of inefficient bureaucratic ways of working (Zuurmond, 1994). Connecting all kinds of networks and files with personal and other data in all sectors of the public administration and the government infocracy promises to create a highly efficient, transparent and machine-like state and also a transparent citizenry. After all, an increasing number of personal data are collected and linking files of these data in computer networks is a growing practice.

The third development also relates to the former ones. Reacting to the same centrifugal forces the state and institutional politics pack together creating some kind of *party state*. Increasingly the people serving the government, the public administration and (regularly governing) political parties exchange their places and policies among each other. This is even true for the big political parties as their active members, standing as candidates in elections, seem to aspire more to a career in government or the public administration than to serve as a representative of citizens in parliament. For many observers in society, political parties appear to have become a collection of office seekers. To reach this goal, parties transform themselves in electoral campaign organizations, exchanging their other traditional roles of being programmatic associations and bodies for citizens to organize themselves politically. Clearly, ICT serves this transformation. It is a powerful election technology (Newman, 1994; Rash, 1997; Selnow, 1994). However, it is not the only way it can serve political parties or candidates. ICT is also able to intermediate between political organizations and their members or voters for the purpose of association, discussion and programme building, that is the other traditional roles just mentioned. This chosen direction highly depends upon the view of democracy one supports.

The central argument in this chapter is that the opportunities and risks people expect from the application of new media in politics crucially depend upon their conception of democracy and upon the communication capacities of the new media. The assessment of the displacement and concentration of politics just described, of the liberating or oppressive characteristics of ICT in general and of the role of government, political parties and citizens in particular is defined by familiar views of democracy and freedom or central control in communications. In the next section the relationship between views on democracy and applications of ICT will be explained by means of six models of democracy. In the subsequent section the relationship between opportunities of communication and particular applications of ICT will be presented as four available patterns of communication.

Models of Democracy

The enormous diversity of conceptions of democracy can only be summarized by analytical means. A successful attempt to do this has been made by David Held in his *Models of Democracy* (1987). It is to be demonstrated that five of his nine ideal type models of democracy in history and a sixth one added are related to particular applications of ICT in politics. Held's other four models no longer apply or they appear to bear no clear contemporary relationship to applications of ICT. (They are called classical democracy, protective democracy, developmental democracy and democratic autonomy.) This means that six models may serve as an explanatory basis for views to be observed in the actual design and use of ICT in politics. These models are ideal types. Nevertheless one can demonstrate their validity in real applications of ICT in politics. See van Dijk (1996, 1997a) for a first attempt of empirical demonstration to be extended in other studies. This demonstration and empirical support typically follow three steps on every occasion. First, one has to analyse the arguments about the pros and cons of the use of ICT in politics among people engaged in the design and use of political applications of ICT. In these arguments they will reveal particular views on democracy to be listed among one or more models of democracy. This is the second step. Finally, one has to observe the favourite applications of ICT among these advocates of a particular model of democracy and see how they (suggest to) design and use these applications.

Two dimensions typify the differences in the models to be explained. First, what should be the goals and the means of democracy? Should its prime goal be *opinion formation* or *decision making*? In other words, is democracy primarily a matter of substantial input or of procedure (an output)? Secondly, should these goals be reached first of all by means of *representative* or *direct democracy*? The six models of democracy to be explained can be located in this two-dimensional analytical space (see Table 3.1).

A third distinction in the conceptions of democracy to be observed in the design and use of ICT in politics is the *political strategy* behind them. ICT may be used as a means to reinforce or reinvigorate the position of institutional politics in the system as a whole (concentration) or as a means to weaken this

TABLE 3.1   *Six models in two dimensions of political democracy*

Primary Goal	Opinion Formation	Decision Making
Primary Means		Legalist
Representative **Democracy**		Competitive
	Pluralist	
	Participatory	
	Libertarian	
Direct **Democracy**		Plebiscitary

position and to spread politics into society or outside the traditional national boundaries of the political system. In the first two models of democracy to be described below, one endorses the first strategy in the usage of ICT and in the last four models one backs the last-called.

Legalist Democracy

The first model is based upon the classical Western conception of democracy arising after the decline of the absolutist state in Western Europe. It is reflected in most contemporary constitutions. The first advocates of the legalist model were Locke (1690) and Montesquieu (1748). It is called legalist as it clearly is a procedural conception, regarding the constitution and the law as the foundations of democracy.

According to most contemporary constitutions the authority of the state is separated into three powers (the so-called trias politica) controlled by a system of checks and balances. Another important principle is majority rule. This rule is taken to be universal except for particular basic (freedom) rights of the citizen also being part of the constitution. In the legalist model democracy is a means to safeguard the freedom of individuals from authoritarian rule. It is not a goal in its own right. A system of representation is proposed. The heart of our political system is the judgement of heterogeneous interests and complex problems by representatives of the people. Direct democracy is rejected. Populism is feared. The power of every political institution and public administration has to be limited by the least possible, but effective rules. The system of politics and public administration has to be small and effective.

The basic assumption in this model concerning the meaning of ICT for the political system, to be observed in the arguments used by the supporters of this model, is that it should solve its presumed most basic problem: *information short-age*. The present crisis of the political system and the nation state is viewed as the crisis of institutions not sufficiently able to deal with the increasing complexity of the environment and the system itself, as information is lacking, caused by, among other reasons, the obstructions of traditional bureaucracy. The so-called gap between governors or administrators and citizens is also conceived as a kind of information shortage on both sides. Finally, all kinds of threats to the separation of powers and checks or balances in the system, most often caused by the rising power of the executive as compared to the legislative state, are accounted to deficiencies of information as well. It is a matter of sharing the power of information. The problem can be solved by an equal supply of the resources of information to the executive and to parliaments, municipal councils, political parties and other representatives.

So, following the legalist model it can be observed that the supporters of this model design and use the applications of ICT as a means to remove information shortages and to reinforce the present political system by more effective and efficient ways of information processing and organization. ICT is also applied to increase the transparency of the political system. By all these means the system would be capable to confront the problems of complexity.

Which are the favourite applications of ICT following this model of democracy? (See Table 3.2 for the list referred to in this chapter.) In this model they should serve two functions. First, they would have to supply more and better information to governors, administrators, representatives and citizens. Secondly, the interactivity of the new media might create a representative government open and responsive to the people, not directly controlled by the people. Both functions can only be fulfilled by applications of ICT under the control of governors, administrators and representatives. The ones preferred (according to van Dijk, 1996, 1997a) are computerized information campaigns, civic service and information centres, mass public information systems, registration systems for the government or the public administration and computer-assisted citizen enquiries. Registration and conversation media such as electronic polls or referenda and electronic debates between citizens are not adopted at all. They are deeply distrusted.

TABLE 3.2   *Applications of ICT in politics and democracy (arranged according to communication concepts explained below)*

ALLOCUTION
- computerized election campaigns
- computerized information campaigns
- computerized civic service and information centres

CONSULTATION
- mass public information systems
- advanced public information systems (the Internet, etc.)

REGISTRATION
- registration systems for government and public administration
- computer-assisted citizen enquiries
- electronic polls
- electronic referenda
- electronic elections

CONVERSATION
- bulletin board systems
- discussion lists
- electronic mail and teleconferencing
- electronic town halls
- group decision support systems

Competitive Democracy

The second model of democracy is also based on a procedural view of representative democracy. The election of representatives is considered to be the most important operation in the political system. The advocates of this model strongly reject the possibility of direct democracy. According to the best known designers of this model, Max Weber (1921) and Joseph Schumpeter (1942), direct democracy is impossible in large, complex and heterogeneous societies. A central role for bureaucracy, political parties and leaders with authority is inevitable. Politics has to be seen as an everlasting competition between parties and their leaders for the support of the voting public. In this way the best leaders and representatives are elected. This is the solution for the problems of complexity and the crisis of the political system. It is also the main difference as compared to the legalist model that is based on a balance of executive and legislative power and on responsive representation. In the competitive model, power is entrusted to leaders and experts in the executive power. They are supposed to rule the apparatus of state, to weigh matters and interests against each other, to solve conflicts with negotiations and to command authority. As leadership is emphasized in this model, it is called competitive-*elitist* by Held. In one respect this is not a good label for it: populism is one of the best known electoral strategies in this model.

The competitive model is practised first of all in presidential states and two-party systems. It is gaining popularity in contemporary politics as the role of persons and personalities in politics grows. This role was reinforced by old media such as television and will be strengthened once again by the audio-visual new media enabling all kinds of techniques in direct mail, marketing, targeting and visual manipulation.

The last-called facilities show the way to the design and use of ICT in politics according to this model. Preferably, ICT will be used in election and information campaigns. The voting public can be reached by a combination of television and interactive media serving as direct channels to target a selective audience of potential voters with differential political messages. In the second place, the interested public and the electoral base of political leaders and parties should have the opportunity to get information about views, stands and voting behaviour of their leaders and representatives. So they need access to mass and advanced public information systems. Finally, the registration systems of the government and the public administration are vital to a strong and efficient state authority. Other means of registration and conversation, such as electronic polls and town hall meetings, are only used for the benefit of the political leadership. Their resemblance to direct democracy is deceptive. For instance, the electronic polls, conferences and interactive television shows in the campaign of the American presidential candidate Ross Perot in 1992 and 1996 were means to boost the popularity of this leader in his competition with other candidates in the first place (Newman, 1994; Selnow, 1994).

Plebiscitary Democracy

The design and use of direct channels of communication between the political leaders and the citizenry can be transformed into an altogether different view on politics and democracy. In this case these channels are not used to strengthen the position of governors, politicians and administrators, but to amplify the voice of the citizenry. This is the central tenet of the plebiscitarian model of democracy. It is based on notions of direct democracy as a way of decision making. In the plebiscitarian model as few decisions as possible should be taken by political representatives and as many as possible by individual citizens by means of plebiscites. For these radical views the supposed democracy of the Athenian agora and the Roman forum, revived in some late-medieval Italian city states, have always been the prime source of inspiration.

The advent of ICT and the new interactive media stimulated a renaissance of plebliscitarian views in the United States from the 1960s onwards. The concept of *teledemocracy* was invented. Many local experiments have been waged (see Arterton, 1987). In these experiments old and new media were (re)designed and used to open channels between the local government or administration and individual citizens. Well-known American experimenters were Becker (1981) and Barber (1984). They set their hopes on the technical capacities of the new media. These would be able to remove the age-old practical barriers of direct democracy in a large, complex society. The political primacy of the government and institutional politics, already in a state of crisis, should not be saved at all costs. A political system based on a continuing registration of the peoples' will and, for some advocates, the will of consumers on the market as well, might be able to replace this role and this primacy.

Following the plebiscitarian model the logical preferences in ICT are registration systems of the votes and opinions of citizens. Telepolls, telereferenda and televotes by means of telephone and computer networks, two-way cable television or future information highways are the favourite applications. As a well-known criticism of this conception of democracy points at the risks of the individualization and atomization of the citizenry and a simplification of issues, conversation applications are added sometimes. This means the design of electronic town halls, teleconferencing and other new discussion channels. Of course, consultation of mass and advanced public information systems by citizens themselves cannot be discarded either. However, all systems filled with information by institutional politics are distrusted.

Pluralist Democracy

In the competitive, legalist and plebiscitarian models of democracy, nothing seems to exist between the state and the political representation on the one hand and the individual citizen on the other. In the pluralist model, to the contrary, attention is called to the role of the intermediary organizations and associations of civil society. Alexis de Tocqueville (1864) observed the conspicuous role of these organizations in the American democracy of his age. Robert Dahl (1956) did the same about a century later, depicting a political system based upon a representation of competing and negotiating interest, pressure, religious and ethnic groups or political parties. According to this view, the political system should consist of many centres of power and administration. A network conception of politics is favoured as opposed to the centralist views in the legalist and competitive models (a pyramid of representation). In the pluralist model, democracy means not the sovereign power of the majority but an always shifting coalition of minorities. The state should act as an arbiter. If it is supposed to put the different parties in an equal position by some kind of social policy, you have a progressive type of pluralist democracy. If it is supposed to refrain from doing this, you meet a conservative type of it. The pluralist model is a combination of direct and representative democracy. Representation is continually made, not only by professional politicians selected every four or five years, but also by organizational representatives. The constitutional state can be accepted, but its real substance and resources are produced by the intermediary organizations of civil society. In Western Europe and Eastern Asia a frequent result was some kind of corporatist system – a system organized into industrial and professional corporations serving as organs of political representation. A less extreme type of corporatist system is based on consensus building between organizations of employers and employees with a strong influence on government. The words 'substance' and 'resource' indicate that substantial democracy is preferred to a procedural conception. Ultimately, opinion formation in civil society, based on interests, discussions and all kinds of views, is more important for democracy than decision making in the central state.

Two characteristics of the new media are very attractive to this model of democracy. First, the multiplication of channels and stand-alone media supports the potential pluriformity of political information and discussion. Every view and every organization or association can have its say. They can reach their own and every other interested audience. Secondly, interactive communication networks perfectly fit to a 'horizontal' network conception of politics, in contrast to current 'vertical' broadcasting networks.

Following these two general preferences, it can be expected that all applications used to reinforce information and communication inside the organizations of civil society or between them will be favoured. These are applications to inform and to register their membership and external audiences like mass and advanced public information systems, registration systems and computerized self-surveys inside organizations. However, the most favourite instruments to a pluralist model of democracy are conversation systems inside or between organizations, associations and individual citizens: electronic mail, discussion lists, teleconferencing and decision support systems for the most complex problems (van Dijk, 1997a).

Participatory Democracy

The fifth model of democracy to be described is close to the pluralist model in several aspects. Just like pluralism it is a combination of representative and direct democracy. It is based on views of democracy emphasizing the substantial aspects and resources of democracy even more than the pluralist model. The big difference is the shift in attention from organizations to citizens. The support of *citizenship* is the central aim in the model of participatory democracy. Jean-Jeacques Rousseau is the first classical advocate of this model. He can be considered as a proponent of direct democracy, but not in its plebiscitarian brand. Rousseau's notion of the will of the people is not based upon the measurement of the views of individual citizens. Its purpose is the *development* of citizenship by means of collective discussion and education. Educating citizens as active members of the community is the primary aim in this model so clearly originating from the Enlightenment. For Rousseau, the peoples' will was not a sum of individual wills but some kind of totality revealing the sovereignty of the people as a collective. This totality had to be created in public meetings and legislative assemblies. One of the latter-day interpretations was the council or Soviet type of democracy covering a large part of the Marxist tradition. Here the totality was most often transformed in totalitarianism.

A necessary condition of this model of democracy is the presence of informed citizens. Present-day proponents of participatory democracy, such as Carole Pateman (1970) and C.B. Macpherson (1971), want to stimulate active citizenship. The centres of political power themselves should become more accessible to citizens. They should be responsive to their questions and certainly not only pose questions to them. The individualist bias of the plebiscitarian and competitive views is firmly opposed. Plebiscites, electronic or otherwise, are feared for the isolation of the individual citizen and the potential of central manipulation. Another threat is a separation of opinion polling and opinion formation. Polling in its own right is considered to be a poor and passive type of political participation directed by simple and prefabricated questions. A complete fragmentation of political practice is expected. Therefore collective opinion formation in discussions and educational contexts is preferred.

The logical consequence of this model of democracy is the option of ICT applications that are able to inform and activate the citizenry. Computerized information campaigns and mass public information systems have to be designed and supported in such a way that they help to narrow the gap between the 'information rich' and the 'information poor', otherwise the spontaneous development of ICT will widen it. Therefore the access and the user-friendliness of the new media should be improved. According to the participatory view this is the only way to really open up the political system to the mass of the citizenry.

Electronic discussion is taken as a second option. It is attractive as it could serve opinion formation, learning and active participation. Discussion lists on public computer networks, teleconferences and electronic town halls might be very useful. However, a first condition is that not only the social and intellectual elite will participate in them. A second one is their design as suitable instruments of discussion. Both conditions are badly fulfilled at this moment (see Chapters 9 and 10 in this book).

Libertarian Democracy

The last model of democracy to be discussed here is not developed by Held. His model of Democratic Autonomy looks similar, but actually it is much more to the political left than the Libertarian views to be described here. Libertarianism has appeared as a dominant model among the pioneers of the Internet community. This does not mean that the political views behind it are entirely new. Many observers have noticed the affinity of the Internet pioneers to the radical social movements of the 1960s and 1970s in most Western countries. These views range from classical anarchism and left-wing socialism to all kinds or brands of libertarianism. The last-called are most important among these views in the 1990s. Most prominently they are backed by the editors of the *Wired* magazine (Katz, 1997a; Kelly, 1994), the progress and Freedom Foundation in a *Magna Charta* written by Dyson and colleagues (1994) and the Electronic Frontier Foundation (Kapor, 1993) in the United States.

The libertarian model is close to the pluralist and plebiscitarian ones in several respects, as the chances of virtual communities, telepolling and teleconversation are hailed. What is special to it is the emphasis of autonomous politics by citizens in their own associations using the horizontal communication capabilities of ICT in general and the Internet in particular. In the most extreme view, it is held that institutional politics are obsolete and can be put aside by a new political reality collectively created in networks. This is the reason why it is often called apolitical or even anti-democratic by its opponents. The basic problem to be solved, according to this model, is the centralism, bureaucracy and obsoleteness of institutional politics which fail to live up to expectations (the primacy of politics) and are not able to solve the most important problems of modern society. A combination of 'Internet democracy' and a free-market economy will serve as a replacement. Some call this combination a 'Californian ideology' (Barbrook and Cameron, 1996), but actually it is a popular view among pioneers of the Internet in the whole Western world. It is well summarized by Katz (1997b: 49):

> In 'The Birth of a Digital Nation' I described a new 'postpolitical' community that blends the humanism of liberalism with the economic vitality of conservatism. I wrote that members of this group consistently reject both the interventionist dogma of the left and the intolerant ideology of the right. Instead, I argued, Digital Citizens embrace rationalism, revere civil liberties and free-market economics, and gravitate toward a moderated form of libertarianism.

To enable citizens to construct this 'New Digital Nation' some applications of ICT are vital. First, citizens have to be well-informed by advanced, free and unprejudiced information systems, particularly on the Internet. Secondly, they must be able to discuss this information in all kinds of teleconversation systems (news and discussion groups, chat rooms, interpersonal e-mail, etc). Finally, they must get in the position to give their opinion or to cast their vote in telepolls and televotes to be followed or at least taken seriously by institutional politics, as long as it has not passed away. These preferences imply that the libertarian model is both a substantial and a procedural conception of democracy and that it is much closer to direct than to representative democracy (see Table 3.1).

Concepts of Communication and the Future Direction of Digital Democracy

In the description of the six models of democracy, it must have become evident that the direction of the relations of information and communication between the actors of the political system is a decisive factor in the interpretation of potential venues in politics and democracy using means of ICT. Some hope and expect that this direction will be much more horizontal than before. Others think that it will remain primarily vertical, as the representation and administration of institutional politics can not be suspended that easily or should not be weakened in principle. Two sets of concepts in communication science are very helpful in the explanation of these potential directions. The first set consists of four so-called information traffic patterns: allocution, consultation, registration and conversation (concepts first coined in Dutch by Bordewijk and van Kaam, 1982 and internationalized by McQuail, 1987) and concepts of interactivity (Hacker and Todino, 1996; Hanssen and et al., 1996; Rafaeli, 1988; van Dijk, 1991/1997, 1999b; Williams et al., 1988). Both sets of concepts contain a dimension of power between (inter)actors. Therefore they might be feasible for political analysis.

The four information traffic patterns are appropriate, first of all, for a classification of the extremely diverging applications of new media in politics (see Table 3.2). *Allocution* is the most typical pattern in the traditional mass media and political communication practices of mass society. It is known as one-way traffic, which does not rule out an audience being active in selection, perception and cognition. Allocution is the simultaneous distribution of information to an audience of local units by a centre that serves as the source and decision agency for the information in respect of its subject matter, time and speed. In a traditional democracy, this pattern is realized in the dominant position of the centres of government or political administration and the mass media of the press and broadcasting. In digital democracy this pattern marks political news or advertising and government information to citizens using ICT (see Table 3.2). However, in its workings ICT produces a clear shift from allocution to consultation.

Consultation is the selection of information by (primarily) local units at a centre that remains its source. In traditional democracy the principal ways are the reference to papers, books, magazines or other sources of print and the oral council of public relations officers and political representatives and governors. In digital democracy a number of new media are added, first of all different kinds of public information systems most often using websites, cable channels, information pillars and CD-Roms.

Registration has always been one of the prime (re)sources of governments and public administrations (principally votes, opinions and basic information of inhabitants and real estate). Registration is the collection of information by a centre which determines the subject matter, time and speed of information sent by a number of local units who are the sources and sometimes take the initiative for this collection themselves to realize a transaction or reservation. In traditional democracy registration is a matter of printed forms, questionnaires, voting ballots, archives and visual observation. In digital democracy the means of registration are considerably stronger. Some views of democracy put their hopes on these new technical means, first of all legalist and plebiscitary democracy, each with a completely different perspective (an effective state versus direct democracy). So, otherwise very divergent applications, such as registration systems of the government and the public administration, computer-assisted citizen enquiries and electronic polls or referenda, are all marked by this pattern of information traffic.

The last information traffic pattern, *conversation*, spurs the imagination of those wishing to improve democracy even more. Conversation is an exchange of information by two or more local units, addressing a shared medium instead of a centre and determining the subject matter, time and speed of information and communication themselves. In traditional democracy conversation is a matter of political or public meetings and oral interpersonal exchanges between or among citizens, representatives and civil servants. In digital democracy the technical conversation systems of electronic mail or billboards, teleconferences and group decision support systems add to or replace these traditional oral exchanges.

The strongest appeal, perhaps, of digital democracy is the potential reinforcement of interactive politics between citizens, representatives, governors and civil servants. But what does interactivity actually mean, this so poorly conceived and often misused concept of social and communication science? Does interactivity equal the pattern of conversation, or are information retrieval (consultation), selection and feedback in digital broadcasting (allocution) and a reply in electronic questionnaires and transactions (registration) also interactive? The most promising explications of this concept in communication science identify a number of *levels of interactivity*. Rafaeli (1988) distinguishes three levels of communication: two-way (non-interactive) communication; reactive (or quasi-interactive) communication in which later messages refer to, or cohere with earlier ones; and finally fully interactive communication requiring that both sides react to each other. Williams and colleagues (1988) define interactivity as the degree to which (inter)actors have control over and are able to exchange roles in a mutual discourse. They link this definition to a degree of interactivity within systems. The lowest degree of interactivity is to be found in information retrieval systems. A higher degree is possible in the communication between people using a medium where both content and context can be manipulated by both sides. The highest degree of interactivity is to be experienced in face-to-face conversation.

Rafaeli (1988) and Hanssen et al. (1996) emphasize that interactivity is not (only) a medium characteristic. The concept should be freed from the classic linear sender-message-receiver model and replaced by a relational model. Mediated environments are created in the context of social and spatial environments. Modern experience is the collective sharing of information in all these environments taken together. van Dijk (1991/1997, 1999b) has made an attempt to dissect such an integrated concept of interactivity combining (objective) medium characteristics and (intersubjective) contextual applications. This model is based on four cumulative levels and dimensions of interactivity which are close to the levels described by Williams et al. (1988).

The first and most primitive level is the sheer existence or possibility of *two-way communication*, that is action and reaction (to reactions). This is the spatial dimension of interactivity. The second level is *synchronous communication*: clearly interactivity is damaged by asynchronous communication with too much time between action, reaction and reaction to reaction. This is the time dimension of interactivity. The third level is the degree of *control of communication* by the (inter)actors involved: the possibility of role exchange (sender and receiver) at will and at every time and a more or less equal determination of the content of communication. This is the dimension of action and control. The last and highest level of interactivity is the *intelligence of contexts and shared understanding* (Suchmann, 1987). This is the contextual and mental dimension. Until now this level has not been attained in the use of media (face-to-interface communication), but only in face-to-face communication.

Clearly, the level of interactivity in online political activities explains a large part of their popularity. In Figure 3.3 the frequency of the most important political activities on the Internet in 1997 are compared to their offline equivalents. In this figure one can see that most online political activities were no serious competitor to their offline equivalents in the year mentioned. This goes first of all for activities taking advantage of face-to-face interaction: attending meetings and rallies, contributing money, influencing others and discussing issues. Only relatively one-sided online acts of information exchange have become a serious alternative: distributing information, writing officials and signing petitions.

All current so-called interactive media get stuck somewhere at the second or third level of interactivity. To serve in a fully developed social interaction they have to be combined with some form of face-to-face communication that is able to attain the fourth level. This also goes for the applications of digital democracy. Most of them only offer asynchronous two-way communication with more control for the supplier, determining all possibilities of choice, than for the user who retrieves and reacts first of all. This has some fundamental consequences for the nature of digital democracy as will be explained in some of the following chapters. For instance, in Chapter 7 Hacker will deal with the question whether the White House CMC system enables 'real' interaction between the government and citizens and in Chapter 9 Jankowski and van Selm will look at the quality of interactivity in electronic debates.

On a higher level of abstraction levels of interactivity are related to a number of potential models of *digital* democracy in the future. With the concepts of interactivity and information traffic patterns in mind we are able to construct three

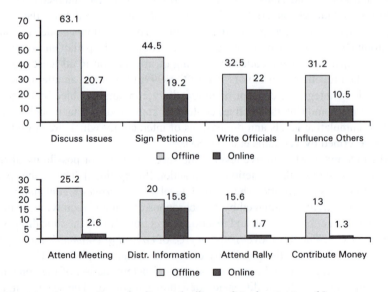

FIGURE 3.3 *A comparison of online and offline political activities of Internet users in 1997 (Source: GVU Centre's WWW Survey)*

possible models of future digital democracy. Once again they are ideal types. Presumably, our real future will be some kind of synthesis of parts of these models, just like real democracy in different political cultures is a shifting combination of or compromise between the six general models of democracy we have distinguished.

In the 1990s the most popular model of the future of democracy in the perspective of the information superhighway may be called the *Internet model*. In this model one expects political communication to become horizontal increasingly. The patterns of information and communication explored on the predominantly public, open, and uncontrolled Internet of the 1990s are viewed as the ones to be developed further. This network of networks is supposed to have no centre but only a countless number of intermediaries in sites and relatively neutral search engines and navigating systems. The patterns of conversation and consultation are dominant in this model. They offer citizens the opportunity to discuss all kinds of social and political affairs (by electronic mail, news and discussion groups or chat boxes) and retrieve all the public information needed on innumerable information sites and systems. A high level of interactivity, reaching at least level three (of control) in conversations is deemed to be possible. See the third model in Figure 3.4 below.

The Internet model is very attractive to people who support the spread of politics into society or who would even like to construct a complete alternative to present day institutional politics like the proponents of plebiscitarian or libertarian democracy. The supporters of a pluralist and participatory society might hope for the future strength of the Internet model as well. However, both accept a strong effort of the state and institutional politics, the first as the protective framework for their favourite field of action, civil society, and the second to protect and stimulate the part of the population that is excluded from participation.

Two other potential models are discussed less often in the perspectives of the future of digital democracy. Nevertheless they might take a much larger part of the design and the practice of politics on the information superhighway to come

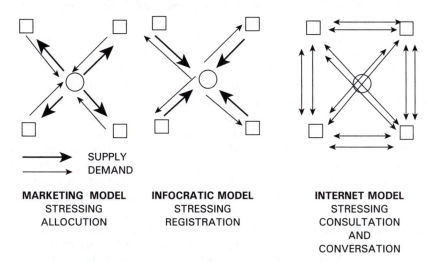

FIGURE 3.4   *Three models of information flow on the information superhighway*

than the supporters of the Internet model hope and expect. In the second part of the 1990s three clear trends are to be observed on the Internet. First, a strongly growing commercial supply and practice. Secondly, a general need for order, structure, transparency and moderation among users overwhelmed by information overload, junk or hate mail and unreliable information. Finally, we conceive strong attempts of governments and corporations to get a grip upon the so-called anarchy of the Internet. All this means that the Internet is on its way to become a 'normal' (mass) medium, with the only difference that it allows a higher level of interactivity than traditional mass media (van Dijk, 1997a). The question is what level of interactivity will be attained?

In the second model of the information superhighway, a *marketing model* we get the predominant commercial supply of interactive television, pay-per-view and advertisements on this highway as a broadband successor to the jamming Internet. This model corresponds much better to the present workings of the mass media in broadcasting, the press or telecommunications and the current practices of institutional politics. In this model only a weak feedback channel is added to the allocution of the traditional mass media, first of all broadcasting. See the first model in Figure 3.4. In this model the source and initiative of the overwhelming part of information produced remains with the (big) suppliers. Controlled feedback channels serve as a marketing tool for them, measuring and targeting selected audiences of consumers and citizens. On the economic market it would mean that so-called interactive services of information, entertainment and transaction take the larger part of traffic on the information superhighway. This is exactly what the large media corporations are trying to achieve at the end of the 1990s offering pay-TV, information services, advertisements, electronic commerce and games on the Internet and other networks. On the political market this model would mean the predominance of information campaigns of the government, the public administration, political parties and, first of all, every kind of corporate and civil pressure group. In times of election, actually almost continually, high-tech political campaigning or advertising would still shape the face of politics by means of a highly selective political marketing of the electorate.

The marketing model might be reinforced by a third one, which is strong as an ideal type of its own: an *infocratic model*. Selectivity and registration both belong to the strongest capacities of ICT. In public administrations, semi-public organizations, large corporations and political organizations powerful infocracies are growing as successors to traditional bureaucracies. Sometimes they compete with each other, sometimes they work together in exchanging information about citizens, consumers, employees and other relations. Together they might shape a surveillance society, not just a surveillance state (Castells, 1997; Gandy, 1994; Loudon, 1986; Lyon, 1994). The largest possible control of the organization and the market is their ultimate aim. In terms of the concept of information traffic patterns they will simply extend the current practice of many applications of ICT who transfer more information about local units to the centre of service and supply than the other way round. See the model in the middle of Figure 3.4. Anyway, this appears to be the case in the application of ICT by the governments and the public administrations of advanced Western countries. In the first place,

ICT is used to register the population and real estate, to collect taxes and to administer social services. Far behind lie the applications designed for public information supply, to open up and make transparent closed ways of government and administration for the citizens and to give them a say in governmental affairs.

The prime attention to registration is to be observed among all kinds of actors, views and interests in the political system. It certainly is not only a matter of surveying states and corporations. It is both present in the aims of direct marketing or market research at the service of institutional politics and in the presumed alternative political views of plebiscitary and libertarian democracy stressing the importance of telepolling and televoting. The substantial differences of political direct marketing and teledemocracy should not hide their structural similarities.

The actual future of politics and democracy on the information superhighway is likely to be a mixture of characteristics of these three ideal types constructed for the purpose of clarification. It is still open which model will acquire the strongest impact, just like this was claimed for the models of democracy above. Specific, national political cultures, like those in North America and Europe, reveal different combinations as will be explained in the next chapter.

This predominantely conceptual chapter started with a definition of digital democracy. Then the context of its growing practice was described. A network structure of the political system has been analysed as part of the structure of the network society at large (van Dijk, 1991/1997, 1999b; Castells, 1996, 1997, 1998). This structure enables a spread and a concentration of politics (and power) both supported by ICT. Both directions indicate evolutionary, rather than revolutionary developments of the political system. ICT amplifies existing tendencies first of all. In this chapter every potential tendency has been related to particular applications of ICT. The same was done with a large number of views on democracy. It was argued that the opportunities and risks assigned to digital democracy are related to longer existing models of democracy. Six models of democracy have been described and an attempt was made to show that they might help to explain particular preferences for applications and purposes of ICT in politics.

Not only views and preferences in politics and power can be related to applications of digital democracy. The same goes for views, patterns and models of communication. Four patterns of information or communication and four levels of interactivity can be related to particular preferences and applications of digital democracy. Together they shape the potential future structures of digital democracy.

References

Arterton, C.F. (1987) *Teledemocracy, Can Technology Protect Democracy?* Newbury Park/Beverly Hills/London/New Delhi: Sage.

Barber, B. (1984) *Strong Democracy: Participatory Democracy for a New Age.* Berkeley: University of California Press.

Barbrook, R. and Cameron, D. (1996) 'A Californian ideology', paper presented at Virtual Democracy: 9th Colloquium on Communication and Culture, 'Virtual Democracy', Prian, 10–14 April.

Beck, U. (1992) *Risk Society*. London/New Delhi: Sage.

Beck, U., Giddens, A. and Lash, S. (1994) *Reflexive Modernization: Politics, Tradition and Aesthetics in the Modern Social Order*. Stanford: Stanford University Press.

Becker, T. (1981) 'Teledemocracy: bringing power back to the people', *Futurist*, 15(6): 6–9.

Bordewijk, J. and Van Kaam, B. (1982) *Allocutie. Enkele gedachten over communi-catievrijheid in een bekabeld land*. Baarn: Bosch & Keuning.

Burnham, D. (1983) *The Rise of the Computer State*. London: Wiedenfield & Nicholson.

Castells, M. (1996) *The Information Age: Economy, Society and Culture Vol. 1, The Rise of the Network Society*. Cambridge, MA/Oxford, UK: Blackwell Publishers.

Castells, M. (1997) *The Power of Identity, The Information Age: Economy, Society and Culture Vol. II*. Cambridge, MA/Oxford, UK: Blackwell Publishers.

Castells, M. (1998) *End of Millennium, The Information Age: Economy, Society and Culture Vol. III*. Cambridge, MA/Oxford, UK: Blackwell Publishers.

Dahl, R. (1956) *A Preface to Democratic Theory*. Chicago: University of Chicago Press.

Dyson, E., Guilder, G., Keyworth, G. and Toffler, A. (1994) *A Magna Charta for the Information Age*. Washington: Progress and Freedom Foundation.

Easton, D. (1953) *The Political System. An Inquiry into the State of Political Science*. Chicago: University of Chicago Press.

Ferguson, M. (1990) 'Electronic media and the redefining of time and space', in M. Ferguson (ed.), *Public Communication, The New Imperatives*. London/Newbury Park: Sage.

Gandy, O. (1994) *The Panoptic Society*. Boulder, CO: Westview Press.

Giddens, A. (1984) *The Constitution of Society: Outline of the Theory of Structuration*. Cambridge: Polity Press.

Guéhenno, J.-M. (1995) *The End of the Nation-State*. Minneapolis: University of Minnesota Press. (Translation from: Guéhenno (1994) *La Fin de la Démocratie*. Paris: Editions Flamarions.)

Hacker, K. and Todino, M. (1996) 'Virtual democracy at the Clinton White House: an experiment in electronic democratization', *The Public/Javnost*, III(1): 71–86.

Hanssen, L., Jankowski, N. and Etienne, R. (1996) 'Interactivity from the perspective of communication studies', in N. Jankowski and L. Hanssen (eds), *Contours of Multimedia*. Luton: University of Luton Press, John Libbey Media.

Held, D. (1987) *Models of Democracy*. Cambridge: Polity Press.

Held, D. (1995) *Democracy and the Global Order, From the Modern State to Cosmo-politan Governance*. Cambridge: Polity Press.

Kaplan, R. (1996) *The Ends of the Earth, A Journey at the Dawn of the 21st Century*. New York: Random House.

Kaplan, R. (1998) *An Empire Wilderness, Travels into America's Future*. New York: Random House.

Kapor, M. (1993) 'Where is the digital highway really heading?' *Wired*, July/August: 53–9, 94.

Katz, J. (1997a) *Media Rants: Postpolitics in a Digital Nation*. San Francisco, CA: Hardwired.

Katz, J. (1997b) 'The birth of a digital nation', *Wired*, April.

Kelly, K. (1994) *Out of Control*. Reading, MA: Addison-Wesley.

Locke, J. (1690/1963) *Two Tracts on Government*. London: Cambridge University Press.

Loudon, K.C. (1986) *The Dossier Society (Comments on Democracy in an Information Society)*. New York: Columbia University Press.

Lyon, D. (1994) *The Electronic Eye: The Rise of Surveillance Society*. Cambridge: Polity Press.

Macpherson, C.B. (1977) *The Life and Times of Liberal Democracy*. Oxford: Oxford University Press.

McQuail, D. (1987) *Mass Communication Theory, An Introduction* (2nd edn). London/ Newbury Park: Sage.

de Montesquieu, C. (1748/1870) *De l'esprit des lois*. Paris: Garnier.

Mowshowitz, A. (1992) 'Virtual feudalism, a vision of political organisation in the information age', in P. Frissen, A. Koers and I. Snellen (eds), *Orwell of Athene?, Democratie en informetiesamenleving*. Den Haag: NOTA/SDU.

Newman, B.I. (1994) *The Marketing of the President. Political Marketing as Campaign Strategy*. Thousand Oaks/ London: Sage.

Pateman, C. (1970) *Participation and Democratic Theory*. Cambridge, UK: Cambridge University Press.

Rafaeli, S. (1988) 'Interactivity: from new media to communication', in R.P. Hawkins, J. Wiemann and S. Pingree (eds), *Advancing Communication Science*. Newbury Park/ Beverley Hills/London: Sage.

Rash, W. (1997) *Politics on the Nets, Wiring the Political Process*. New York: Freeman.

Schumpeter, J. (1942/1976) *Capitalism, Socialism and Democracy*. London: Allen & Unwin.

Science and Technology Options Assessment (1999) *Development of Surveillance Technology*. Brussels: Office for Official Publications of the European Communities.

Selnow, G.W. (1994) *High-tech Campaigns: Computer Technology in Political Communication*. Westport/London: Praeger.

Suchmann, L. (1987) *Plans and Situated Actions: The Problem of Human–Machine Communication*. Cambridge, NY: Simon & Schuster.

de Tocqueville, A. (1864) *De la Démocratie en Amérique*, Oeuvres Completes, Part 1–3. Paris: Alexis de 4 Lévy Frères.

van Dijk, J. (1991/1997) *De Netwerkmaatschappij, sociale aspecten van nieuwe media*. Houten, Zaventem: Bohn, Stafleu van Loghum (1st and 3rd edns; see 1999b for English edn).

van Dijk, J. (1996) 'Models of democracy, behind the design and use of ICT in politics', *The Public/Javnost*, III(1): 43–56.

van Dijk, J. (1997a) *Nieuwe Media en Politiek* (New Media and Politics). Houten/ Zaventem: Bohn, Stafleu van Loghum.

van Dijk, J. (1997b) 'The reality of virtual communities', *Trends in Communication*, 1: 39–63.

van Dijk, J. (1999a) 'The one-dimensional network society of Manuel Castells', *New Media and Society*, 1(1): 127–38.

van Dijk, J. (1999b) *The Network Society, Social Aspects of New Media*. London/ Thousand Oaks/New Delhi: Sage.

Weber, M. (1921) *Gesammelte Politische Schriften*. Tübingen: Mohr.

Williams, F., Rice, R.E. and Rogers, E. (1988) *Research Methods and the New Media*. New York: Free Press.

Zuurmond, A. (1994) 'The infocracy, a theoretical and empirical reorientation on Weber's idealtype of the rational legal bureaucracy in the information age', English summary of a Dutch PhD dissertation. The Hague: Phaedrus. pp. 318–28.

4

Digital Democracy and Political Systems

Martin Hagen

In 1989, at the end of his seminal work *Democracy and its Critics*, Robert Dahl suggested using an electronic 'minipopulus' to fight two of modern democracy's biggest problems, a less and less informed citizenry and a decline in political participation. With the help of telecommunications, a representative sample of citizens could meet online to deliberate major policy issues and thus create an 'attentive public' (Dahl, 1989: 338–41). Since then, the rapid development of computer-based information technology and its political applications have transformed this afterthought to democratic theory into a full-scale discussion of merits and problems of 'digital democracy', both in the US and Europe (as discussed in this book).

In this chapter, it will be asked how the specific national contexts in three countries, the United States, the United Kingdom and Germany, have an influence on how these nations think and feel about digital democracy and what this means for constructing concepts of digital democracy. The three nations are all democracies characterized through a representative form of government and a separation of powers between different branches of government. All three nations share a very high standard of socio-economic development and have experienced the 'information revolution' in similar ways (Kubicek et al., 1997).

However, despite sharing central features of democratic political systems, there are considerable differences in the structure and the culture, e.g. the values, norms and traditions, between the American, British and German political systems. One such difference is that the US is a presidential democracy, while the UK and Germany are parliamentary democracies. This means that in the latter case the executive branch is ruled by a prime minister or chancellor presiding over a cabinet elected by the majority faction in the legislature. Germany and the US are federal republics, while the UK is a constitutional monarchy. In Germany, the public administration system is a 'classic' one, marked by its strong adherence to the Weberian principles of modern public administrations, hierarchy, differentiation of labour and tasks, and competence. The public administration sector has been very stable and has outlived quite a few different political regimes, e.g. monarchy, totalitarian dictatorship and democracy. Alternatively, the US and the UK have political cultures formed by a stable political regime, in which public administrations have developed differently from that in Germany. In the first two countries, the 'citizenry regards the bureaucracy as performing in a service capacity and being properly subjected to firm political control, however expert the bureaucrat may be, and however intimately he may be involved in the consideration of policy alternatives. Partial myth though it is, the bureaucracy is viewed as the neutral agent of the political decision-makers' (Heady, 1995: 239).

Another difference exists with reference to the age of the democracy. The United States declared independence from Britain in 1776 and is one of the oldest democracies in the world. The contemporary British system of government has even older roots, dating back at least into the seventeenth century. Germany's democratic system of government is much younger, established in its present form only after the Second World War in 1949 for the western part and in 1990, after re-unification, for the eastern part, the former communist German Democratic Republic. The first democratic state in Germany, the Weimar Republic, was short-lived: established in 1919 after the First World War, it ended in political turmoil following the economic crisis of the late 1920s/early 1930s and was abolished with the take-over of the Nazi regime in 1933.

The Importance of National Contexts for the Theoretical Debate on Digital Democracy

Against simplistic views that the Internet will 'save' democracy (Clift, 1998: 20) most scholars agree that ICT will not change *per se* a political system (see, for example, Kubicek et al., 1997). Defenders of the latter can point to a long history of new ICT developments and raised hopes for a better-fitted democracy which have not been fully successful. Cable television sparked a similar debate about technically supported democracy very much like today's in the early 1970s (see Pool and Alexander, 1973; Smith, 1972), which continued until the 1990s, when the Internet fuelled the debate on digital democracy again.

By the end of the 1980s it was clear that democracy had not benefited much from cable TV or video cassettes (among others, see Arterton, 1987; Elshtain, 1982). Research on IT applications in politics and government has found overwhelming evidence that political, cultural, economic and social factors shape the forms and extents of political uses of computer technology. ICT do not change political institutions and processes by virtue of their mere existence. Rather, their use may amplify existing social behaviours and trends. This can be contributed to the fact that the development of technological applications is controlled by specific dominant interests. With its instrumental character, ICT becomes a trend-amplifier in a given area of application (Reese et al., 1979).

The role of actors and their interests has been decisive in the development of new applications (see Rogers and Malhotra, Chapter 2 in this book). Arterton concluded from an early survey on teledemocracy that a project's design and success is determined not by the technology employed but from the organizational choices made by the project initiators and their respective values and presumptions about participation (1988: 623).

The consequence which follows from this is that computer technology is not an independent force working for the better or worse of democracy, but it is amplifying other political trends at work or reinforces existing institutions. This also explains why on the whole, mostly those projects which have aimed to support traditional, well-established structures and processes of democratic systems have been more successful than those which have tried to employ new, transformative democratic ways and means (for examples see Abramson et al., 1988 and Tsagarousianou et al., 1998).

Because ICT is a trend-amplifier, concepts of digital democracy have to take into account current social, political, economic and cultural trends 'working' on the political system if they are to serve politicians and citizens in assessing benefits and costs of ICT-supported democratic structures and processes. This is as important as relating concepts of digital democracy to various normative models of democracies, such as competitive, plebiscitary, pluralist and participatory democracy (see van Dijk, Chapter 3 in this book). A comparison of different national contexts shows how specific political institutions and cultural trends shape various concepts of digital democracy.

The Political System in the US and Concepts of Digital Democracy

Political Participation and Institutional Reform

In the US, a continuous crisis in political participation lays the basis for most concepts of digital democracy (see Hagen, 1997). At the end of the twentieth century, voter turn-out has been very low. Not even half of the total population is participating in presidential elections and during off-year elections, the turn-out is even lower (see Flanigan and Zingale, 1998). To address this problem many scholars agree that one needs to foster the civic education of the individual and re-invigorate public discourse. The proponents of digital democracy have taken up this line of argument. Electronic means of communication can help the citizen become active in many different roles, when it transforms an ordinary citizen into 'a publisher, an eyewitness reporter, an advocate, an organizer, a student or teacher, and potential participant in a world-wide citizen-to-citizen conversation' (Rheingold, 1993).

Civic education, but also new forms of direct democracy, can help transform the *weak democracy* of the representative democracy into a strong democracy, as Benjamin Barber has argued in his influential book *Strong Democracy*. He suggested using electronic media to support the necessary re-vitalization of citizenship. In 1984, he called for electronic town meetings, a civic videotex service and a system of electronic balloting. Today, he has turned his attention to the use of the World Wide Web for similar purposes (Barber, 1997a).

In addition, 'futurologist' Alvin Toffler has long been arguing that only a series of direct-democratic institutional reforms can help overcome the sclerosis of the representative system: 'Using advanced computers, satellites, telephones, cable, polling techniques, and other tools, an educated citizenry can, for the first time in history, begin making many of its own political decisions' (Toffler, 1980: 430). First stated in 1980, these ideas were widely popularized in 1995, when they were championed by the then newly elected Speaker of the House, Newt Gingrich (Toffler and Toffler, 1995; see also PFF, 1994).

The US has seen a long series of practical experiments in electronically supported institutions of direct democracy. Political scientists and activists Ted Becker and Christa Daryl Slaton have been experimenting with them in various locations (Slaton, 1992); James Fishkin has been holding 'National Issues Conventions' in collaboration with PBS (Fishkin, 1995); and various scholars have tried different formats of electronic town meetings (Abramson, 1992; Elgin, 1993). Lastly, Ted Wachtel has suggested establishing a third chamber of Congress, through which the citizenry can involve themselves in the legislative process with the help of electronic media (Wachtel, 1992).

All of these ideas and applications can be interpreted as expressions of a long American tradition, which has accommodated several reforms inspired by direct democratic ideas. These can be traced from Jacksonian Democracy via the Progressive Movement to the modern presidential primaries and the recent popularity of direct democratic forms of participation, such as ballot initiatives and referenda. These movements reflect a hands-on perspective, which sees the democratic system as a long experiment or a laboratory which can be altered and modified according to changing circumstances.

Direct Communication Between Constituency and Representatives

A second reason for the appeal of new media in the political process is the overarching importance which is contributed to the direct communication between constituents and representatives. In the absence of strong parties, the representatives (including senators, mayors, governors and the President) are more or less independent 'political entrepreneurs', whose chances for re-election rely heavily on how well political accomplishments are communicated to the constituents. This is why techno-savvy representatives are very likely to experiment with every kind of new media. For example, senators Patrick Leahy and Edward Kennedy were very quick to adopt electronic bulletin boards, discussion groups and the World Wide Web to communicate with their constituencies (see Casey, 1996 for a detailed account). Very rapidly, the new way of communicating via the Internet has become one of the standards in the US Congress. This comes as no surprise as today about 40 per cent of the American public can be addressed effectively via the Internet (see Pew Research, 1999).

Part of the motive in using these means of communication comes from the representatives' intentions to portray themselves as being 'close to home'. ICT gives them a chance to bridge the gap many Americans see between themselves and the government. Even more so, politicians appreciate the symbolism of cyberspace. The Internet, the symbol of decentralization, anarchy and self-regulation is the perfect antithesis to the federal government, which is often pictured as the essence of centralization and hierarchy.

Absence of Public Broadcasting System

Next to the crisis in political participation and the need for institutional reforms, American concepts of digital democracy criticize the role mass media currently play in the American political system. The latter have always been viewed as an integral part of the American political system and its system of *checks and balances*, frequently justifying their description as the fourth branch of government.

In recent days, however, mass media coverage has been held responsible for the above mentioned crisis in political participation (Diamond and Silverman, 1995; Patterson, 1996). Television is accused of inappropriate, negative and cynical reporting of election campaigns and there is some evidence that broadcast mass media (including media formats such as *talk radio*) have caused an alienation of the American public from the political process. Some have argued that TV is to blame for the erosion of 'social capital', e.g. the willingness of people to engage in commonly shared, public activities – once the heart of the American polity, as many scholars since Alexis de Tocqueville have maintained (see Putnam, 1995). While empirical corroboration for this thesis is contestable, there can be no doubt that disenchantment with the role of traditional mass media in the political process is widespread in the US. Within this climate, the arrival of a new communication technology, such as the Internet, is prone to become a crystallization point of hope for a better and more meaningful political discourse in the public sphere.

Two of the more influential writers on concepts of digital democracy have made the call for public service broadcasting the core of their political agenda. Instead of letting political coverage be the subject of an exclusively commercial system, Benjamin Barber has suggested a 'Civic Communications Cooperative' (Barber, 1984: 277f.) and Lawrence Grossman, who was both the president of NBC News and PBS, would like to create a 'Federal Commission on Citizenship' (Grossman, 1995: 243), which would help to organize political arenas of discourse and to develop universally receivable, high-quality and civic-minded features. What these scholars are proposing in effect is a public broadcasting system, much like that which has been in place in Britain and Germany for a long time.

Technological Optimism, the Founding Fathers and the Frontier

The political culture of the United States has been very open to technology. Since the founding of the US, technology and democracy have always been regarded as being deeply intertwined, if not complementary to each other. The *founding fathers* regarded the creation of the republic as the creation of a governmental technology. Just as science helped to manage and control the forces of nature, democracy in its American conception was meant to be the appropriate means of managing and controlling the political life of the young republic. From its beginning, the newly created nation was a 'technological republic' (McWilliams, 1993). For this reason, new technologies have always been welcomed as 'technologies of freedom' (Pool, 1983) much more readily in the US than in Europe. This optimistic view toward technology helps the cause of digital democracy champions: 'If nothing else, America is a nation of button pushers. We love gadgets, dials, digital displays, mechanical operations', as Richard Hollander (1985: 29), a journalist interested in the use of interactive TV for direct democratic purposes, has observed.

In addition, concepts of digital democracy in the US refer to the *American creed*, a peculiar mixture of political theory and history of the US. The strong emphasis with which Thomas Jefferson underscored the importance of the availability of universal media for the creation of an 'informed citizenry' has been invoked by many proponents of digital democracy (see, for example, Arterton, 1987: 14; Dahl, 1989: 339; Grossman, 1995: 239). What is more, when new communication technology creates a 'cyberspace', it becomes a new 'frontier'. As with the West, it is natural for many proponents of digital democracy to believe that this new space needs to be 'civilized'. Steven Miller (1996), a communication policy specialist, named his analysis of relevant policy issues associated with the information revolution 'Civilizing Cyberspace', and an interest group championing freedom of speech and protection against privacy invasion as its political cause calls itself 'Electronic Frontier Foundation'. Thus, digital democracy in the US can trace a cultural link back to the *founding fathers* and the Westward expansion, which has helped it in gaining support among the American public.

Prevalence of Communitarian Ideals

Concepts of digital democracy have to be seen in close connection with a revitalization of communitarian ideals popularized by Michael Walzer, Amitai Etizioni and others. To a great degree, authors writing about community networks and their significance for democratic politics have underscored what they see as a mutually reinforcing relationship between networks and community organizing (Doheny-Farina, 1996; Ogden, 1994). Howard Rheingold, who described how members of the Bulletin-Board-System 'The WELL' (Whole Earth 'Lectronic Link) built their own community, which created not only a wealth of new friendships, but helped its members 'IRL' – in real life, too, believes that this creation of community can build the much missed *social capital* so yearned for by American political scientists and politicians:

> I suspect that one of the explanations for this phenomenon [i.e. virtual communities] is the hunger for community that grows in the breasts of people around the world as more and more informal public spaces disappear from our real lives. I also suspect that these new media attract colonies of enthusiasts because CMC enables people to do things with each other in new ways, and to do altogether new kinds of things – just as telegraphs, telephones, and televisions did. (Rheingold, 1993)

Following suit to the communitarian ideas, particular strands of democratic thought are also a motor behind the debate on digital democracy in the US. Much of it has originated in California, where two dreams of a new 'virtual class' have converged: the 'hippie' dream for a direct, self-empowered citizen government, and the 'yuppie' dream for material wealth, generally measured in dollars and stock values. Both dreams are an interpretation of the individual pursuit of happiness and meet in an anti-statist outlook on politics: the state is viewed as a potential threat both to individual freedom and the maximization of wealth. This normative outlook was labelled 'Californian Ideology' by Richard Barbrook and James Cameron (1996). The San Francisco-based authors James Brook and Ian Boal compare the shift from the material political sphere to *cyberspace* as a central reference point for political theory as a *virtual flight*, paralleling in cause and aim the *white flight* from the inner cities and their problems to a more 'civilized' – and ordered – suburbia:

The wish to leave body, time and place behind in search of electronic emulation of community does not accidentally intensify at a time when the space and time of everyday life have become so uncertain, unpleasant, and dangerous for so many – even if it is the people best insulated from risk who show the greatest fear. (Brook and Boal, 1995: IX)

The Political System in the UK and Concepts of Digital Democracy

Decentralization of Political and Administrative System

One of the biggest reforms in UK politics at the end of the twentieth century is the decentralization of the political system and the establishment of the Scottish Parliament and the Welsh Assembly. With the new institutions being implemented, it comes as no surprise that public interest groups have drawn up visions on how to use ICT in conducting parliamentary business. Recommendations by the John Wheatley Centre's report, 'A Parliament For the Millennium', suggest public access to parliament information, online possibilities for petitions, Parliamentary Television, and similar initiatives to support the representative institution of the Scottish Parliament (quoted in Coleman, 1998). In Wales, the New Wales Research Group has produced a report called 'A Vision For Wales: The Welsh Assembly, Electronic Government and Participatory Democracy in the Twenty First Century', with even farther reaching proposals, such as the remote linkage of Assembly Members in their Regional Offices, creating a digital parliament. Most important, the recommendations regarding the provision of information and public service delivery have resurfaced in the comprehensive study by the Parliamentary Office of Science and Technology, 'Electronic Government: Information Technology and the Citizen'.

Much of Britain's institutional politics in the 1990s is centred around a far-reaching effort to restructure the public service, mainly through separation between policy making and executive functions of agencies and subsequent privatization. The Thatcher administration initiated this far-reaching effort; but it is being continued under the 'New Labour' government of Tony Blair. This has led to an emphasis on market principles in the way government conducts business. Most significantly, the 'Citizen's Charter' issued by John Major did not spell out civil, but consumer rights, it aimed to extend 'access to official information, and to respond to *reasonable* requests for information except where disclosure would not be in the public interest' (Connell, 1996: 94; emphasis added). British electronic government initiatives, such as 'Government.direct' (Major administration) and 'Better Government' (Blair administration), are clearly more interested in the economic than in the democratic potential of ICT (Coleman, 1998). As is the case with their US counterpart, the 'Access America' initiative of Vice President Gore, these reform papers basically support the representative system of government and do not want to change institutions of political participation. Rather, they want to increase customer service, thus echoing the strong public *service* attitude of their respective public administration systems. This is also true for the Blair administration's initiative to deliver 25 per cent of all government transactions electronically by 2002. In a recent report on 'modernizing government', a further goal was stated that all dealings with government should be deliverable electronically by 2008 (*Modernising Government*, 1999). However, it is far from clear what this will actually mean and – if the goal is not reached – which services will really be delivered electronically.

It is characteristic of British work on the 'information polity' that they mix 'electronic service delivery' with issues of 'electronic democracy capabilities' (see Loader, 1997; Raab et al., 1996). Most notably, Christine Bellamy and John Taylor have developed a vision of 'consumer democracy' (Bellamy and Taylor, 1998: 90–118). Instead of organizing and instigating an already alienated and often cynical public for more participation, they suggest to deliver public services in the best way possible; this can be achieved through market-like powers, such as rights to choose between government products. The delivery of public services and the publication of government information to create improved customer–vendor relations between the government and public become crucial elements of the political process. The significance of this theory is the fact that the consumer democracy thesis neglects the sovereign capabilities of the people, which as citizens and voters can determine 'who gets what, when and how'. By voting or participating in political activities, social and other policies are decided. A mere 'customer' of public services might have some power in determining the quality of these services, but will not be able to decide normative and distributive questions, for example, who will be entitled to which benefits and how high these will be.

This kind of reasoning marks a decisive switch in perspective on the view of the democratic potential of new communication technology. While in the US concepts of digital democracy are developed in response to (perceived) deficiencies of the political system on the input side, e.g. that the representative system is not responsive enough to citizens' demands ('inputs'), in the UK, digital democracy is more closely linked to the perception that the democratic system and especially the public administration can no longer serve the needs of the customer, as the members of the population are predominantly thought of, e.g. that the political system is not responsive on the 'output' side.

Access to Information

Unlike in the US, where the 'freedom of information' paradigm has mandated the publication of numerous government publications, ranging from bills and reports of Congress to lists of financial contributors, and to candidates' campaigns, there has been a rather long history of government 'secrecy' in the UK. As many observers note, it is very hard in Britain to control or observe the inner working of the political system from the outside. Recent reforms of the Official Secrets Act have not changed this in principal (Sturm, 1996). The attempts to introduce 'Freedom of Information' legislation by the Blair government are an advance, but it is unclear if they will have a strong impact. As a result, the debate on digital democracy in the UK is concentrated on issues of access to information. This has inspired one of the more publicly noticeable initiatives, the UK Citizen Online Democracy project, which set up a web-site to discuss the Freedom of Information Act proposed by the Labour Government. Although public information is a prerequisite of political participation, by itself it is not likely to foster it. Also, as public information is viewed more and more as an asset and new ways are looked for to 'sell' this information to the private sector in order to generate more revenue, the focus on access to information lends itself more to output-oriented discussions of digital democracy than to input-oriented ones, focusing on voting or political activism.

Public Broadcasting System

In Britain there is a similar disenchantment with mass media as in the US, thus creating a similar incentive to discuss the use of alternative media (see Coleman, 1998; Connell, 1996). However, the hope US writers associate with public broadcasting systems cannot be replicated here. The BBC has been a public broadcasting system for a long time. In recent years, it has lost substantial market-share to private broadcasters, such as BSkyB and ITV. The commercialization, which is full-blown in the US, is thus a dominant trend in the UK as well. In this regard, hopes that a public broadcasting system can help the democratic process sound almost ironical, since the major problem of public broadcasting in the UK is how it can attract its viewership in competition with commercial TV and radio broadcasters and their more entertainment-oriented programmes.

US Influences

That digital democracy is a topic in the UK, then, is mostly due to the fact that the American debate has inspired attempts to copy practical initiatives. For example, UK Citizen Online Democracy is organized by people closely connected with 'Minnesota E-Democracy', a US online-forum which has pioneered online discussions and debates with candidates for office since the 1994 election (see Clift, 1998). Also, there have been some attempts to organize community networks, but they have never had the same focus on citizen participation as was seen in early US or other European, such as Dutch or Italian, projects (see Bryan et al., 1998). One should also note that Fishkin's experiments with 'Issues Conventions' were also practised in the UK, but his efforts seem to have gone by largely unnoticed by current discussions of online democracy in Britain. Bellamy and Taylor conclude: 'We have seen the electronic assistance to the processes of democracy has so far done little to disturb the politics of the UK. It is far easier to discern the deployment of the new technologies in the shoring up of old practices than it is to see that they offer profound challenges to established political institutions' (1998: 116).

The Political System in Germany and Concepts of Digital Democracy

Static Political System

The German parliamentary democracy, inaugurated in its present form after the Second World War, is a static polity. Whereas the US Constitution established only basic principles and left a lot of room for a dynamic evolution of democracy, the German political institutions set forth in the *Grundgesetz* are described in detail and have hardly ever been modified. After the ill-fated experience with the first German democratic state, the Weimar Republic, Germans are rather satisfied with their current system of government, commonly viewed as having guaranteed them an exceptionally peaceful and prosperous time for the last 50 years. After the fall of the Berlin Wall, this system was applied one-to-one to the five new 'Eastern' states (*Länder*); with virtually no constitutional reform (even though such changes were debated at the time, but with no subsequent action). Thus, any initiative trying to instil new practices of democracy in Germany will have to fight widespread reluctance against it.

After the failure of the Weimar Republic, which had comparatively strong elements of direct democracy, the founders of the West German state deliberately excluded any form of it in the basic law. Referenda had been abused in the Weimar Republic in a populist manner and did little to foster trust in democratic institutions. Therefore, the scepticism against direct democratic means on a national level is even more widespread in Germany than in the US and possibly the UK. (This, of course, is hard to measure in quantifiable terms, for data see Gabriel and Falter, 1996.)

It was left up to the *Länder* to include some possibilities for ballot initiatives and forms of direct democracy. Only in recent times, though, have these forms been used more widely, following a wake of successful campaigns on the *Länder*-level to institutionalize referenda (Roth, 1997). Local governments, which have been one of the experimental grounds for democracy in Germany, just like the states have been in the US, have almost all introduced the direct election of the mayor, as well as new instruments for public referenda. However, this comes at a time when the effective policy ground of local government has been severely limited by government budget cuts. It should also be noted that the German *Länder* have less authority than the US states. The result is that major policy decisions, such as taxes, are not left to be decided by any direct democratic means.

Party System and its Requirements for Political Communication

German elected representatives do not rely as heavily on direct communication with their constituency as their US counterparts. In a very complicated system, candidates for parliaments are almost exclusively chosen by parties, for which candidates run. This applies to candidates which represent a regional district in parliament, too. Parties are generally able to decide which candidate they will run in any district. The process of primaries and exclusive single-member representation in the US are unknown in Germany. The result of this system is that members of parliament have to communicate their achievements primarily to their own party leadership, who then will communicate it to the general public. Thus, there is less incentive for single representatives to communicate directly with the constituents.

Concepts of digital democracy developed in the US have not taken into account the problem ICT poses for strong political parties. American concepts of digital democracy almost universally view the power of ICT to help organize interest groups as a positive force. Yet, they fail to theorize about what happens when existing institutions, such as the parties in Germany and the UK, use this technology to foster their own political effectiveness, or, alternatively, when these parties fear losing political power to new, media-savvy political actors. Accordingly, German scholars have concentrated their analysis of the potential roles of ICT in a democracy on its effects on party government and political communication (Gellner and von Korff, 1998; Jarren, 1998).

As parties have to manage the transition from the industrial to the information age, they see themselves confronted with declining memberships and less and less social cohesion. Therefore, they must view attempts to empower citizens directly with the help of ICT with suspicion. This is especially true since a new type of politician, such as Chancellor Gerhard Schröder, is very effective in 'playing' the mass media, where, a lot of times, content follows second to style. ICT is mostly used to help the parties in their PR efforts and to provide a means of effective internal communication. Mainly, the large parties in Germany have been able to spend significant resources on Internet projects. Their effectiveness has not been evaluated with substantial empirical evidence, however. And since the Internet helps political extremists in their organizing too, there is an ambivalent attitude towards new media within the established parties.

Technological Scepticism
In addition, Germans in general are very sceptical about the benefits of new technology. While the information revolution is heralded much in the same way as it is in the US and the UK by politicians and business leaders, democratic uses of ICT play an insignificant role in their visions of the information age. New ICT in particular is not viewed as working to foster democracy only. Instead, Germany realized from firsthand experience how media can also be used for reinforcing less benign systems of government. The Nazi dictatorship employed the *Volksempfänger*, a radio set produced cheaply and readily available in the 1930s, very effectively to relay Hitler's propaganda directly to the people.

US Influences
Of course, political apathy and a decline in voter turn-outs create the same seedbed for concepts of digital democracy in Germany as in the US and the UK. The few theoretical works about digital democracy are inspired mostly by the American debate on digital democracy. They either point out negative consequences of ICT, such as information inequality, which have to be balanced against their positive effects (Buchstein, 1996), or they take the US debate as a cue to call for either more direct democratic practices (Leggewie, 1997) or more transparency of the political process (Kleinsteuber and Hagen, 1998).

Practical experiments with the use of ICT in democratic processes have been far and few between. One of the earliest examples of digital democracy projects in Germany, when Helmut Krauch used television to broadcast political debates and then tallied a public vote on the issue with the help of the telephone, was inspired by a similar project at Berkeley in which Krauch had participated before (see Krauch, 1972). Community networks which have helped so much to publicize the debate on digital democracy in the US, have not successfully been established on a larger scale. This can also be attributed to the different political cultures in both countries, most significantly the absent culture of community organizing in Germany (Kubicek and Wagner, 1998).

Conclusions

The basic problem all concepts of digital democracy address is the perceived crisis in political participation and the dysfunctional role of mass media in the political process. While in the UK and Germany there are similar problems with political participation and the role of mass media as in the US, concepts of digital democracy have not played the same part in the public discourse on the information age as they have in the US. This is because there are different institutional and cultural particularities in each political system, which either lend themselves favourably to ideas of digital democracy as in the US or are adverse to such debates as in the UK and Germany.

So far, the reality of the information age in all three countries is leading the majority of experts to very critical assessments of the high hopes proponents of digital democracy have raised. Community networks have given way to commercial Internet service providers. Citizen-oriented Web sites play an increasingly marginalized role compared to entertainment-oriented Web sites (see also Barber, 1997b). And in none of the three countries have digital democracy projects been implemented on a larger scale. The majority of political communication scientists in the US, the UK and Germany do not share the normative assumptions and values of digital democracy nor do they instil high hopes in the use of new communication technologies.

The explanation for the meagre results of practical experiments with ICT in terms of fostering political participation can be found in a large body of research which has shown that the extent to which an individual is politically active is largely dependent on socio-economic status and age, factors which cannot be affected easily by ICT. This is the so-called 'standard model' of political participation, formulated by Verba and Nie (1972). However, the form of the political activity is a function of the institutionally mandated and socially accepted forms of political participation, which range from voting across party and interest group membership to campaign work to participation in demonstrations and similar activities. If the political system is modified with the help of ICT, it can play a role in how, but not how much, people participate in the political process.

As technology does not cause, but merely amplifies social trends, the basic assumption of many concepts of digital democracy that traditional media, such as TV and newspapers, cause political disillusionment, much be rejected. The reason why all three nations are concerned with a sense of political disillusionment and mistrust in government to cope with current problems is more likely to be found in larger social trends of globalization. Two of these world-wide trends, the free flow of capital, resources and people around the globe and a multiplying of ideas, norms and values, present new challenges to existing political institutions which once were created to administer the industrial nation state and are now imperfectly suited to deal effectively with the consequences of globalization (see Beck, 1997).

ICT is welcomed warmly in the US, since there exists a culture which has long believed in the 'technological fix' of the political system. High value is seen in direct communication between political representatives and constituents, and the absence of a public broadcasting system is an additional impetus for hopeful concepts of digital democracy. When traditional media, such as TV and radio, cannot be 'un-commercialized', maybe new media can be used in more 'civic-oriented' ways, whatever this actually means. Also, the anti-statist political culture and the prevalence of communitarian ideas are congruent with the non-hierarchical uses of computer networks, which prevailed in American universities and community networks at least in the early and mid-1990s.

In the UK, the decentralization of the political system, the creation of more independent regional parliaments and a deliberate attempt by the administration to use ICT in its campaign to better the customer service quality of public administrations are the only trends to which concepts of digital democracy can connect. Therefore, the debate on digital democracy is not focused on creating new possibilities for political participation. New forms of citizen's input are hardly discussed in the framework of direct vs. representative democracy, but mostly in association with its public service delivery orientation. Also, since the public broadcasting system is facing serious competition from commercial media and has to cope with the comparatively less appeal of 'informative' programming, there is hardly any reason why there should be hope in new ICT as alternative media.

In Germany, a more state-centrist culture and especially the central role parties play in governing the country create yet a third political–institutional context for concepts of digital democracy. Here, they seem to be only relevant in so far as they refer to possibilities of strengthening (or weakening) large organizations, such as parties or unions. From its historical experience, abuse of new media is very well known in Germany, and thus scepticism about the democratic uses of new media prevails.

Therefore, as was shown in this chapter, in discussing digital democracy one needs to place concepts of digital democracy in the context of national political systems and cultures. Key contexts to consider are the institutional forms of representation, the role of political parties, current and past roles of mass media, especially in regard to public broadcasting systems, and attitudes toward technology. The better promoters of concepts of digital democracy try to take into account theories of democracy and actual political systems, the more such concepts are likely to become guiding principles for democratic uses of ICT in the information age.

Note

The author would like to thank the editors, all participants of the Euricom Colloquium in Piran, Hans J. Kleinsteuber and Herbert Kubicek for criticizing earlier versions of this article, as well as his wife, Kelly Hagen, for correcting it.

References

Abramson, J. (1992) *Democratic Designs for Electronic Town Meetings*. Washington, DC: The Aspen Institute Communication and Society.

Abramson, J.B., Arterton, F.C. and Orren, G.R. (1988) *The Electronic Commonwealth: The Impact of New Media Technologies on Democratic Politics*. New York: Basic Books.

Arterton, F.C. (1987) *Teledemocracy: Can Technology Protect Democracy?* Newbury Park: Sage.

Arterton, F.C. (1988) 'Political participation and "Teledemocracy"', *PS: Political Science and Politics*, 620–7.

Barber, B.R. (1984) *Strong Democracy: Participatory Politics for a New Age*. Berkeley: University of California Press.

Barber, B.R. (1997a) 'A state of "electronically enhanced democracy": a survey of the internet', report for the Markle Foundation submitted by the Walt Whitman Center for the Culture and Politics of Democracy. New Brunswick: Rutgers University.

Barber, B.R. (1997b) 'The new telecommunications technology: endless frontier or the end of democracy?', *Constellations*, 2: 208–28.

Barbrook, R. and Cameron, A. (1996) 'The Californian ideology', manuscript, University of Westminster. (Presented at EURICOM conference, Piran, Slovenia, 10–14 April.)

Beck, U. (1997) *Was ist Globalisierung?*, Frankfurt/Main: Suhrkamp.

Bellamy, C. and Taylor, J.A. (1998) *Governing in the Information Age*. Buckingham: Open University Press.

Brook, J. and Boal, I.A. (eds) (1995) *Resisting the Virtual Life: The Culture and Politics of Information*. San Francisco: City Lights.

Bryan, C., Tsagarousianou, R. and Tambini, D. (1998) 'Electronic democracy and the civic networking movement in context', in R. Tsagarousianou, C. Bryan and D. Tambini, *Cyberdemocracy: Technology, Cities, and Civic Networks*. London: Routledge. pp. 1–17.

Buchstein, H. (1996) 'Bittere bytes: cyberbürger und demokratietheorie', *Deutsche Zeitschrift für Philosophie*, 4: 583–607.

Casey, C. (1996) *The HILL On The NET: Congress Enters the Information Age*. Boston: AP Professional.

Clift, S. (1998) 'Democracy is online', *OnTheInternet* (Internet Society), March/April: 20–7.

Coleman, S. (1998) 'Can the new media invigorate democracy?', manuscript, London.

Connell, I. (1996) 'Cyberspace: the continuation of political education by other means', *Javnost/The Public*, 1: 87–102.

Dahl, R.A. (1989) *Democracy and its Critics*. New Haven, London: Yale University Press.

Diamond, E. and Silverman, R.A. (1995) *White House to Your House: Media and Politics in Virtual America*. Cambridge, MA/London: MIT Press.

Döring, H. (1996) 'Bürger und politik – die "Civic Culture" im Wandel', in H. Kastendiek, K. Rohe and A. Volle (eds), *Länderbericht Großbritannien*, Schriftenreihe Band 326. Bonn: Bundeszentrale für politische Bildung.

Elgin, D. (1993) 'Revitalizing democracy through electronic town meetings', *Spectrum. The Journal of State Government* (Lexington, KY), Spring: 6–13.

Elshtain, J.B. (1982) 'Democracy and the QUBE tube', *The Nation*, August 7–14: 108–10.

Flanigan, W.H. and Zingale, N.H. (1998) *Political Behavior of the American Electorate* (9th edn). Washington, DC: CQ Press.

Fishkin, J. (1995) *The Voice of the People: Public Opinion and Democracy*. New Haven: Yale University Press.

Gabriel, O.W. and Falter, J.W. (1996) *Wahlen und politische Einstellungen in westlichen Demokratien*. Frankfurt/Main: Lang.

Gellner, W. and Korff, F. von (eds) (1998) *Demokratie und Internet*. Baden-Baden: Nomos.

Grossman, L.K. (1995) *The Electronic Republic: Reshaping Democracy in the Information Age*. New York: Viking (20th Century Fund).

Hagen, M. (1997) *Elektronische Demokratie: Computernetzwerke und politische Theorie in den USA*. Hamburg: Lit-Verlag.

Heady, F. (1995) *Public Administration: A Comparative Perspective* (5th edn). New York: Marcel Dekker.

Hollander, R. (1985) *Video Democracy: The Vote-From-Home Revolution*. Mt Airy, MD: Lomond.

Jarren, O. (1998) 'Internet – neue Chancen für die politische Kommunikation?', *Aus Politik und Zeitgeschichte*, B40/98: 13–21.

Kleinsteuber, H.J. (ed.) (1996) *Der 'Information Superhighway': Amerikanische Visionen und Erfahrungen*. Opladen: Westdeutscher Verlag.

Kleinsteuber, H.J. and Hagen, M. (1998) '"Elektronische Demokratie": Ansätze und Argumente in USA und Deutschland', *Zeitschrift für Parlamentsfragen*, 1: 128–42.

Krauch, H. (1972) *Computer-Demokratie*. Düsseldorf: VDI Verlag.

Kubicek, H., Dutton, W.H. and Williams, R. (eds) (1997) *The Social Shaping of Information Superhighways*. Frankfurt/New York: Campus/St Martin's Press.

Kubicek, H. and Wagner, Rose M.M. (1998) 'Community networks in a generational perspective', paper presented at the workshop 'Designing Across Borders: The Community Design of Community Networks', Participatory Design Conference (PDC), Seattle, WA, USA, 12–14 Nov.

Leggewie, C. (1997) 'Netizens oder: der gut informierte Bürger heute. Ein neuer Strukturwandel der Öffentlichkeit?', *Transit*, 13, Medien und Demokratie: 3–25.

Loader, B. (ed.) (1997) *The Governance of Cyberspace: Politics, Technology, and Global Restructuring*. London: Routledge.

McWilliams, W.C. (1993) 'Science and freedom: America as the technological republic', in A. Melzer, J. Weinberger and M.R. Zinman (eds), *Technology in the Western Political Tradition*. Ithaca, NY: Cornell University Press. pp. 85–108.

Miller, S.E. (1996) *Civilizing Cyberspace: Policy, Power, and the Information Superhighway*. New York: ACM Press.

Modernising Government (1999) Cm 4310. London.

Ogden, M.R. (1994) 'Politics in a parallel universe. Is there a future for cyberdemocracy?', *Futures*, 26(7): 713–29.

Patterson, T.E. (1996) 'Bad news, bad governance', *Annals*, AAPSS, 546, July: 97–108.

Pew Research (The Pew Research Center For The People & The Press) (1999) 'The Internet News Audience Goes Ordinary', manuscript, Washington, DC: Pew Research Center.

PFF (Progress and Freedom Foundation [E. Dyson, G. Gilder, G. Keyworth and A. Toffler]) (1994) *A Magna Charta for the Information Age*. Washington: Progress and Freedom Foundation.

Pool, I. de Sola (1983) *Technologies of Freedom*. Cambridge, MA: MIT Press.

Pool, I. de Sola and Alexander, H.E. (1973) 'Politics in a wired nation', in I. de Sola Pool (ed.), *Talking Back*. Cambridge, MA: MIT Press.

Putnam, R.D. (1995) 'Bowling alone: America's declining social capital', *Journal of Democracy*, 6(1): 65–78.

Raab, C. et al. (1996) 'The information polity: electronic democracy, privacy, and surveillance', in W. Dutton (ed.), *Information and Communication Technology*. Oxford: Oxford University Press. pp. 283–99.

Reese, J., Kubicek, H., Lange, B., Lutterbeck, B., Reese, U. (1979) *Gefahren der informationstechnologischen Entwicklung*. Frankfurt/New York: Campus.

Rheingold, H. (1993) *The Virtual Community*. New York: HarperCollins.

Roth, R. (1997) 'Die kommune als ort der bürgerbeteiligung', in A. Klein and R. Schmalz-Bruns (eds), *Politische Beteiligung und Bürgerengagement in Deutschland*, Schriftenreihe Band 347. Bonn: Bundeszentrale für politische Bildung. pp. 404–42.

Slaton, C.D. (1992) *Televote: Expanding Citizen Participation in the Quantum Age.* New York: Praeger.

Smith, R.L. (1972) *The Wired Nation. Cable TV: the Electronic Communications Highway.* New York: Harper & Row.

Sturm, R. (1996) 'Staatsordnung und politisches system', in H. Kastendiek, K. Rohe and A. Volle (eds), *Länderbericht Großbritannien*, Schriftenreihe Band 326. Bonn: Bundeszentrale für politische Bildung. pp. 185–212.

Toffler, A. (1980) *The Third Wave.* New York: Bantam.

Toffler, A. and Toffler, H. (1995) *Creating a New Civilization: The Politics of the Third Wave.* Atlanta: Turner.

Tsagarousianou, R., Tambini, D. and Bryan, C. (1998) *Cyberdemocracy: Technology, Cities, and Civic Networks.* London: Routledge.

Verba, S. and Nie, N. (1972) *Participation in America: Political Democracy and Social Equality.* Chicago: University of Chicago Press.

Wachtel, T. (1992) *The Electronic Congress: A Blueprint for Participatory Democracy.* Pipersville, PA: Pipers Press.

5

Structural Transformations of the Public Sphere

John Keane

The term 'public sphere' is among the most popular within contemporary studies of media and politics – indeed, it is so much part of their common sense that its genealogy is normally overlooked. Broadly speaking, in modern times there have been three overlapping historical phases in the invention, refinement and popularization of the concept and such 'partner' terms as public opinion, public life and the public good. It is imperative to recall this genealogy, for an understanding of the history of these terms deepens our appreciation of their multiple meanings, empirical utility and normative potential – and the political pitfalls of using early modern terms such as 'the public sphere' in the much-changed circumstances of the late twentieth century.

The modern prominence of the public sphere concept was initially bound up with the struggle against despotic states in the European region. The language of 'the public', 'public virtue' and 'public opinion' was a weapon in support of 'liberty of the press' and other publicly shared freedoms. Talk of 'the public' was directed against monarchs and courts suspected of acting arbitrarily, abusing their power, and furthering their 'private', selfish interests at the expense of the realm. During the seventeenth and eighteenth centuries, the normative ideal of the public sphere – a realm of life in which citizens invented their identities within the shadows of state power – was a central theme of the republican politics of the middling classes. Republicans like the 'Commonwealthmen' simultaneously looked back to the Roman republic (and sometimes to the Greek polis) and forward to a world without mean-spirited executive power, standing armies and clericalism (Robbins, 1961). Republicans were sharply critical of the ways in which absolutism induced apathy among its subjects, promoted conformity in matters of religion and statecraft, and corrupted its rulers, to the point (as Molesworth complained in his attack on Danish absolutism) where even the town clocks of Copenhagen chimed in unison with the time-pieces of the palace. Republicans accordingly emphasized the importance of cultivating public virtue and public spirit. They yearned for the radical reform of existing polities by means of the right of free expression of citizens and constitutional devices to secure the rule of law, mixed government and freedom from 'party' and 'faction' – especially that promoting internal dissension and the 'private' designs of monarchs, ministers and ambitious men of wealth.

With the growing power and dynamism of modern capitalist economies, the ideal of the public sphere came to be used principally to criticize the monopoly grip of commodity production and consumption upon areas of life considered to be in need of protection from considerations of rationally calculated profit and loss. *Public Life and Late Capitalism* (Keane, 1984) traced the growing concern within twentieth-century German political thought, especially after the death of Max Weber, to define and to protect a public sphere against the expanding power of organized capitalism, advertising agencies and other professional bodies bent on divining 'public opinion' and making it speak in their favour. Ferdinand Tonnies' *Kritik der öffentlichen Meinung* (1922) highlighted the dangers of deifying public opinion in an era in which organized interests, especially the capitalist press, profited from its manipulation. Karl Jaspers (1969) defended the value of 'unlimited communication' in an age of market-driven, rational calculation. Hannah Arendt's *Vita Activa* (1960) mourned the modern loss of public life, understood as the capacity of citizens to speak and to interact for the purpose of defining and redefining how they wish to live together in common; according to Arendt, such public interaction has been gradually corroded in modern times by the acid of consumerism trickling through a society of labourers ignorant of the joys and freedoms that result from communicating in public about matters of public importance. Jürgen Habermas' *Strukturwandel der Öffentlichkeit* (1962) refined and extended this pessimistic thesis by tracing the rise in early modern Europe of a bourgeois public sphere and the subsequent 'replacement of a reading public that debated critically about matters of culture by the mass public of culture consumers' (1962: 162). Common to each of these interpretations of public life is the insistence that commodity-structured economies encourage moral selfishness and disregard of the public good; maximize the time citizens are compulsorily bound to paid labour, thereby making it difficult for them to be involved as citizens in public life; and promote ignorance and deception through profit-driven media manipulation.

The first two phases of defining and defending the public sphere highlighted, respectively, the uniquely modern problems of territorially defined state power unaccountable to its citizens and the business-biased egoism of organized market capitalism. During the third, most recent phase of usage of the public sphere concept, these twin problems, characteristic of modern societies, are simultaneously emphasized and the public sphere ideal is linked to the institution of public service broadcasting. This is seen to have an elective affinity with public life and to be the best guarantee of its survival in the era of state-organized, consumer capitalism.

The 'Westminster School' of Nicholas Garnham, Paddy Scannell and other researchers has arguably done most to invent, refine and popularize this third version of the theory of the public sphere. Among its most influential contributions is a series of essays by Nicholas Garnham, who has proposed the thesis that debate about broadcasting policy has hitherto been conducted too narrowly in terms of the state/market dualism (Garnham, 1990). Borrowing explicitly from Habermas (who curiously ignored the public service broadcasting model), Garnham argues for a third term, 'the public sphere', for the analytic-empirical and normative purpose of identifying a 'space for a rational and universalistic politics distinct from both the economy and the state' (1990: 107). Garnham insists that the best guarantor of such a politics is the public service broadcasting model, which is designed to mediate and counterbalance state and corporate power and can in fact do so because it is bound by neither the imperatives of maximization of political power nor the maximization of profit. While Garnham admits that the actual practice of public service broadcasting is an imperfect realization of the Habermasian ideal of a public sphere of deliberating citizens, he is adamant about its superiority.

> to the market as a means of providing all citizens, whatever their wealth or geographical location, equal access to a wide range of high-quality entertainment, information and education, and as a means of ensuring that the aim of the programme producer is the satisfaction of a range of audience tastes rather than only those tastes that show the largest profit. (1990: 120)

Market-driven media, Garnham insists, are inimical to public life. In stark contrast to public service broadcasting, market-driven media narrow the scope of what it is possible to say publicly. The number of enterprises which control (or strongly influence) the production and circulation of information and culture is reduced; inequitable power relationships develop between dominant, metropolitan enterprises and cultures and subordinate and peripheral identities; and these market-produced inequalities in turn reinforce deep-rooted social inequalities, which future market-driven technological change in the field of communications will almost certainly deepen – unless the castles of public service broadcasting are protected through guaranteed tax-based funding.

The Decay of Public Service Broadcasting

The proposed defence of the public sphere through public service media accurately spots the limits of market rhetoric and practice. It is moreover an important contribution to the task of clarifying and amplifying publicly felt concern about the future of electronic media in the old democracies of such countries as Britain, France and the Netherlands. The proposed defence of public life also serves as a vital reminder of the important practical achievements of public service media. The twentieth-century project of providing a service of mixed programmes on national radio and television channels, available to all citizens, often in the face of severe technical problems and pressing financial constraints – as Garnham and others have argued – has kept alive public spirit and widened the horizons of citizens' awareness of the world. For half a century, the 'provision of basic services' (*Grundversorgung* as the German Federal Constitutional Court put it) helped to decommodify electronic media. It reduced the role of budget-conscious accounting and corporate greed as the principal qualities necessary to media management.

The public service model also enforced specific national rules covering such matters as the amount and type of advertising, political access, 'balanced' news coverage, and quotes of foreign programming. It succeeded for a time in protecting employment levels in the national broadcasting industries of countries such as the Netherlands, Canada, Norway, Britain and the Federal Republic of Germany. The public service model – partly in response to challenges posed by market-based tabloid media – also legitimized the presence of ordinary citizens in programmes dealing with controversial issues. It helped to make respectable vernacular styles by publicizing the pleasures of ordinariness and creating entertainment out of citizens playing games, talking about their private experiences, or immersing themselves in events as disparate as tennis matches, skiing competitions, religious ceremonies, and dancing to rap, rock and reggae.

While these achievements of the public service model are impressive, there are major problems inherent in the argument that existing public service media are a bulwark of the public sphere. For reasons of space, I shall set aside questions about the fault lines evident in Garnham's attempt to synthesize an originally seventeenth- and eighteenth-century ideal with the peculiarly twentieth-century practice of electronic broadcasting. I also want deliberately to overlook another bundle of problems, internal to Garnham's account, such as his silence about the rise and survival of public controversy within the market-dominated sector of print and broadcasting media, or the question of whether a 'rational' and universalistic politics was descriptive of either the intended aim or the actual practice of public service broadcasting in its heyday. I shall instead concentrate for a moment on the mounting difficulties faced by contemporary public service broadcasting and, hence, on the perilous strategy of attempting to tie the fortunes of the public sphere ideal to an ailing institution.

There is today a long-term crisis settling on the public service model. The status quo is ceasing to be an option. Public service media in Europe and elsewhere are slipping and sliding into a profound identity crisis – the same identity crisis that from the beginning has dogged American public service media, which have suffered permanent insecurities about their financial basis, legal status and public role. Deeply uncertain about their sources of funding and the scope and nature of their contemporary political role, European public service media are enmeshed in a wider political problem, evident in all the old democracies, in which political parties, professional associations, trades unions, churches and other means of defining, projecting and representing citizens' opinions to decision makers are either losing their vibrance or prompting new disputes about their own degree of 'representativeness'. Such controversies about the best means of publicly representing citizens' opinions are symptomatic of an upswing in the modern democratic revolution first outlined by Tocqueville; contrary to many Western observers, the defeat of the Soviet Empire, the chief enemy of parliamentary democracy, is leading not to spontaneous outbursts of self-satisfied applause within the old democracies but to loud questioning of the legitimacy and effectiveness of the entrenched procedures of liberal democracy.

The contemporary malaise of public service broadcasting has several deep-seated causes, three of which bear directly on the theory of the public sphere:

1 *Fiscal squeeze* The financial footings of public service broadcasting in the European region are tending to crack and crumble. As Nowak (1991), Blumler (1995) and others have shown, licence fee income increases, which resulted during much of the post-war period from the steady diffusion throughout civil society of black-and-white and then colour sets, peaked during the 1970s. With the saturation of households with televisions and radios, the onset of inflation, the proportionately steeper increases in programme production costs, and government cutbacks, licence fee revenue then began to decline in real terms – for example, by 30 per cent during the period from 1972/73 until 1983/84 in Sweden. This fiscal squeeze not only pinched the prospects for a vigorous public service response to those critics favouring 'deregulation', for whom market competition and more advertising are the key conditions of press and broadcasting freedom, understood as private broadcasters' freedom from state interference. The long-term fiscal squeeze also ruled out any sustained involvement of public service broadcasters in the current technological revolution – except here and there, as exemplified by modest teletext initiatives or satellite services operated by BBC and the German broadcasters, ARD and ZDF. Most of the pioneering interventions in the field of communications were consequently left in the hands of national and international private entrepreneurs – an instructive symbol of which was the inability of BSB, the British satellite operation licensed as a public service venture by the Independent Broadcasting Authority, to survive cut-throat financial competition from Rupert Murdoch's Sky television. Finally, the long-term fiscal squeeze on public service broadcasters has forced them to intensify co-production deals, to privatize or subcontract parts of their programming and production facilities, to engage in international marketing ventures, and in general to speak the language of profit-conscious business executives. Such trends toward 'self-commercialization' arguably weaken the legitimacy of the public service model by diluting its programming distinctiveness and heartening deregulators in their crusade to marginalize public media.

2 *Legitimacy problems* Public service broadcasters could in principle exercise the option of publicly campaigning to renew the appeal of their activities, but in practice such fightbacks tend to be hamstrung by a growing legitimacy problem. Defenders of the existing public service model typically understate the ways in which the alleged 'balance', 'quality' standards and universalism of existing public service media are routinely perceived by certain audiences as 'unrepresentative'. For their part, public service broadcasters routinely perceive that the repertoire of programmes channelled through existing public service media cannot satisfy the multitude of opinions in a complex (if less than fully pluralist) society in motion. In other words, both audiences and broadcasters sense that the public service claim to representativeness is in fact a defence of virtual representation of a fictive whole, a resort to programming which simulates the actual opinions and tastes of some of those at whom it is directed.

The fate of music programming on public service radio well illustrates this legitimation problem. Although, for obvious reasons, music has always occupied the bulk of radio time, it has proved impossible in the long run to provide programming with general appeal on public service radio because in any one country a nationally shared musical culture has never existed in the past, and certainly does not exist in the present. Different forms of music appeal to different publics, whose dislikes are often as strong as their likes, and that is why the twentieth-century history of public service radio has been the history of the gradual recognition of the fragmentation of mass audiences into different taste publics. Trends in the world of music illustrate the key point here: the public service model corsets its audiences and regularly violates its own principle of equality of access for all to entertainment, current affairs and cultural programming in a common public domain. The corset is tightened further by the fact that, for reasons of government pressures, threatened litigation and a stated commitment to 'balance', the public service representation of such topics as domestic life, sexuality and political dissent is perceived by some audiences as too timid. It is routinely thought that certain things cannot be transmitted, or not in a particular way; or that when they are transmitted, their troublesome or outrageous implications are choked off. The sense that public service media are prone to 'bias' is further reinforced by the fact that public service media – here they are no different from their commercial competitor – unevenly distribute entitlements to speak and to be heard and seen. They too develop a cast of regulars – presenters, reporters, academic experts, professionals, politicians, business people, showbiz figures whose regular appearance on the media enables them to function as accredited representatives of public experience. The combined effect of these corseting effects is to decrease the legitimacy of public service media. Audiences tend to become restless; as broadcasters know, they gradually lose their 'ontological' status by becoming less predictable in their tastes and more receptive of commercial forms of media (see Ang, 1991).

3   *Technological change*   A third difficulty faced by the public service model – the advent of cable, satellite television, community radio, computerized networks – is arguably the most serious, since it has destroyed the traditional argument that the scarcity of available spectrum blesses public service broadcasting with the status of a 'natural monopoly' within the boundaries of a given nation state. Contemporary technological change is not simply encircling public service broadcasting and forcing it to compete with privately owned firms within a multi-channel environment. Less obviously, it is exposing the spatial metaphor deeply encoded within the public sector model, according to which citizens, acting within an integrated public sphere, properly belong to a carefully defined territory guarded by the sovereign nation state, itself positioned within a wider, englobing system of territorially defined states.

The assumption that public service media properly function as servants and guarantors of territorially fixed nation states preserved intact a similar geographic metaphor encoded within nationally demarcated stems of print journalism (as Benedict Anderson's study of print capitalism and nation states has shown (Anderson, 1982)). It nevertheless had to be fought for politically during the infant stage of broadcasting, as evidenced not only in the global struggle of European fascism and Soviet communism to tailor radio and film to their respective expansionist states, but also in the desperate efforts of early public service broadcasters to justify publicly why broadcasting media could be organized in a 'third way' – incorporating them into a parliamentary democratic state in which electronic media could serve to generate and sustain public life within a given territory. The famous document prepared for the Crawford Committee in 1925 by John Reith, the first Director-General of the BBC, made the point explicitly. Public service broadcasting, Reith argued, should function as a national service. It should act as a powerful means of social unity, binding together groups, regions and classes through the live relaying of national events, such as the first broadcast by King George V at the previous year's Empire Exhibition, which had the effect of 'making the nation as one man' (Reith, 1925: 4). A half-century later, Sir Michael Swann, chairman of the BBC's Board of Governors, argued before the Annan Committee that an 'enormous amount of the BBC's work has in fact social cement of one sort or another. Royal occasions, religious services, sports coverage and police series all reinforce the sense of belonging to our country, being involved in its celebrations and accepting what it stands for' (Annan Committee, 1977: 263). Still today this same assumption that the public service model is the principal forum which enables the whole nation to talk to itself is sometimes stated explicitly, as when French Presidents dub their television and radio services 'the voice of France' and BBC policy documents reiterate the principle that 'publicly funded broadcasters have a primary obligation to the public' and style the corporation as 'the national instrument of broadcasting'. The point is echoed in virtually every recent academic study of the public service/public sphere nexus (see Curran, 1991; Peters, 1994; Scannell, 1989).

I want to argue that such talk – the talk of those who suppose an elective affinity between public service broadcasting and 'the public sphere' – is hardening into dogma, precisely because the leading spatial metaphor upon which it rests is now out of touch with long-term media trends in the old parliamentary democracies. We are living in times in which spatial frameworks of communication are in a state of upheaval. The old dominance of state-structured and territorially bounded public life mediated by radio, television, newspapers and books is coming to an end. Its hegemony is rapidly being eroded by the development of a multiplicity of networked spaces of communication which are not tied immediately to territory, and which therefore irreversibly outflank and fragment anything formerly resembling a single, spatially integrated public sphere within a nation state framework. The ideal of a unified public sphere and its corresponding vision of a territorially bounded republic of citizens striving to live up to their definition of the public good are obsolete. In their place, figuratively speaking, public life is today subject to 'refeudalization', not in the sense in which Habermas' *Strukturwandel der Öffentlichkeit* used the term, but in the different sense of the development of a complex mosaic of differently sized, overlapping and interconnected public spheres that force us radically to revise our understanding of public life and its 'partner' terms such as public opinion, the public good and the public/private distinction.

Although these public spheres emerge within differently sized milieux within the nooks and crannies of civil societies and states, all of them are stages of power and interest-bound action that display the essential characteristics of a public sphere. A public sphere is a particular type of spatial relationship between two or more people, usually connected by a certain means of communication (television, radio, satellite, fax, telephone, etc.), in which non-violent controversies erupt, for a brief or more extended period of time, concerning the power relations operating within their given milieu of interaction and/or within the wider milieux of social and political structures within which the disputants are situated. Public spheres in this sense never appear in pure form – the following description is a typical example – and they rarely appear in isolation. Although they typically have a networked, interconnected character, contemporary public spheres have a fractured quality which is not being overcome by some broader trend toward an integrated public sphere. The examples selected below illustrate their heterogeneity and variable size, and that is why I choose, at the risk of being misunderstood, to distinguish among *micro-public spheres* in which there are dozens, hundreds or thousands of disputants interacting at the sub-nation state level; *meso-public spheres* which normally comprise millions of people interacting at the level of the nation state framework; and *macro-public spheres* which normally encompass hundreds of millions and even billions of people enmeshed in disputes at the supranational and global levels of power. I should like to examine each in turn – and to explore their implications for a revised political theory of the role of public spheres within democratic republics.

Micro-Public Spheres
The coffeehouse, town-level meeting and literary circle, in which early modern public spheres developed, today find their counterparts in a wide variety of local spaces in which citizens enter into disputes about who does and who ought to get what, when and how. John Fiske's *Power Plays* (1993) has made a convincing case for the importance of bottom-up, small-scale locales in which citizens forge their identities, often in opposition to top-town 'imperializing' powers bent on regulating, redefining or extinguishing (or 'stationing') public life at the local level. While Fiske (following Foucault) correctly emphasizes that these micro-public spheres take advantage of the fact that all large-scale institutions ultimately rest on the co-operation of their subordinates, and that challenges and changes at the micro-level therefore necessarily have broader macro-effects, he underestimates the importance of internal disputes within these locales – instead preferring to emphasize the contestatory relationship between 'imperializing power' and locales – and unfortunately ignores the rich significance of these localized disputes for the conventional theory of the public sphere. Two examples will help to clarify these points – and to illustrate what is meant by a micro-public sphere.

Micro-public spheres are today a vital feature of all social movements. As Paul Mier, Alberto Melucci and others have observed, contemporary social movements are less preoccupied with struggles over the production and distribution of material goods and resources and more concerned with the ways in which post-industrial societies generate and withhold information and produce and sustain meanings among their members (Melucci, 1989). The organizations of the women's movement, for instance, raise important questions about the material inequalities suffered by women. They also, at the same time, challenge dominant masculinist codes by signalling to the rest of society the importance of symbolically recognizing differences. While the movements have millenarian tendencies, their concentration on defining and redefining symbolic differences ensures that they are not driven by grand visions of a future utopian order. The supporters and sympathizers and actors within the movements are 'nomads of the present'. They focus upon the present, wherein they practise the future social changes they seek, and their organizational means are therefore valued as ends in themselves. Social movements normally comprise low profile networks of small groups, organizations, initiatives, local contacts and friendships submerged in everyday life. These submerged networks, noted for their stress on solidarity, individual needs and part-time involvement, constitute the laboratories in which new experiences are invented and popularized. Within these local laboratories, movements utilize a variety of means of communication (telephones, faxes, photocopiers, camcorders, videos, personal computers) to question and transform the dominant codes of everyday life. These laboratories function as public spaces in which the elements of everyday life are mixed, remixed, developed and tested. Such public spheres as the discussion circle, the publishing house, the church, the clinic and a political chat over a drink with friends or acquaintances are the sites in which citizens question the pseudo-imperatives of reality and counter them with alternative experiences of time, space and interpersonal relations. On occasion, these public spheres coalesce into publicly visible media events, such as demonstrations in favour of gay male and lesbian rights or sit-ins against roadbuilding or GM crop projects. But, paradoxically, these micro-public spheres draw their strength from the fact that they are mostly latent. Although they appear to be 'private', acting at a distance from official public life, party politics and the glare of media publicity, they in fact display all the characteristics of small group public efforts, whose challenging of the existing distribution of power can be effective exactly because they operate unhindered in the unnewsworthy nooks and crannies of civil society.

Micro-public spheres may also be developing among children within households, as the disputed example of video games illustrates. For many adults, particularly those without children, the widespread appeal of video games remains incomprehensible; contemplating a four-button keypad leaves them with a powerful sense of wasted time, ignorance based upon innocence, even disgust at the thought that the current generation of children will grow up as the first ever in modern times to learn to compute before they learn to read and write. But for most children, at least most boys between eight and eighteen, the experience of playing video games and creating an everyday culture of schoolroom stories, swapping and sharing videos, and a new critical lexicon (filled with codewords like 'crap', 'smelly', and 'cacky') that generates tensions with adults has become a routine part of childhood – as routine as old-fashioned ways of hating parents or squashing a worm or overfeeding a goldfish to death.

The growth within households of micro-public spheres of this kind has been dramatic. During the first half of the 1990s in the United Kingdom, for example, the video games market, dominated by the Japanese companies Sega and Nintendo, grew from virtually nothing to a turnover of around 800 millions per annum. Eight out of ten children between 11 and 14 now play video games; six out of ten have their own game consoles (the hardware needed to play games on television monitors); while in 1992 alone, around two million new consoles were sold. Industry figures like to cite the power of advertising 'hook' to explain their marketing success, but this underestimates the way in which the popularity of video games among children is chosen by subjects striving, if only intuitively, for the power to co-determine the outcomes of their electronically mediated play. It is true that the currently marketed form of video games normally thwarts children's choices. The sex-typing of women as figures who are acted upon, and often victimized as kidnap victims in need of rescue, is a typical case in point (Provenzo, 1991). Video games nevertheless challenge children to come to terms with the new media of digital communication. Their appeal stems not only from the fact that for brief moments children can escape the demands of household and school by becoming part of an alternate world of bionic men, damsels in distress, galactic invasions and teenage mutant turtles. Video games also promise interactivity and actually encourage users to improve their hand–eye co-ordination and interpretative skills by browsing through texts in an orderly but non-sequential manner. Unlike the process of learning to read books, which reduces children initially to mere readers with no freedom but that of accepting or rejecting the rules of a text, the playing of video games confronts children with a form of hypertext (Nelson, 1987). Players are required to choose their own pathways through texts composed of blocks of words, images and sounds that are linked electronically by multiple paths, chains or trails that are unfinished and open-ended. Video games blur the boundaries between readers and writers by encouraging their users to determine how they move through a forest of possibilities to do with rescue and revenge, and good versus evil, constrained only by the permitted household rules governing playtime, the manufacturers' mise en scene, and the child's capacity for inventiveness in the face of persistent adult suspicion or outright opposition to the phenomenon.

Meso-public Spheres

The treatment of meso-public spheres can be comparatively brief, since they are the most familiar of the three types of public sphere examined here. Meso-public spheres are those spaces of controversy about power that encompass millions of people watching, listening or reading across vast distances. They are mainly co-extensive with the nation state, but they may also extend beyond its boundaries to encompass neighbouring audiences (as in the case of German-language programming and publishing in Austria); their reach may also be limited to regions within states, as in the case of the non-Castilian-speaking regions of Spain like Catalonia and the Basque country. Meso-public spheres are mediated by large circulation newspapers such as the *New York Times, Le Monde, die Zeit,* the *Globe* and *Mail*, and the Catalan daily, *Avui*. They are also mediated by electronic media such as BBC radio and television, Swedish Radio, RAI and (in the United States) National Public Radio and the four national networks (CBS, NBC, ABC and FOX).

Although constantly pressured 'from below' by micro-public spheres, meso-public spheres display considerable tenacity. There is no necessary zero-sum relationship between these differently sized public domains, in part because each feeds upon tensions with the other (readers of national newspapers, for instance, may and do consult locally produced magazines or bulletins, precisely because of their different themes and emphases); and in part because meso-public spheres thrive upon media which appeal to particular national or regional language groupings, and which have well-established and powerful production and distribution structures that sustain their proven ability to circulate to millions of people certain types of news, current affairs, films and entertainment that daily reinforce certain styles and habits of communication about matters of public concern. The strength of reputation, funding and distribution is certainly an important reason why public service media, not withstanding their self-commercialization, are unlikely to disappear as props of public life. There is another, more surprising reason why public life at the meso-level is unlikely to disappear. The above-mentioned examples of the media sustaining meso-public spheres highlight the point – foreign to recent attempts to tie the theory of the public sphere to the fate of public service media – that public controversies about power are also regularly facilitated by privately controlled media of civil society. There is plenty of evidence that just as public service media are ever more subject to market forces, market-led media are subject to a long-term process of self-politicization, in the sense that they are forced to address matters of concern to citizens capable of distinguishing between market 'hype' and public controversies. The entry into official politics of commercial media figures such as Ronald Reagan and Silvio Berlusconi are extreme instances of this trend. The British tabloids' ruthless probing of the private lives of monarchs and politicians during the past decade is symptomatic of the same trend. So also are popular current affairs programmes such as CNN's Larry King Live and the remarkable proliferation of fast-cut television talk shows like Ricki Lake, which, amid advertisements for commodities such as mouthwash, chocolates, inner-spring mattresses and pizza, simulate raucous domestic quarrels about such matters as teenage sex, pregnancy and child abuse, in front of selected audiences who argue bitterly among themselves and, amid uproar, talk back to the presenter, experts and interviewees, contradicting their views, calling them 'real assess', urging them to 'get real', and insisting that something or other 'sucks with a capital S'.

Macro-public Spheres
The recent growth of macro-public spheres at the global or regional (e.g. European Union) level is among the most striking, least researched developments running contrary to the orthodox theory of the public sphere. Macro-publics of hundreds of millions of citizens are the (unintended) consequence of the international concentration of mass media firms previously owned and operated at the nation state level. A prior form of concentration of media capital has of course been under way for a century, especially in the magazine and newspaper industries and in the core group of news agencies, dominated by American, British, German and French firms that carved up the world within the spheres of

influence of their respective governments. The current globalization of media firms represents a projection of this process of concentration onto the international plane. It involves the chain ownership of newspapers, cross-ownership of newspapers, the acquisition of media by ordinary industrial concerns, and significantly, the regional and global development of satellite-linked communications systems. The development of globe-girdling communications firms such as News Corporation International, Reuters, Time-Warner and Bertelsmann was not driven by the motive of funding the development of international publics. Although research on the perceived motives and benefits of globalization remains limited, it is clear that the process, which is virtually without historical precedents, is driven by reasons of political economy. Media firms operating at the global level have certain advantages over their nationally-based counterparts. Headed by a tiny group of people who have become adept at 'turning around' ailing media firms and fully utilizing their assets, transnational firms take advantage of economies of scale. They are able to shift resources of expertise, marketing skills and journalistic talent, for instance, from one part of the media field to another; they can also reduce costs and innovate by tapping the specialist work forces of various societies. These firms can also effect synergies of various kinds, such as trying out a novel in one country and producing a movie based upon it in another, or releasing a work successively through such media as cable, video, television, magazines and paperback books, without the difficult rights-negotiation and scheduling problems that inevitably arise when a diversity of competing national companies is involved. Highly important as well is the advantageous fact that transnational media firms are often able to evade nation state regulations and shift the core energies of the whole operation from one market to another as political and legal and cultural climates change. Among the central ironies of this risk-driven, profit-calculating process is its nurturing of the growth of publics stretching beyond the boundaries of the nation state. Most of these public spheres are so far fledglings. They operate briefly and informally – they have few guaranteed sources of funding and legal protection, and are therefore highly fragile, often fleeting phenomena. International media events, which are now staged virtually every week, are cases in point. As Daniel Dayan and Elihu Katz (1992), Daniel Hallin (1994) and others have shown, global media events like summits are highly charged symbolic processes covered by the entire media of the world and addressed primarily to a fictive 'world audience'. In the three major summits hosted by Reagan and Gorbachev – at Geneva in 1985, Washington in 1987 and Moscow in 1998 – audiences straddling the globe watched as media channels such as CNN, ABC's Nightline and the Soviet morning programme 90 Minutes relayed versions of a summit that signalled the end of the Cold War. It is commonly objected that such coverage spreads rituals of pacification, rendering global audiences mute in their fascination with the spectacle of the event. That could indeed be legitimately said of the heavily censored Malvinas War and Gulf War coverage, but still there are signs that the global casting of summits and other events tends to be conducted in the subjunctive tense, in that they heighten audiences' sense that the existing 'laws' of power politics are far from 'natural' and that the shape of the world is therefore dependent in part on current efforts to refashion it according to certain criteria. The dramatic emphasis upon the subjunctive, combined with the prospect of reaching a world-wide audience, can incite new public controversies about power stretching beyond the limited boundaries of meso-public spheres. During the Reagan–Gorbachev summits, for example, political arguments about the dangerous proliferation of nuclear and conventional weaponry here commonplace among the citizens and governments of various countries at the same time; and in the Soviet Union, where autonomous public life had long been considered a counter-revolutionary crime, the supporters of Boris Yeltsin were heartened by the way in which the demoted party leader's interviews with CBS and the BBC during the Moscow summit forced Mikhail Gorbachev to respond with a televised press conference; meanwhile, Soviet religious dissidents successfully lobbied President Reagan to grant them a public meeting, at which there was a frank airing of conflicting views about elections, the future of religion and the comparative 'standards of living' of America and the Soviet Union.

Probably the most dramatic example so far of the way in which global media events can and do incite public controversies about power before audiences of hundreds of millions of people is the crisis in Tiananmen Square in China during the late spring of 1989. Broadcast live by CNN, 24 hours a day, the Tiananmen episode was a turning point in the development of global news. Not only was it perceived as the most important news story yet to be covered by international satellite television; it was also (according to Lewis Friedland (1992) and others) the first occasion ever when satellite television directly shaped the events themselves, which unfolded rapidly on three planes: within national boundaries, throughout global diplomatic circles and on the stage of international public arguments about how to resolve the crisis. CNN's wire-service-like commitment to bring its viewers all significant stories from all sides of the political spectrum helped to publicize the demands of the students, many of whom had travelled abroad and understood well the political potential of the television medium in establishing public spheres in opposition to the totalitarian Chinese state. Not coincidentally, they chose 'The Goddess of Democracy' as their central symbol, while their placards carried quotations from Abraham Lincoln and others, all in English for the benefit of Western audiences. The students reckoned, accurately, that by keeping the cameras and cellular telephones (and, later, 8 mm 'handicams' carried around on bicycles) trained on themselves they would maximize the chances of their survival and international recognition. Their cause certainly won international recognition from other states and citizens. By damaging the international reputation of the Party, the global coverage of the Tiananmen events may also have boosted the long-term chances of a non-violent self-dismantling of the communist regime (along the lines of Kádar's Hungary). In the short run, the coverage almost certainly prolonged the life of the protest, which ended in the massacre of between 400 and 800 students. According to CNN's Alec Miran, who was executive producer in China during the crisis 'People were coming up to us in the street, telling us to "Keep going, keep broadcasting, that they won't come in while you're on the air". That turned out to be true. The troops went in after our cameras were shut down' (cited in Friedland, 1992: 5).

The pathbreaking development during the past two decades of an international system of computerized communication networks provides a final illustration of macro-public spheres. Based upon such techniques as packet switching developed during the 1960s by the Advanced Research Projects Agency (ARPA) for the United States Department of Defense, a world-wide network of computers funded by governments, businesses, universities and citizens, is beginning to draw together users from all continents and walks of life. The Internet, the most talked about and talked through network, comprises millions of computers serving as hosts that are in turn directly connected to other computers used by over 200 million people. The number of Internet 'citizens' is growing rapidly (by an estimated 1 million users a month), in part because of heavy subsidies that keep access costs to a minimum, partly because of peer pressure to get an e-mail address, and in part because of the lack of constraints, globality and informality currently enjoyed by users communicating for a variety of self-chosen ends. Some 'surf' the Internet, logging on to servers throughout the world just for the hell of it. Companies and other organizations conduct banking transactions and transmit financial and administrative data by means of it. Live telecasts of speeches and transmissions of scanned images of weather maps, paintings and nude photographs are commonplace. Still others use 'the net' to obtain detailed print-outs of data downloaded from libraries or to 'chat' with a friend on another continent.

The manifold purposes for which the Internet can be used at reasonable cost or free of charge has led some observers (e.g. Krol, 1994) to liken its users, in neo-Romantic terms, to eighteenth-century travellers seeking food and shelter in houses they reach at nightfall. While correctly drawing attention to the contractual or voluntary character of electronic interactions, the simile is arguably misplaced. It not merely understates the way in which the often clumsy organization of information sources generates confusion among users who are posting items – with the consequence that travellers on the information highway find themselves hazy about their routes, their means of travel, their hosts' house rules, and (insofar as messages are frequently forwarded several times, often by unknown receiver/senders) their ultimate destinations. More pertinent is the fact that the simile fails because the Internet stimulates the growth of macro-public spheres. There is a category of users with a 'net presence' who utilize the medium not as travellers but as citizens who generate controversies with other members of a far-flung 'imagined community' about matters of power and principle. The Association for Progressive Communications (APC), for example, functions as a world-wide partnership of member networks dedicated to providing low-cost and advanced computer communication services for the purpose of network-strengthening and information-sharing among organizations and individuals working for environmental sustainability, economic and social justice, and human rights. Within the APC framework, spheres of public controversy ('public discussion forums') stretching to all four corners of the earth have a permanent presence. So too do reflections upon the power relations operating it – the global networks themselves. 'Netizens' whose approach to the public forums of the Internet exudes selfishness – taking rather than giving – can generally expect to be abused ('flamed'), as unsolicited advertisers find to their embarrassment.

Controversies are erupting about the merits of state-subsidized, cost-free access of citizens to the Internet; proposals are surfacing (in the United States) for the formation of a Corporation for Public Cybercasting that would serve as a clearing house for federal funds, help to increase the density and tensility of the network, and lobby for citizens' access; and fears are expressed that the telecommunications and entertainment industries are building advanced communications systems that would enable them to control parts of the Internet and thereby levy considerably higher access charges.

Research Implications

The above attempt radically to rethink the theory of the public sphere, like all lines of enquiry that transgress the limits of conventional wisdom, opens up new bundles of complex questions with important implications for future research in the fields of politics and communication. The most obvious implication is that the neo-republican attempt to tie the theory of the public sphere to the institution of public service broadcasting has failed on empirical and normative grounds and that, more positively, there are empirical reasons alone why the concept of 'public spheres' should be brought to bear on phenomena as disparate as computer networking, citizens' initiatives, newspaper circulation, satellite broadcasting and children playing video games. Public spheres are not exclusively 'housed' within state-protected public service media; nor (contrary to Habermas) are they somehow tied, by definition, to the zone of social life narrowly wedged between the world of power and money (state/economy) and the pre-political group associations of civil society. The political geography supposed by both the Habermasian and public service model theories of 'the public sphere' is inadequate. Public spheres can and do develop within various realms of civil society and state institutions, including within the supposed enemy territory of consumer markets and within the world of power that lies beyond the reach of nation states, the Hobbesian world conventionally dominated by shadowy agreements, suited diplomacy, business transactions, and war and rumours of war. Whether or not there is a long-term modern tendency for public spheres to spread into areas of life previously immune from controversies about power is necessarily a subject for a larger enquiry. Yet among the implications of this reflection upon the theme of public life in the old democracies is the fact that there are no remaining areas of social or political life automatically protected against public controversies about the distribution of power. The early modern attempt to represent patterns of property ownership, market conditions, household life, and events like birth and death as 'natural' is gradually withering away. So too is the older, originally Greek assumption that the public sphere of citizenship necessarily rests on the tight-lipped privacy (literally, the idiocy) of the *oikos*. As the process of mediated publicity spreads – television talk shows like Ricki Lake and children playing video games suggest – supposedly private phenomena are being drawn into the vortices of negotiated controversy that are the hallmark of public spaces. The realm of privacy disappears. The process of politicization undermines the conventionally accepted division between 'the public' (where power controversies are reckoned to be the legitimate business of others) and 'the private' (where such controversy is said to have a legitimate role before the thrones of 'intimacy' or individual choice or God-given or biological 'naturalness'). Politicization exposes the arbitrariness or conventionalism of traditional definitions of 'the private', making it harder (as various figures of power are today painfully learning) to justify any action as a private matter. Paradoxically, the same process of politicization also triggers a new category of public disputes about the merits of defining or redefining certain zones of social and political life as 'private' – and therefore as nobody else's business. Legal authorities publicize the problem of rape while insisting upon the need to keep private the identities of those who have suffered the crime; gay males and lesbians campaign publicly for their right to live without intrusions by bigots and gawking journalists; advocates of the right to privacy press publicly for data protection legislation; meanwhile, embattled politicians and scandalized monarchs insist publicly that the media has no place in their bedrooms.

Such developments cannot adequately be understood from within the orthodox perspective on the public sphere, wedded as it is to a version of the early modern division between 'the public' and 'the private'. Its defenders might reply that at least some of the public spheres mentioned above are bogus public spheres, in that they are neither permanent nor structured by rational argumentation, or what Garnham calls 'a rational and universalistic politics'. Certainly – as the *impermanent* public controversy generated by social movements shows – not all the examples of public life cited above display longevity, but that arguably signals the need to question the conventional assumption that a public sphere is only a public sphere insofar as it persists through time. The point about rational argumentation is more difficult to answer, although it is again clear that there is no reason in principle why the concept of the public sphere must necessarily be wedded to the ideal type of communication oriented toward reaching consensus based upon the force of the best argument (or what Habermas calls *verständigungsorientierten Handelns* (Habermas, 1976)). In their study of television talk shows, Sonia Livingstone and Peter Lunt (1991) usefully highlight the several ways in which audience discussion programmes defy the dominant philosophical notion of rationality, derived from deductive logic, according to which there exists a set of formal reasoning procedures that express tacit inference rules concerning the truth or falsity of assertions independently of the content or context of utterances. Following Wittgenstein's *Philosophische Untersuchungen* (1958), Livingstone and Hunt defend the legitimacy of lay or 'ordinary reasoning', such as quarrels (characterized by emotional intensity and a commitment to assert one's point of view at all costs) and preaching, political oratory and storytelling, in which points are built up in a haphazard manner by layering, recursion and repetition. Their move is convincing, but their conclusions remain a trifle too rationalist. Early modern public spheres – as I proposed from a post-Weberian perspective in *Public Life and Late Capitalism* (Keane, 1984) and Oskar Negt and Alexander Kluge (1972) insisted from a neo-Marxian standpoint in *Öffentlichkeit und Erfahrung* did not conform to the Habermasian ideal type of rational discussion. Music, opera, sport, painting, dancing were among the forms of communication propelling the growth of public life, and there is therefore no principled reason, aside from philosophical prejudice, why their late twentieth-century popular counterparts – the rambunctiousness of MTV's annual video awards, the simulated uproar of Ricki Lake shows, or the hypertext of video games – should not be understood as legitimate potential media of power conflicts.

To suppose that public controversies about power can and should unfold by means of a variety of modes of communication is not to fall into the relativist trap of concluding that any and every power struggle counts as a legitimate public sphere. Violent confrontation among subjects does not do so, since, as the originally Greek understanding of war as external to the polis maintained, it seeks physically to silence or destroy outright its antagonists. The essential point (detailed in Keane, 1988, 1991) is this: the plea for a pluralistic understanding of the variable forms of communication that currently constitute public life shares an elective affinity with a non-foundationalist understanding of democracy as a type of regime which enables a genuine plurality of individuals and groups openly to express their solidarity with, or opposition to, others' ideals and forms of life. By abandoning the futile and often dangerous high roads of supposed transhistorical Ideals and definite Truths, the plea for a pluralistic account of public life implies that there is no ultimate criterion for determining which particular type of public controversy is universally preferable. The most that can be said, normatively speaking, is that a healthy democratic regime is one in which various types of public spheres are thriving, with no single one of them actually enjoying a monopoly in public disputes about the distribution of power. In contrast, a regime dominated by television talk shows or by spectacular media events would compromise its citizens' integrity. It might prove to be as stifling as a regime in which seminar-style 'rational discussion' or demagogic political preaching served as the sole 'civilized' standard of disputation about who gets what, when and how.

The emphasis here upon pluralism brings us back to the subject of space, which was the point of departure of this broad reconsideration of the structural transformations of the public sphere in the old democracies. Within the republican tradition of political thinking that extends through to the recent attempt to tie public life to the public service model, it is normally assumed that power is best monitored and its abuse most effectively checked by means of ongoing argumentation within the international framework of the nation state. Republicanism supposes that public-spirited citizens can best act together within an integrated, politically constructed space that is ultimately rooted in the physical place occupied by state power. This supposition needs to be rejected, since a growing number of public spheres – the Internet and global media events, for instance – are politically constructed *spaces* that have no immediate connection with physical territory. Public life, one could say, is presently subject to a process of de-territorialization which ensures that citizens' shared sense of proximity to one another in various milieux bears a declining relationship to the places where they were actually born, where they grew up, fell in love, worked and lived, and where they will eventually die.

It might be objected that the attempt to categorize contemporary public life into spaces of varying scope or 'reach' is mistaken on both empirical and normative grounds. Empirically speaking, it could be said that the public spheres discussed in this essay are not discrete spaces, as the categories micro-, meso-, and macro-public sphere imply; that they rather resemble a modular system of over-lapping networks defined by the lack of differentiation among spheres. Certainly, the concept of modularization serves as a useful reminder of the dangers of reifying the distinction among micro-, meso- and macro-public spheres. It is also helpful in understanding the growing complexity of contemporary public life. But this does not mean that the boundaries among variously sized public spheres are obliterated completely. To the contrary, modular systems thrive on internal differentiation, whose workings can thus only be understood by means of ideal type categories that highlight those systems' inner boundaries. The recent development of computerized communication is illustrative of this point. Computer networks originally linked terminals to mainframes for time-sharing, but during the past two decades a pattern of distributed structures at the micro-, meso-, and macro-levels has come to predominate. During the 1980s, local area networks (LANs) providing high-speed data communication within an organization spread rapidly; they have subsequently been linked into metropolitan area networks (MANs) that are often associated with a 'teleport' of satellite dishes, and into wide area networks (WANs) that may cover several continents – and yet still the differentiation between micro-/meso-/macro-domains remains a vital feature of the overall system.

The triadic distinction among differently sized public spheres can also be contested on normative grounds. During the early years of the twentieth century, at the beginning of the era of broadcasting, John Dewey's *The Public and its Problems* famously expressed the outlines of the complaint that modern societies are marked by the fragmentation of public life. 'There are too many publics and too much of public concern for our existing resources to cope with,' wrote Dewey. 'The essential need,' he added, 'is the improvement of a unified system of methods and conditions of debate, discussion, and persuasion, that is the problem of the public' (1927: 142). This kind of appeal (repeated more recently by Robert Bellah (1967) and others) to revive republicanism is questionable. It fails to see that the structural differentiation of public spaces is unlikely to be undone in the coming decades, and that therefore the continued use of 'the' public sphere ideal is bound to empty it of empirical content and to turn the ideal into a nostalgic, unrealizable utopia. We are moving, as Henri Lefebvre predicted, from a society in which space is seen as an 'absolute' toward one in which there are ongoing 'trials of space' (1974: 116). Orthodox republicanism also ignores the undemocratic implications of its own hankering after a unified public sphere. The supposition that all power disputes can ultimately be sited at the level of the territorially bounded nation state is a remnant from the era of state-building and the corresponding struggles of its inhabitants to widen the franchise – and, hence, to direct public controversies primarily at the operations of the sovereign state. In the present era of the universal franchise, by contrast, it is not so much who votes but *where* people vote that is becoming a central issue for democratic politics. From this perspective, the proliferation of mosaics of differently sized public spheres ought to be welcomed and practically reinforced by means of political struggles, law, money and improved modes of communication. Exactly because of their capacity to monitor the exercise of power from a variety of sites within state and social institutions, public spheres ensure that nobody 'owns' power and increase the likelihood that its exercise everywhere is rendered more accountable to those whom it directly or indirectly affects.

The trends described in this chapter are admittedly only trends. Within the old democracies, there are plenty of anti-democratic countertrends, and it should therefore not be supposed that we are at the beginning of the end of the era of unaccountable power. All political classes, Harold Innis (1991) once remarked, have sought to enhance their power by utilizing certain media of communication to define and to control the spaces in which their subjects live. Statues of military and political heroes sited in public squares are only the most obvious example of a much older and highly complex history of rulers' attempts to define space in their honour, and thereby to inspire devotion among their subjects by making the exercise of power seem unblemished – and unchallengeable. When reflecting upon the twentieth century, Innis doubted whether this struggle by dominant power groups to regulate their subjects' living space could be resisted. He supposed that space-biased media such as newspapers and radio broadcasting, despite their promise to democratize information, in fact entrench new modes of domination.

Was Innis right in this global conviction? Is modernity, just like previous epochs, distinguished by dominant forms of media that absorb, record and transform information into systems of knowledge consonant with the dominant institutional power structures? Is the era that lies beyond public service broadcasting likely to prove unfriendly toward public life? Is the vision of a democratic plurality of public spheres nothing more than a bad utopia? Or is the future likely to see a variety of contradictory trends, including not only new modes of domination but also unprecedented public battles to define and to control the spaces in which citizens appear? In the disciplines of political science and communication studies, such questions are at present poorly formulated, while the tentative answers they elicit are by definition either not yet available or highly speculative. Perhaps the most that can be said at present is that a theory of public life that clings dogmatically to the vision of a unified public sphere in which 'public opinion' and 'the public interest' are defined is a chimera – and that for the sake of democracy it ought not to be jettisoned.

References

Anderson, B. (1982) *Imagined Communities: Reflections on the Origin and Spread of Nationalism*. London: Verso.

Ang, L. (1991) *Desperately Seeking the Audience*. London: Routledge.

Annan Committee (1977) *Report of the Committee on the Future of Broadcasting*. London: HMSO.

Arendt, H. (1960) *Vita Activa*. Stuttgart: W. Kohlhammer.

Bellah, R.N. (1967) 'Civil religion in America', *Daedalus*, 96 (Winter): 1–21.

Blumler, J. (1995) 'Broadcasting finance and programme quality: An international review', *European Journal of Communication* 1(3): 343–64.

Curran, J. (1991) 'Rethinking the media as a public sphere', in P. Dahlgren and C. Sparks (eds), *Communication and Citizenship: Journalism and the Public Sphere in the New Media Age*. London/New York: Routledge. pp. 27–57.

Dayan, D. and Katz, E. (1992) *Media Events: The Live Broadcasting History*. Cambridge: Harvard University Press.

Dewey, J. (1927) *The Public and its Problems*. New York: H. Holt & Co.

Fiske, J. (1993) *Power Plays, Power Works*. London: Verso.

Friedland, L.A. (1992) *Covering the World: International Television News Services*. New York: Twentieth Century Fund.

Garnham, N. (1990) *Capitalism and Communication: Global Culture and the Economics of Information*. London: Sage.

Habermas, J. (1962) *Strukturwandel der Öffentlichkeit: Untersuchungen zu einer kategorie der bürgerlichen Gesellschaft*. Neuwied: Luchterhand. (English edn, 1989: *The Structural Transformation of the Public Sphere: An Inquiry into a Category of Bourgeois Society*. Cambridge: MIT Press.)

Habermas, J. (1976) 'Was heisst Universalpragmatik?', in K.O. Apel (ed.), *Sprachpragmatik und Philosophie*. Frankfurt am Main: Suhrkamp.

Hallin, D.C. (1994) *We Keep America on Top of the World: Television Journalism and the Public Sphere*. London/New York: Routledge.

Innis, H. (1991) *The Bias of Communication*. Toronto: University of Toronto Press.

Jaspers, K. (1969) *Philosophy is for Everyman. A Short Course in Philosophical Thinking*. New York: Harcourt, Brace.

Keane, J. (1984) *Public Life and Late Capitalism*. Cambridge/New York: Cambridge University Press.

Keane, J. (1988) *Democracy and Civil Society*. London: Verso.

Keane, J. (1991) *The Media and Democracy*. Cambridge: Polity Press.

Krol, E. (1991) *The Whole Internet: Users Guide and Catalogue*. Sebastopol, CA: O'Reilly & Associates.

Lefebvre, H. (1974) *La production de l'espace*. Paris: Editions Anthropos.

Livingstone, S. and Lunt, P. (1991) *Talk on Television: Audience Participation and Public Debate*. London: Routledge.

Melucci, A. (1989) *Nomads of the Present: Social Movements and Individual Needs in Contemporary Society*, P. Mier and J. Keane (eds). London/Philadelphia: Temple University Press.

Negt, O. and Kluge, A. (1972) *Öffentlichkeit und Erfahrung: Zur Organisationsanalyse von bürgerlicher und proletarischer Öfferntlichkeit*. Frankfurt an Main: Suhrkamp.

Nelson, T.H. (1987) *Computer Lib: Dream Machines*. Redmond, WA: Tempus Books.

Nowak, K. (1991) 'Television in Sweden: position and prospects', in J. Blumler and T.J. Nossiter (eds), *Broadcasting Finance in Transition: A Comparative Handbook*. New York: Oxford University Press. pp. 235–59.

Peters, B. (1994) 'Der Sinn von Öffentlichkeit', *Kölner Zeitschrift für Soziologie und sozialpsychologie*, 34: 42–76.

Provenzo, E.F. (1991) *Video Kids: Making Sense of Nintendo*. Cambridge/London: Harvard University Press.

Reith, J. (1925) 'Memorandum of information on the scope and conduct of the broadcasting service'. Caversham, Great Britain: BBC Written Archives.

Robbins, C. (1961) *The Eighteenth-century Commonwealthmen: Studies in the Transmission, Deployment and Circumstance of English Liberal Thought from the Restoration of Charles II until the War with the Thirteen Colonies*. Cambridge: Harvard University Press.

Scannell, P. (1989) 'Public service broadcasting and modern public life', in *Media, Culture and Society*, 11(2): 135–66.

Tonnies, F. (1922) *Kritik der öffentlichen Meinung*. Berlin: Springer.

Wittgenstein, L. (1958) *Philosophical Investigations*, G. Anscombe and R. Rhees (eds). Oxford: Blackwell.

6

The Controversies of the Internet and the Revitalization of Local Political Life

Sinikka Sassi

Every time the media landscape changes – as with the emergence and extension of the information networks today – the utopia of the capacity of new media for improving democracy and empowering citizens arises anew. In Rosen's words (1994), we confront the real but unrealized possibility of a communicating public. A relevant theory of democracy presupposes a notion of the public sphere as a space where the diversified and critical conversations are conducted along with the notion of a communicating public. Recently, transformations of economic and political power structures have given rise to lively debates on the forms of political action and, conjointly with it, the qualities of the public sphere, mostly confined to national borders. A fair share of the current global and national changes can be attributed to the emergence of the digital networks, nicknamed the Matrix (Gibson, 1984), but although the source may be easily identified, its implications are much more difficult to determine. The Internet, the best known part of the network, is intermingled with the changes and is a reason for at least some of the present reconfigurations of the public sphere. It encompasses controversial qualities and elicits conflicting tendencies such as fragmentation and unification of the various sectional publics. Furthermore, it has the capacity to mould the boundaries between the private and the public, that is to essentially redefine the realm of the common concerns.

The Dual Origin of the Network

The dual roots of the network can be found through its early history (see Rogers and Malhotra, Chapter 2 in this book; Hauben, 1990), one originating in the basic processes of modernization and the other in the sphere of sociality and spontaneous need for communication. This dual heritage has consequences both in the methodological choices in conducting network research, and in understanding the constraints and potential of citizen political action. First, the fundamental trends of modernization, rationalization in particular, have given rise to the network as a necessary means of controlling and managing complex systems of production (see, for example, van Dijk, 1993). The economy and the administration, the system in Habermas' terms (1987), make use of the digital networks largely to get better results or more surplus value with fewer inputs. Today the effects of rationalization appear as acceleration and intensification of immaterial and material flows and the general speeding up of life. Thus, no matter how casual the emergence of the network may seem, it nevertheless has its historical causes and precedents.

Secondly, while military and economic interests by and large brought the network into existence, the human needs of intercourse and sharing have shaped the Internet and account for its specific social qualities and, for two decades, its ethos of equality. At the same time as our social interaction has been invigorated and communication facilitated, everyday living, the lifeworld in Habermas' vocabulary (1987), has been negatively affected by some functions of networked economics and administration. In the political sphere, the established institutions seem to become disabled in responding to the effects of the globalizing economy and new transnational organizations, and the surveillance functions of the state seem to shrink the citizens' realm of privacy. It is fair to say that while the Internet opens up an entirely new sphere of citizen activities, the options are dependent on the way the whole network structure is constituted and managed. Here the governments are not neutral parties, however much the autonomous and uncontrolled nature of the Internet is celebrated.

All these interdependencies, the effects of the macro-systems upon the micro-systems of social and political life, make it necessary to apply a multi-dimensional approach to the study of the Internet (Sassi, 1995). Accordingly, given its democratic potential and especially its impact upon the public sphere a double strategy has been chosen here. The Internet will be looked at here both from the structural point of view, from above, and from below, from the perspective of the citizen's everyday life. Finally, these two pictures are put together in order to get some idea of what happens at the juncture between systemic constraints and everyday concerns. This chapter will also focus on neighbourhood, since it is in a particular locality that political initiatives and democratic practices emerge, or at least should do so. In all, the aim is to explain some central features of the Internet with an eye to their relevance to theorization of the public sphere.

The Varying Senses of the Public Sphere

To begin with, the basic concept of public sphere has to be examined and made familiar. At one end of the spectrum of definitions is the academic notion of the public sphere, commonly associated with Habermas. He has become largely responsible for its current interpretation, even though the discussion on the public sphere as part of the democratic tradition had arisen long before him. In fact, he has returned the concept to where it originally belonged, namely the liberal Anglo-American tradition (Peters, 1993). Habermas (1989) gives a thorough account of the history and sociological institutions of public communication which included newspapers, novels, letters, conversation, debate, salons and coffeehouses, concerts and the theatre, secret societies, living rooms and public parks, and parliaments. Crucial to the bourgeois public sphere was the articulation of principles of rational-critical debate conducted primarily through face-to-face discussion and the print media.

Peters (1993) shows how translations of Habermas' term help to remove some of its exotic aura. *Öffentlichkeit*, the German term translated as public sphere, combines two of the most ordinary and fundamental political terms of the Anglo-American tradition: 'publicity' in the sense of openness and access; and 'the public' as a sovereign body of citizens. In current German, it means pretty much what English-speakers mean by 'the public': a sociological aggregate of readers, viewers or citizens, that excludes no one a priori and is endowed with key political and critical powers. The English equivalent, *publicity*, which similarly once meant the condition of being public, has been incapacitated for political or theoretical usage and today only suggests public relations. The semantic change in *publicity* thus mirrors Habermas' thesis about structural transformation from critical participation to consumerist manipulation. As Peters says, the language of public and private thereby participates in the structural transformation of the public sphere.

At the other end of the conceptual spectrum, another sign of the transformation is revealed by the current commonsense understanding of the public sphere. Popular opinion generally associates the public sphere with the media and, in particular, dominant mainstream media, simply ignoring or forgetting the other institutions. Common sense often equates the public sphere with publicity and associates it with the doings of celebrities. From the perspective of everyday life, the academic considerations may seem distant and even uninteresting, if known at all. The narrow understanding of the term reflects a fundamental aspect of the contemporary public sphere: it is not public. If publicness is conceived as the equivalent of openness, it is exactly what this sphere is currently not, and common sense has got it right. Although we still have a rich variety of places and events to converse, these discussions largely miss the chance of being connected with the political sphere and mostly affect it only indirectly, under the public surface.

Here the public sphere is broadly understood in Habermas' sense as a space where common matters become public and are discussed and thus become the objects of politics. The public sphere is important because it is the space where the individual and collective interests of the lifeworld will be mediated to the administration, and vice versa. In principle, it is a site governed neither by the authority of the state, nor the exchange of the market, but by public reasoning, reaching for the best possible arguments. In its present form, as a media publicity, it is a site where the interests of elites generally prevail.

The Debate about the Concept

While it is commonly agreed that Habermas has done a great service by reconstructing a largely forgotten concept that still lies at the foundation of constitutional government, his conceptualization and historical account have met with sharp criticism. Feminist scholars, among others, have paid critical attention to the concept and elaborated it in a radical way (see McLaughlin, 1993). Some relevant elements of the reformulations will be presented here and considered together with the apparent effects of the Internet upon the public sphere. For a number of feminist scholars the general idea of the public sphere is indispensable to critical theory, but they are concerned about the underlying presumptions. The original bourgeois public sphere, according to Fraser (1992: 110), rested on and was importantly constituted by a number of significant exclusions, especially the exclusion of women, the proletariat and popular culture. Instead of a single public sphere she argues for a multiplicity of publics in stratified societies (1992: 115). The problem of Habermas' notion is not only that it idealizes the liberal public sphere but also that he fails to examine other competing, non-liberal, non-bourgeois, public spheres. Revisionist historiography demonstrates that the bourgeois public was never *the* public. A host of counter-publics like those of the feminist and labour movements arose simultaneously, contesting the exclusionary norms of the bourgeois public and elaborating alternative styles of political behaviour and alternative norms of public speech. Fraser sees that counter-publics can partially offset the unjust participatory privileges enjoyed by members of dominant social groups, although not wholly eradicate them.

Secondly, she argues for the inclusion of private interests and issues instead of a universal common concern defined in advance of the discourse. Only participants themselves can decide what is and what is not of common concern to them. Fraser's point is that there are no naturally given, a priori boundaries between the public and the private domains. Democratic publicity requires positive guarantees of opportunities for minorities to convince others that what was not public in the past should be so now. Habermas' stress on a common good transcending the mere sum of individual preferences can work against the principal aim of deliberation; namely, to help participants clarify their interests. In particular, the less powerful may not find ways to discover that the prevailing sense of 'we' does not adequately include them. In general, Fraser invites a more critical look at the terms 'private' and 'public' since they are cultural classifications used to repress some interests, views and topics and to valorize others. Instead of a coherent, homogeneous public, feminist scholars propose multiple public spheres, where differences are recognized and appreciated. There is a common understanding among the critics that the concept of the public sphere should be read as plural and decentred, constituted by conflict, and combining the notions of interest and identity.

In the light of various feminist critiques, Habermas (1992: 458) has conceded that his earlier formulation of the public/private distinction may have failed to note how this distinction was gender-specific. This critique has led him to suggest that it may be more appropriate to speak of public spheres rather than simply the public sphere. His later formulation of the concept constitutes it in a more fragmented and unorganized form (Habermas, 1992: 445). Baynes (1994) also emphasizes that Habermas' conception does not anticipate the idea of a homogeneous public which excludes difference or diversity. Neither does it rely on a model of face-to-face interaction that has become increasingly irrelevant for modern forms of social integration. Baynes defines the public sphere broadly as a vast array of institutions in which a wide variety of practical discourses overlap.

Thus it ranges from the more or less informal movements and associations in civil society where solidarities are formed, through the various institutions of the public mass media, to the more formal institutions of parliamentary debate and legal argument.

The Net as a Public Sphere

From the structural point of view, what might the effects of the Internet upon the public sphere be? First, while it has certain implications for the media-centred public sphere, it can justifiably be called a public sphere itself. With private business and governmental services growing in volume on the Net, it still is typically a realm of public communication and debate. As to the reformulation of the concept, the Net now seems to realize, almost too well, the suggested qualities of pluralization and inclusion of private interests and issues.

While the multiplicity of publics is strongly emphasized as a necessary extension of the established public sphere, the tendency is very ambiguous in essence. Multiplicity and plurality, both of the same origin, point to a deeper process of modern social life. In general, to understand modernity is to understand the dialectical interplay between its disintegrating and reintegrating forces. Individualism is commonly accepted as a specific feature of modern societies and regarded as an important source of diminishing social cohesion. Seligman (1992: 120) claims that it was the autonomy of the individual citizen stressed throughout the nineteenth century that led to a decrease in solidarity between citizens, and gradually to the fragmentation of social life. In Lii's (1998) view, the idea of the individual and individualism grew with the changing forms of social gathering and it did not emerge until the beginning of the modern era. A common concern about whether a general interest designed to serve as a foundation of social life can still emerge is expressed today. Because of the plurality of competing interests it is doubtful in our highly complex societies in any case, but the Net now seems to be responsible for even more intensified fragmentation. The public, previously a national entity, is presently dispersed into smaller groups which reach across national borders and have casual relations to each other if any. Paradoxically, the prospects of the Net lie precisely in its capacity to create these new publics since, by definition, a plurality of opinions should be appreciated in a democracy. Thus, the quality of pluralization is found at the same time truly promising and very alarming.

To respond to the disintegrating tendencies, the notion of a global public sphere with its corresponding public has arisen. In today's world there are other forces acting against fragmentation of social life but they often are distressing in essence such as wars and ecological disasters. It is suspected that, because of the negative attitudes involved, they may not produce strong affiliations and what we are left with instead is, as Tomlinson (1994) says, an attenuated sense of global commonality. In his view, the simple perception of common risks is liable to be fragile and easily displaced from the foreground of consciousness. What is required in the current situation is a much stronger sense of commonality. Because there is nothing like a global public sphere it is not surprising for Tomlinson that we see the global context largely as a set of determining structures, not of a potential political and cultural community.

We can further ask whether the notion of a global public or global public sphere is itself an anomaly, because it would have to include all of humanity. In such a case, social movements and the institutional arena of their interaction would have to be of international scope and not limited to the confines of a particular nation state. In the sense of a communicating public, the requirements seem to be unattainable, although international organizations as well as mass audiences created by the media have existed for a long time. The former are still too restricted and the latter too fragile and imaginary to act as a world-wide public. However, something like a sense of commonality has grown on the Net and although it is technologically mediated, it differs significantly from the mass-mediated one. The simple reason is that the mode of communication on the Net is mixed, containing interpersonal and group interaction in addition to the 'one to many' type. The Net public sphere can alternately operate dialogically and hence the environment can actually produce conditions for a public to be born. Does the sense of commonality reach a level that is in some respects global?

To answer the question we can examine the global public sphere, not from the perspective of a structure, but from that of a process and flow. While there is a rapidly growing number of non-governmental organizations and their transnational networks creating the institutional structure of a global public sphere, it still more often emerges around a topic, evolving for a moment and then fading away. Currently many social movements take the form of a campaign to appeal against a national government or a multinational corporation and, although these campaigns may be prolonged and renewed, they are generally transitory and their publics occasional. Campaigns against MacDonalds, Shell and Monsanto may serve as examples of the new activism, continuing to proceed virtually even when the activities seem publicly to cease. A slogan of the consequences of the Net public sphere might be that the publics are fragmenting, the issues are uniting. The Net will give birth to an abundance of new publics which, due to the world-wide process of modernization, increasingly share the same topics. Where the Net is concerned the truth, however, is not as simple as that. While the publics fragment, they may simultaneously be global, that is, stretching across the continents. And while the topics may be local, they can acquire a global public. All kinds of combinations of issues and publics, local and global, become possible on the Net, and this is the most obvious difference between it and the previous, more stable public sphere.

The Private and Public Dilemma

The second reformulation of the public sphere concerns the inclusion of interests and issues formerly part of the private sphere and the questioning of a fixed notion of the common good. The above discussion of the plurality of publics and the fear of disintegration of social life fall entirely within the confines of politics. To make the distinction between private and public is to determine the subjects of common discussion and decision and thus the borders of politics. Communication media can actually be viewed as the site of continual disputes over the boundary between the public and private spheres and it is commonly accepted that precisely these shifting interactions should be explored (Murdock, 1993). Moreover, it has also been suggested that in relation to the Net the whole division is simplistic and unhelpful and should be dismissed. However, the distinction is of primary importance here because the whole concept of the public sphere rests on it.

First, it is argued that the public sphere is constituted of exclusions, some of which are based on this division. A set of objections against the model of the public sphere focuses on the hierarchical ordering of reason over affection, the universal over the particular, and male over female (Benhabib, 1992; Pateman, 1988; van Zoonen, 1991). As a consequence of this ordering a model of the public sphere was established which was homogenizing in its effects. Conventionally, these pairs can be combined as one set incorporating reason, the universal and male, and the other incorporating affection, the particular and female. Even if this description is simplifying, the public sphere can be said to be constituted largely as a privileged area of man whereas the private sphere was reserved for woman. Accordingly, the domain of the household, of meeting the daily needs of life, of sexuality and reproduction, and of care of the young, the sick and the elderly, was not defined as a public issue.

Benhabib (1992) argues that contemporary political theory still continues to neglect these issues and ignores the transformation of the private sphere resulting from massive changes in women's and men's lives. She sees the traditional modes of drawing this distinction as part of a discourse of domination that legitimizes the locking of women's interests into the private realm. This gendered subtext of the public sphere is now slowly being recognized by scholars, but in everyday routine and political practice the division will presumably survive for years to come. In Baynes' view (1994), however, it is not the concept itself that is problematic because it is inherently structured to exclude heterogeneity or particularity. Though the public sphere presupposes some distinction between the public and the private, he ascribes it a self-referential character that opens it up to self-transformation. The boundaries between the public and the private are then not fixed but rather remain open to criticism and possible renegotiation. In recent years, there has also been positive change at this borderline, concerning for example physical integrity and issues of private ownership both of which used to belong to the private realm. Family violence and pollution of private land property have become issues of common concern and measures have been taken to prevent and punish malpractices.

However, the distinction has given rise to another concern, contrary to the fear of an issue becoming excluded from the public sphere. It is expressed as a concern about the potential emptying of the public sphere caused by the extension of the private. The notion had already appeared in Habermas' analysis when he was tracing the reduction of the public sphere to an arena of private interests, incapable of representing the whole. Seligman (1992: 132) points to the way the relations between public and private spheres are currently conceived. In his view, the shared public realm, within which the citizen is constituted, has itself disappeared. What has taken its place is the individual existing in public only in the most abstract and generalized form. Seligman suggests that today the private is projected into the public arena and made public. Although the arguments are rather radical, they are not difficult to agree upon looking at the content of many media.

Admittedly, both of the suggestions mentioned here, that of including formerly excluded publics into the public sphere, and that of transforming the boundaries between private and public issues, are justified. What makes the position difficult is that through the Net, it seems, some undesirable tendencies inherent in contemporary society such as disintegration and privatization may be intensified. An example may demonstrate the dilemma we face: a few years ago, the Council of Masturbation Educators proclaimed an anniversary on the Net, dedicated to solitary or mutual masturbation world-wide on New Year's Eve. They expected millions of people to participate in the event both through the Net and in other local celebrations. Was the action a joke, sheer exhibitionism or an example of new politics? Being sexual by nature, it is hard to ascribe this to any other than the intimate sphere, but since it was intended to raise money for safe sex programmes, it was clearly political. The organizers called on people to participate in an international orgy, that is, in a collective event. How should this action be evaluated? Obviously not only by rational-critical criteria but, perhaps, according to the intentions and potential consequences. While it certainly annoys many, leaves others untouched, and makes still others enjoy it, it is symptomatic of the implications of breaking the conventional borders between public and private.

In all, we have to get acquainted with forms of politics that evade established codes and study the contemporary transformations between private and public carefully. In today's politics, matters involving emotions and relations of care, issues of the traditionally female lifeworld, can come under discussion, meaning a welcome enlargement of the political realm and vocabulary alike. However, it also seems clear that some issues remain private in essence even when they enter publicity and should at least partly be repulsed. Moreover, we should pay attention to the sphere of privacy as the necessary ground of our political life since if we lose it, everything becomes political and we have lost the refuge. The borderline between these two spheres is neither fixed nor universal, but needs to be rethought. The implications of the Net are confusing in many ways, to say the least. The perspectives opened up are very promising, but often underused, and still more often very embarrassing. It seems that prominent features, both negative and positive, of the contemporary culture are liable to gain strength on the Net. What we are left with is not a choice between alternatives but an endeavour to balance contradictory trends and a wish to avoid the extremes.

The Lost Glory of Politics

The essence of the public sphere is supposed to be politics, implying that common concerns are discussed and contested in public. In the democratic tradition, the notion of political life without a well-established public sphere would be unthinkable, and Habermas in effect used to call it the political public sphere. The very low esteem generally enjoyed by politics in Western countries, however, reveals the decreasing legitimation of political systems in the minds of the citizens. In Rosen's view (1994), the dominant trend of contemporary society is to downgrade citizens more or less to the role of spectators. In fact, in the circumstances of representative democracy and the mass media, the idea of a widely accessible, critical-rational political discourse also seems extremely utopian.

Murdock (1993) sees it as a problem of representation touching upon the relationship between the discourses of major parties and the institutions of public communications available. In Arendt's view (1958), the principle of representation has led to the emergence of an oligarchic class and the privileged governing of the majority by the few. The current democratic system does not really encourage the systematic and active participation of citizens in matters that affect our everyday living such as city planning or work organization. Industrial modernization has been accompanied by a strong planning system taking care of social arrangement to the extent that it seeks to render citizens meaningless to the system except on voting day. The prevailing model of political thought seems to anticipate a citizen who is detached from intermediary social groups and communities, traditions, special interests, class attachments and prejudices. Consequently, the present conditions resemble a serious break between politics and the people. In the Habermasian sense, however, politics should be realized as the interplay between a constitutionally formed system and spontaneous flows of citizen communication.

In the absence of citizen deliberation, conversation and decision making, the public world will tend to dissipate. If this condition should be corrected by reinstalling the public as the subject of politics, how will the Net contribute to it? In recent years, the exponential growth of the Net seemed to come about in any area except that of politics, if defined as initiatives taken by citizens. Today the view has shifted, largely because of a new generation of political projects that has evolved, but also because of better understanding of emerging forms of politics (Beck, 1994, 1997; Melucci, 1996). These considerations have helped to discern political activism where previously there seemed to be nothing. New social and cultural groups utilize the Net to create media-type action and to invent discourses unfamiliar to the media public sphere. Thus, it can be stated that the principle of representation has to some extent given way to the possibility of participation, although the new activities have not yet much influenced the institutional forms of politics.

Here we come to the relation between the Net public sphere and the media public sphere which has to be examined because in the new communication environment it is precisely their interaction that is interesting. While the micro-public spheres draw their strength, paradoxically, from the fact that they are mostly latent (Keane, 1995), to become known to a wider public and be politically more effective they need the major media. The productivity of new political projects is largely dependent on them and whatever their goals they have to consider their media strategies. The fact that micro-public spheres aim to establish direct contacts with major media is also in accordance with the commonsense understanding of the media as the real public sphere. In the long run, their predominance over publicity could be reduced by the micro-public spheres linking with one another. In addition, the reverse interaction also exists between the Net and the media. The information circulated on the Net, previously often ignored by the media, has now become largely acceptable. Now the Net has become a mass medium itself and journalists have started to employ it to gather information and to compile their stories. However, it is more than just a tool: it has also changed the dominant discourses of the media either by offering counter-information or by eliciting entirely new issues.

Locality and Everyday Life

Having considered basic structural features of the public sphere and the Net, the focus will now turn to the social life of a locality. What might the functions of the Net as a public sphere be for someone living in a suburban neighbourhood?

First, it is presumed that the widespread indifference to politics exposed by Gallup polls and elections is proportional and is, most of all, directed to political parties and established institutions. Bringing politics closer to everyday life and locality would probably increase interest in it (see Beck, 1994). In urban belts, suburbs and neighbourhoods, people would obviously have their say on matters of the immediate environment and everyday arrangements. Everybody lives somewhere and therefore develops a relationship with the neighbourhood, often a weak and temporary one, but still meaningful. From the neighbourhood perspective, public sphere and politics, which at the national level often are experienced as remote and beyond individual control, could become significant again. Bookchin (1987: 245) further claims that there can be no politics without community. His vision of the authentic unit of political life is the municipality, whether as a whole, if it is humanly scaled, or as its various subdivisions, notably the neighbourhood. He finds the significance of the municipality all the greater because it constitutes the discursive arena in which people can intellectually and emotionally confront each other, indeed, experience each other through dialogue, body language, personal intimacy and face-to-face modes of expression in the course of making collective decisions.

Apparently, democratic participation cannot be based on the delegation of power and the principle of representation in a neighbourhood. Procedures of local politics, to be meaningful, should in principle include everyone. Arendt (1958) has examined the dimensions of power and structures of the political world in a way that can assist us to reconfigure the situation. In her view, power is essentially communicative by nature, evolving both as action and discourse, and inseparable from politics. She interprets it as a potential for something. In this sense, it is not repressive but a necessary quality especially for those without a share of entitlements and wishing to pursue change. Characteristic of Arendt's political world is its irreversibly open and processual nature: it is always a sphere of differences and ambiguity, and conflict and dispute are exactly the forces creating progress. The representative model still has a strong influence upon our minds, and both scientific and practical objections are soon raised against a more participatory model. They range from the inability of citizens to deal with complex issues to the controversies bound to be stirred up among local inhabitants.

If a stronger commitment to the participatory model of democracy is inevitable, where do we find the local public spheres to carry out the essential public discussions in the first place? There are, in fact, a wide variety of local spaces in which citizens enter into discussions. These micro-public spheres are today a vital feature of all social movements (Melucci, 1996) although their local connections may be obscure and diffuse. For Keane (1995), the discussion circle, the publishing house, the church, the clinic and a political chat over a drink with friends or acquaintances represent such public spheres. They are the sites in which citizens question the pseudo-imperatives of reality and counter them with alternative experiences of time, space and interpersonal relations. Keane finds them effective simply because most of the time they work unnoticed by the media and the authorities. However, their chance of challenging the existing divisions of power remain largely latent and their radical role hidden from most of the participants. We do not usually consider conversations with our neighbours or friends as political acts challenging the status quo. Moreover, there are no established ways to interpret and mediate these conversations to the political institutions.

Sociality as a Basis of Politics

The political nature of the present micro-public spheres looks rather faint if compared to the early modern public spheres as known from Habermas' account. An influential space of consumption has now grown, evolving along the public sphere and flourishing as a rich realm of mass-produced images and symbols. This imaginary sphere is shared by the members of a culture who thus become related one to another through it, though in a weak and remote way. The question then arises of how to link the far-removed worlds of consumption and everyday concerns and politics together when there seems to be just an empty space between them. How would the concern for common matters and solidarity with others arise in a late modern neighbourhood? The classical Athenian polis might give us an insight by serving us with a notion of citizenship which consisted not only of political, but of social and cultural dimensions alike. To be a citizen in Athens implied an array of personal qualities, various fora of discussion, and a range of educational means and aims. Today the model can show us the way to politics: to go beyond the political sphere to the social sphere, or sociality in Bauman's sense (1992).

Beyond politics, all societies, including previous ones, have had their specific ways of organizing themselves. Lii (1998) employs the term 'social sphere' to deliberately distinguish this mode from the public sphere. Bookchin (1987: 39) explains the difference between the two by the growth and development of the social into the political. Political life has developed out of social life to acquire a distinct identity of its own, which itself presupposes social forms as its underpinnings. The social sphere can be conceptualized as a form of societal self-organization and the creation of a cultural landscape in which private individuals can be brought together into a social collectivity. In a neighbourhood, we can find many such occasions, like lectures, concerts, bazaars, excursions, voluntary work days, sport and gymnastic exercises that bring people together and through which, finally, public life is made possible.

While the public sphere strives to rise above particular interests to achieve a common mind, the social sphere, Lii says, creates a shared living context from which a social fabric develops among its members. This social fabric then creates an ethical relation which is essential for the maintenance of public life. In this context, city planning seems vital since the way our physical environment is constructed can either prevent rich social relations arising or greatly assist in forming them. Throughout history, people have showed themselves capable of creating their own political institutions and forms of organization outside the official realm, but the physical and social structures can become a constraint. The origin of the Net should therefore be recalled, as the cause of its emergence, aside from the military ones, was precisely human sociality and the desire of its early developers to share the information, ideas, opinions and innovations they had at disposal with each other. Today it is still the need for communication and intercourse that largely accounts for its extension. In this sense, the Net is contributing to establishing the social basis of future politics. Indeed, it would be useless to found permanent political fora unless people had no other opportunity to get together and share their everyday experiences. Local public spheres could then be intentionally created on the Net and their interrelations be strengthened. Wider contacts are also as vital as the horizontal connections: the local public spheres should exploit the existence of the de-nationalized public spheres of the Net to become more influential and to avoid the parochialism inherent in a local context.

In recent years, some basic elements of societal life, in particular the forms of family and work, have been radically changing. The concomitant diversification has turned what used to be an expectional mode into a norm. A new demand for civil society to take more responsibility for social arrangements and well-being is therefore growing, implying, in Beck's words (1997), the emergence of a new political society. On the presumption that the modern public has to a great extent lost its solid and collective character and individuals have instead emerged as the centres of social relations, we cannot expect an easy revival of the political public sphere. However, there are ongoing processes, seemingly paradoxical, which can be pointed out here as components of the political society aspired to. Although individuals are today pulled away from their traditional modes of social connection, such as family lineages, occupational categories and classes, it does not lead to the end of all kinds of society but to new modes of social connectedness (Beck, 1997: 94–5).

The young of today and the expressions of puberty are an example. In Western countries this period of disengagement from the family ties has in general become rather exhausting to the parties concerned because of the very strong aspiration to autonomy and a self-centred way of life led by the young. Puberty is at the very heart of the individuation process, revealing plainly some basic qualities of our culture. In some European countries with well-established welfare arrangements and a secularized culture, youth behaviour has taken asocial forms which are generally found undesirable. The young tend to form a tribe of their own with specific codes and rites, and with a remote relation to the other society. Paradoxically, it was the welfare state that created the conditions for ego-centred ways of life (Beck, 1997: 97), consumer capitalism assisting significantly in expressing them.

Presumably there is also something good in the extreme phase of individuation. By identifying and separating persons as different bodies, individuation becomes a precondition of subjectivity (Lii, 1998: 127), meaning a growing awareness of and responsibility for individual choices. With these notions in mind, we might start constructing more diversified urban structures providing the young with their own social spaces and spheres of responsibility and enlarging the possibility of separate age groups coming together. Here we can combine the old idea of the polis with the new innovation, the Net. The latter is needed to produce a sense of universalism and to help to overcome the sometimes too close relations of a locality.

Contradictions on the Net

The Net is by no means a neutral zone of citizen activities or a realm of freedom. The examination of the network structure and functions suggests that citizens are not even free to choose whether they want to use the Net. The current push towards the information society is realized through transfers of operations of administrations and economies alike to the Net – of our request, it is often said. Moreover, to remain outside the Net means to remain outside civil society, which is also increasingly constituted upon it. For future prospects, we should not just react to systemic imperatives, but should take our own initiatives and invent new approaches concerning the Net.

A burning question today is whether we can have any experience of community in our fully individualized societies. While academic debate on the controversy between individualism and communitarianism continues, people become spontaneously committed to civic action in everyday matters. These include responses and reactions to deterioration of neighbourhoods, heavy drinking by teenagers, and neglect of old people, among other things. These modes of local co-operation, already known from many communities, have been accompanied by new efforts at employing the Net. Local associations have started to establish Web sites, informing people for example on coming social events and on city planning, and various cultural or social groups are supporting their interests and identities through the Net. Not only individual, but also collective identities are encouraged by collecting and exposing histories and personal memories on the Net. These activities touch upon a problem Tomlinson (1994) called 'the audience lacking a past in common'. He examined the constitution of a global community via the global media and was concerned about it lacking a shared basis. In urban neighbourhoods, it seems that history is now emerging as an important source of identity. Recently, in a meeting of African librarians great enthusiasm was also expressed about their newly acquired access to the cultural heritage of mankind, available on the Net. These examples show how a new technological innovation is often employed by the people in unexpected ways or for reasons not anticipated in advance.

The new activities, both inside and outside the Net, have also aroused concern among some commentators. The aims and motives involved are thought dubious because of the fear that they may promote particularistic and private interests.

The activities are seen as defensive and parochial, promoting selfish ends, and social movements are accused of being responsible for creating discord instead of harmony and solidarity. Admittedly, both present and past experiences partly prove these accusations justified. However, we cannot simultaneously make a claim for more diversified publics and judge them, when they appear, as worthless, not at least without discussing the principles of judgement.

If we consider politics as public empowerment and participatory action, we are bound to encounter controversies and disputes. What would the alternative be – a return to the homogenized public sphere, in the singular? Let us recall Arendt's view on politics as thoroughly open and processual and as a sphere of differences and ambiguity, of conflicts and disputes. For her, these were the qualities that create progress. Hegel (1973), known for his commitment to the idea of a unified collective will, argued for the particularist interests of a community as its prerequisite. He put strong emphasis on the hermeneutic nature of the general interest, originating in the process of temporary public opinions being developed and interpreted as a more generalized one. The disintegration of a community into atomized individuals could be avoided by interpretative discussions and as Hegel (1973: 294) pointed out, in the course of history freedom of speech has turned out to be far less dangerous than enforced silence. Finally, since the specific interests of a community have to be balanced against more general ones, there is a need for the existence of international political organs (Peters, 1993) and global public spheres. We can call it the perspective of cultural universalism, in contrast to that of cultural relativism, implying the democratic criteria by which to charge racist, neo-fascist or chauvinist movements, and exclude them. In all, the Net projects our self-portrait before us, with its beautiful and ugly traits, and can thereby help us to choose the direction to take.

Note

The article is based on a case study on local politics and ecological urban planning employing the Net as a tactical medium. Since the project aims at changes in the agendas and procedures of local democracy, how the concept of public sphere is defined and how the role of politics is conceived are important factors. Although the Web site of the project originally represented the particular interests of a few – the researcher and her husband – and was confined to a specific geographical area, they were meant to advance the public good more generally (Sassi, 1997).

References

Arendt, H. (1958) *The Human Condition*. Chicago: University of Chicago Press.

Bauman, Z. (1992) 'A sociological theory of postmodernity', in Z. Bauman, *Intimations of Postmodernity*. London: Routledge.

Baynes, K. (1994) 'Communicative ethics, the public sphere and communication media', *Critical Studies in Mass Communication*, 11: 315–26.

Beck, U. (1994) 'The reinvention of politics: towards a theory of reflexive modernization', in U. Beck, A. Giddens and S. Lash, *Reflexive Modernization*. Cambridge: Polity Press.

Beck, U. (1997) *The Reinvention of Politics. Rethinking Modernity in the Global Social Order.* Cambridge: Polity Press.

Benhabib, S. (1992) 'Models of public space: Hannah Arendt, the liberal tradition, and Jurgen Habermas', in C. Calhoun (ed.), *Habermas and the Public Sphere*. Cambridge: MIT Press.

Bookchin, M. (1987) *The Rise of Urbanization and the Decline of Citizenship*. San Francisco: Sierra Club Books.

Fraser, N. (1992) 'Rethinking the public sphere: a contribution to the critique of actually existing democracy', in C. Calhoun (ed.), *Habermas and the Public Sphere*. Cambridge: MIT Press.

Gibson, W. (1984) *Neuromancer*. London: Grafton Books.

Habermas, J. (1987) *The Theory of Communicative Action. Volume 2. Lifeworld and System: A Critique of Funtionalist Reason*, translated by Thomas McCarthy, first published in 1981. Cambridge: Polity Press.

Habermas, J. (1989) *The Structural Transformation of the Public Sphere: An Inquiry into a Category of Bourgeois Society*. Cambridge: MIT Press. (Originally published 1962.)

Habermas, J. (1992) 'Further reflections on the public sphere', in C. Calhoun (ed.), *Habermas and the Public Sphere*. Cambridge: MIT Press. pp. 421–61.

Hauben, R. (1990) 'From Arpanet to Usenet News. On the nourishment or impediment of the NET.Common wealth'. Paper presented at the IAMCR conference in Dublin, June 1990.

Hegel, G.W.F. (1973/1852) *Hegel's Philosophy of Right*, translated with notes by T.M. Knox. Oxford: Oxford University Press.

Keane, J. (1995) 'Structural transformations of the public sphere', *The Communication Review*, 1(1): 1–22.

Lii, D. (1998) 'Social spheres and public life. A structural origin', *Theory, Culture & Society*, 15(2): 115–35.

McLaughlin, L. (1993) 'Feminism, the public sphere, media and democracy. Review essay', *Media, Culture and Society*, 15: 599–620.

Melucci, A. (1996) *Challenging Codes. Collective Action in the Information Age*. Cambridge: Cambridge University Press.

Murdock, G. (1993) 'Communications and the constitution of modernity', *Media, Culture and Society*, 15: 521–39.

Pateman, C. (1988) 'The fraternal social contract', in J. Keane (ed.), *Civil Society and the State*. London: Verso. pp. 101–27.

Peters, J.D. (1993) 'Distrust of representation: Habermas on the public sphere', *Media, Culture and Society*, 15: 541–71.

Rosen, J. (1994) 'Making things more public: on the political responsibility of the media intellectual', *Critical Studies in Mass Communication*, 11: 362–88.

Sassi, S. (1995) 'A self-willed and odd thing called the Net. Remarks on the quality of the network world', *Nordicom information*, 2: 49–58.

Sassi, S. (1997) 'The Internet and the art of conducting politics: considerations of theory and action', *Communication*, 22(4): 451–69.

Seligman, A. (1992) *The Idea of Civil Society*. New York: Free Press.

Tomlinson, J. (1994) 'A phenomenology of globalization? Giddens on global modernity', *European Journal of Communication*, 9: 149–72.

van Dijk, J. (1993) 'Communication networks and modernization', *Communication Research*, 20(3): 384–407.

van Zoonen, L. (1991) 'A tyranny of intimacy? Women, femininity and television news', in P. Dahlgren and C. Sparks (eds), *Communication and Citizenship. Journalism and the Public Sphere in the New Media Age*. London: Routledge. pp. 217–35.

PART III

PRACTICE

7

The White House Computer-mediated Communication (CMC) System and Political Interactivity

Kenneth L. Hacker

As we have seen in the previous chapters of this book, there are many and varied claims made regarding digital democracy. Unfortunately, many of them lack rigorous theoretical and/or empirical grounding. Often, the results of computer-mediated political communication technologies fall behind the rhetorical claims made regarding their role in new forms of political communication and changing democratic systems. Moreover, observers may neglect to acknowledge the possible negative effects of computer-mediated communication systems.

This chapter acknowledges these issues while addressing some specific practice issues in regard to the role of the Clinton White House computer-mediated communication (CMC) system. Since 1993, this system has had the potential of making contributions to democratization, political interactivity and new forms of political communication. As with most emerging systems and technologies, it has done some good, while it has also fallen short of accomplishing its stated objectives.

The White House CMC (WHCMC) system goals are described in this chapter in relation to the claims made by the White House concerning how this technology would facilitate democracy in the United States. The White House claims are evaluated in light of data gathered (by system evaluators) on system users reported in 1996 (the last year that such data have been available for public scrutiny). They are also compared to the standards of democratic communication suggested by a typology of democracies and various perspectives of democratic communication. The conclusions reached in this chapter focus on what the system planners promised and what the system has delivered as a new means of political communication. Finally, some early groundwork for initiating some theoretical constructs and models of political interactivity is presented in an effort to usefully relate democracy and communication in ways that can influence future WHCMC development and evaluation.

The White House (WHCMC) Technology/System

The Clinton WHCMC system (http://www.whitehouse.gov) began as an extension of the intensive uses of new communication technologies by the Clinton presidential campaign in 1992. Of the three major campaigns (Bush, Clinton, Perot) in 1992, only the Clinton campaign made early use of computer networks to disseminate its messages. The distribution of Clinton campaign documents began with the use of CompuServe (Chapman, 1993). In time, all three campaigns eventually used computer networking for such purposes (Hacker et al., 1996).

After the election victory, the Clinton–Gore team moved into the White House in 1993 and installed new phone lines, computers, modems, FAX machines and e-mail technology (Diamond and Silverman, 1997). The staff perceived that they were ending a Dark Ages of communication technologies used by the Bush administration. For example, President Bush did not get direct dial tone on his own phone; he had to place his calls with the assistance of his operator. Whether or not the Clinton WHCMC system ever accomplished its stated objectives for democracy, its designers can legitimately claim that the Clinton administration was the first to make CMC part of US government communication with its citizens (Davis and Owen, 1998).

The WHCMC system has numerous components including document retrieval, World Wide Web (WWW) pages and electronic mail which makes it possible for citizens to write to the president and other government officials. The people who have designed and managed the WHCMC system are confident that American democracy will be enhanced with CMC. Although they acknowledge that this will take time, they say that the increasing use of the system will encourage greater citizen participation in the political system (Hacker, 1996a).

In its earliest days, White House e-mail was printed on paper and treated as paper correspondence by postal personnel (Chapman, 1993). Today the e-mail sent to the White House is scanned by subject lines and from there forwarded to a specific agency in the federal government. The sender of the mail usually receives a computerized acknowledgement and thank-you note. The White House system had received over 60,000 messages by September 1993 (Bradley and Frederick, 1994). In the year 1996, the mail had reached nearly 800,000 notes for the year, the first time that e-mail letters were exceeding the number of paper mail letters at times (Rothman, 1997). By April 1999, the system had received over 2.8 million messages since its inception.

The White House Office of Communications obtained assistance from the Artificial Intelligence (AI) Laboratory at MIT to construct software that would analyse the contents of e-mail messages reaching the White House. The assistance of MIT AI experts was necessary because of the enormous volume of e-mail reaching the White House (Chapman, 1993). As stated earlier, this program reads key words in messages addressed to the president or vice president and routes the incoming messages to the most appropriate federal agencies. For example, a message with repeated references to 'Bosnia' or 'Kosovo' will be routed to the State Department (Chapman, 1993). Development of the technology has been said to include natural language processing in the AI program which will allow the computer programs to ascertain the tone of incoming messages. In time, this system will be able to provide a cumulative attitudinal tracking system for the president and his/her advisers (Diamond and Silverman, 1997). The White House will be able to use the system to track public concerns on a variety of issues and policies over time.

The White House Web site has links to various federal agencies, White House photo archives, press releases of presidential statements or press secretary, and a virtual tour of the White House. The Web site is part of the White House electronic publications service which distributes transcripts of speeches, executive orders and other presidential documents. By 1996, the site was getting nearly a million hits per month (Davis and Owen, 1998). The site was constructed in 1994 under the supervision of political scientist David Lytel (Rothman, 1997). Average daily hits for the site in 1997 were 72,000 per day (Rothman, 1997).

The White House argues that the central objective of its CMC system is to connect government and people. Through its high-profile advocates, President Clinton and Vice President Gore, and its host of lower-profile advocates like the system designers and evaluators, the WHCMC system has been repeatedly touted as an instrument of revolutionary change in American political communication. Even the autoresponder message sent back to people who send e-mail to the White House declares, 'Online communication has become a tool to bring government and the people closer together.'[1]

The Claims made by the White House

In 1993, the Clinton administration announced plans for the National Information Infrastructure (NII), which they said would eventually provide all Americans with affordable access to a national system of communication and information (Hacker, 1996a). In August 1993, an announcement from the White House said that the White House e-mail system was part of its efforts to 'reinvent government'.[2] A component of the NII would be the White House communication system. In various press releases, speeches, interviews and documents, the administration claimed that the WHCMC system would lead to more citizen participation, less top-down information dissemination, and a lowering of the feelings of disconnection that many Americans feel in relation to the federal government (Hacker, 1996a). They also argued that the White House e-mail system would make the new presidential administration more accessible to the people (Jones, 1995).

In September 1993, the Clinton administration revealed its NII 'Agenda for Action'.[3] This document claimed that more government information would be made available to people over the Internet, that communication with government officials would be facilitated, that network usage would improve how Americans participate in democracy, that accessibility of government information would improve, and that the NII would result in a 'more open and participatory democracy'.

On 21 December 1993, Vice President Al Gore said that communication networking can build communities whereas advancements in transportation had contributed to a fracturing of communities. Gore claimed that new means of communication including the Internet would provide a healthier, more educated and more prosperous American society ('Remarks by the Vice President...', 1993).

Other than the president and vice president, the conceptual planners of the White House CMC system appear to have been Jock Gill, Mark Bonchek, Roger Hurwitz and John Mallery. I will refer to these people as the WHCMC system analysts.

Jonathan 'Jock' Gill, the director of the WHCMC system and former Clinton 1992 campaign e-mail director, addressed the Political Communication division of the International Communication Association in 1993. He said that the administration was working with a new communication model that would facilitate more two-way and lateral communication.[4] Gill argued the previous top-down, one-way models of political communication worked against community and interactivity. He also argued that the empowerment of citizens involves helping people make better personal decisions and helping them with personal responsibilities.

In 1994, I went to the Old Executive Office Building offices of the White House to interview Jock Gill. He told me that the new president had oriented his election campaign around three main themes: community, opportunity and responsibility. Part of this, he said, is getting people to be more interactively involved with their government. Relationships between government and citizens would build community which would make opportunities and responsibilities more possible. More specifically, Gill said that President Clinton wanted to get more people involved with the political system and that over time people will learn from their positive experiences with the WHCMC system, as well as how to communicate more with government (Hacker, 1996a).

In other interviews, Jock Gill argued that President Clinton wished to inform people directly of political events as they occurred and thus to create communication that would result in a more informed electorate and possibly one that is less disaffected (Bradley and Frederick, 1994). He also argued that the White House CMC planners were trying to put more control into the hands of its users ('Electronic communication at the White House', 1994). Gill made it clear that the previous administration had no CMC infrastructure at all and that the Clinton administration has established one ('Electronic communication at the White House', 1994).

A 1995 document released by the National Information Infrastructure Advisory Council made the following claims about enhancing participatory democracy with CMC. They claimed that the NII would improve communication between government and constituents, enhance delivery of information, provide user-friendly information sources such as the White House Web page, encourage more responsive and efficient government, and enable citizens to actively participate in political processes (NII, 1995). The document argues that Internet communication offers an 'unprecedented opportunity' to enhance participatory democracy. The NII Council says that as Americans learn to use CMC to communicate with their government, government will become more responsive. In turn, there will be a flourishing of participatory democracy (NII, 1995).

Mark Bonchek (1995) argues that CMC facilitates political activity by reducing costs of moving information, forming groups, co-ordinating actions and recruiting members. He notes that in 1994, about 10,000 people were visiting the White House Web site each day. With less cost, there is more likelihood of activity. More importantly, Bonchek (1995) draws attention to the fact that the many-to-many nature of the Internet allows people to tap into knowledge bases and online communities while possibly participating in constructing some political networks of their own.

Mark Bonchek and Jock Gill argue that Internet communication is superior to mass communication because the former can more easily facilitate group communication and co-operation among citizens (Bonchek and Gill, 1996). They also assert that there are many false claims about Net users being politically different from non-Net users. They argue that users and non-users are the same in terms of party identification, who they voted for in the 1992 presidential election, and concern for government helping the disadvantaged (Bonchek and Gill, 1996).

In 1997, Mark Bonchek, Roger Hurwitz and John Mallery argued that the WHCMC system had mixed results and that Internet communication in general may improve democratic processes by making it easier to be informed, making it easier for citizens to communicate with each other, and by facilitating communication among citizens and leaders or agencies. However, they also note that inequalities block many of these benefits from being widespread (Boncheck et al., 1997).

A recent addition to the White House Web site is a page labelled 'Customer Service'. This page makes the claim that the White House is 'leading a revolution to give you better service from your government'.[5] While this may sound like Total Quality Management rhetoric, it is consistent with previous claims about bringing government and citizens closer together. The White House site continues to offer documents, images, scrapbook photos, a virtual tour of the White House and audio messages. It also facilitates the e-mail system by providing note writers with a menu of options regarding the subject of their message to the president (Davis and Owen, 1998). All of this reflects design efforts to make the WHCMC system easier to use.

With qualifications, we see that over the years, the White House has claimed that its CMC system would do the following: make government information easily and more widely available to citizens; increase citizen participation in democracy; decrease political disaffection; make government more accessible; and lessen top-down political information dissemination.

Before assessing the strength and validity of the White House claims about increasing or improving citizen–leader communication through the WHCMC system, it is instructive to briefly examine some sociological data about Internet and World Wide Web usage in general since these are the main platforms of the WHCMC system.

Sociological Data

Information from the US Department of Commerce indicates that only about 3 million people used the Internet in 1994, fewer than 40 million people around the world were using the Internet in 1996 and by the end of 1997 more than 100 million in the world were using it (Margherio et al., 1998). The report indicates that traffic on the Internet has been doubling every 100 days. Some experts argue that as many as 1 billion people in the world will be using the Internet by the year 2002 (Margherio et al., 1998). As of 1999, Internet user statistical estimates varied from 64 million Americans online (Mediamark Research, 1999) to 83 million Americans online (Intelliquest, 1999). In 2000, estimates of world usage were over 300 million (NUA Surveys, March 2000). Such estimates are generally for all people with any type of net access. All of the individual survey numbers are subject to validity problems, but the trend data is what counts most. The trends across surveys indicate that both the Internet and World Wide Web have reached critical mass and are being adopted at rates so fast that there are clearly no indications of digital communication lessening or not becoming as widely used, by those who can afford access, as previous communication technologies of the past. Just about 20 years ago, there were about 50,000 computers in the entire world. Today, that many computers are sold every 10 hours around the world (Gladieux and Swail, 1999). In 1985, there were about 300,000 e-mail users world-wide. Today, Americans alone account for about 80 million e-mail addresses (Gladieux and Swail, 1999). Over 40 per cent of the US population had some form of net access by the year 2000 (Nielsen Net Ratings, February 2000). As shown in the Rogers and Malhotra chapter of this book, the growth of the Internet and World Wide Web has exceeded early expectations and we truly have a new medium of political communication.

While in 1996 only 6.4 per cent of US households had one or more Internet users, the number of Internet users increases exponentially every year (Whillock, 1997). Despite this rapid adoption of the Internet as another channel of communication, the political uses of the Internet are not as substantial as one might surmise from the statistics regarding dramatic increases in general network usage. Studies indicated that in 1996, about 50 per cent of Internet users claimed to be online at least 10 hours per week (Davis and Owen, 1998). Those who get news on the Internet are most likely the same people who seek out news in traditional media such as print and television (Davis and Owen, 1998). Pew Research Center data indicated that about 12 per cent of the American voting age population used online sources for political information in 1996. The same data set indicated that only about 4 per cent of the same population used online sources during the election of 1996 (Davis and Owen, 1998). Of the Usenet groups on the Internet, only about 12 per cent of them concern politics (Hill and Hughes, 1998).

According to the GVU 5th Survey done in 1996, Web users tend to be interested in politics as reflected in the finding that 92 per cent of those who completed questionnaires are registered to vote and 60 per cent of them report participating in recent elections. The data also indicated that over 40 per cent of the Web users self-report being more involved with political issues since coming online (GVU, 1996a). Hill and Hughes (1998) argue that survey data indicate that Internet activists are more politically active than both non-Net users and Internet users who are not activists. By activism, they refer to political communication on the Net. Of course, we must remember that causal directions are still at issue regarding these types of generalizations. Do activists become more politically active due to their use of the Internet or do they merely add the Internet to their ongoing activism?

While the Internet user and World Wide Web users tend to be more affluent and more educated than average Americans, these are the people that are most likely to vote, and are, therefore, target audiences for candidates and leaders. Some data indicate that Net users are more informed that non-Net citizens. Whillock (1997) argues that this suggests that Net users are more active than passive in information seeking and they are reinforced in their use of information.

Data on the White House CMC System

An MIT Artificial Intelligence Lab survey of WHCMC users in 1996 (1472 respondents) indicates that by July 1996, over 6400 documents were distributed and archived. White House documents were distributed to over 4000 e-mail subscribers. The White House Web site was being referred to by more than 30,000 Web pages (Bonchek et al., 1997). Some key data about users and usage are shown in Tables 7.1, 7.2 and 7.3.

As seen in Table 7.1, the most prominent kinds of bias (positive differences scores in the table) for the WHCMC system are for gender, income and education. The survey's data indicate that present users of the White House CMC system are wealthier than the general population, more educated than most Americans, younger than most of the population, and that the system is used by people who are more politically active than other citizens (Bonchek et al., 1997). There is also a gender advantage for males (80 per cent of the total users). However, the White House CMC analysts argue that when you compare the bias of the system toward Anglos, males, wealthier people, more educated and younger people, that the trends are similar to the Web patterns found in the GVU surveys. This includes a gradual diminishing in these biases (Bonchek et al., 1997). Perhaps oddly, they suggest that women may be lower in user percentage because women have a lower interest in public affairs. The GVU data for 1996 indicated that Web usage appeared to be approximately 69 per cent male and 31 per cent female (GVU, 1996b).

In Table 7.2, there are data regarding the uses of the White House CMC system. These data are much more promising than the demographic figures just discussed because they indicate that there may be some information-seeking resources available to users.

The uses data (Table 7.2) indicate that WHCMC users find politically useful functions for documents that they retrieve. The system analysts' inference from this observation, whether defensible or not, is that the ease of retrieval and the

TABLE 7.1   *1996 WHCMC user data/users*

Factor	WHCMC	US	Difference
Male users	80%	49%	+31
Income over $50,000/year	47%	27%	+20
Anglo users	82%	75%	+7
Over 55 years of age	8%	21%	−13
Under 35 years of age	46%	39%	+7
College-educated	69%	28%	+41

TABLE 7.2   *1996 WHCMC user data/system uses*

Factor	Data
White House documents used as first-hand news	48%
Have sent e-mail to White House	50%
Get more information about political processes	35%
Redistribute documents online	68%

TABLE 7.3   *1996 WHCMC user data/attitudes*

Factor	Data
Web helps connect with similar people	37%
Web makes government more personal and accessible	62%
More involved with issues now	61%
More involved with personally relevant issues now	43%

fact that many users forward information to other citizens helps citizens become more connected with their government (Bonchek et al., 1997). They argue that the WHCMC system is a useful mechanism for 'connecting citizens directly with their government'. It may be more accurate to conclude that the system appears to facilitate citizen retrieval of government-posted documents.

The 1996 data also show interesting findings about user attitudes about the utility of the system. Key findings are shown in Table 7.3.

These data reveal that 62 per cent of the WHCMC system users find government becoming more personal and accessible as they use the system and the WWW. They also indicate that 61 per cent perceive themselves as becoming more involved with important issues (Bonchek et al., 1997).[6] The survey also shows that some users report that they engage in communication with government officials, distribution of political data, and involvement with political initiatives online while not doing so offline (Bonchek et al., 1997). The data also show that the WHCMC system users employ retrieved documents to use in interpersonal or CMC conversations.

The system analysts acknowledge that '... the citizens who are utilizing the new media are predominantly those who are already privileged and politically active' (Bonchek et al., 1997: 7). Despite this admission, however, they say that the system, along with the Internet and World Wide Web, is contributing to improved feelings of political efficacy. This goes well beyond the simple observations by others that WHCMC users are doing more with this type of information than with that obtained from traditional mass media (Whillock, 1997).

TABLE 7.4 *Verbatim reactions of student WHCMC users*

Positive Reactions	Negative Reactions
'It is very important if the White House considers the messages.'	'I think this e-mail is a waste of time … In this way voters can think Clinton is paying attention to communities.'
'It is very important in letting the people participate with their opinions and making them feel that they are part of the government.'	'Get a team of REAL people to reply – it's still we the people, right?'
'A good idea if it is taken seriously. A good first step. The next step is to get politicians to act upon this new system.'	'It will help people who have access to e-mail and who have an interest in becoming more informed. Since it doesn't allow for people to express feelings, thoughts, opinions, etc. this is more like a one-sided conversation.'
'It makes me feel that I can build a closer relationship with the federal government.'	'It is not as personal as I anticipated.'
'It is very important in giving people information about government.'	'… it's just bureaucracy as usual… Our messages are not even read by the President, so what's the use?'
'I can't recommend any improvements to the system until I get familiar with it.'	'It seems like a waste of time and money. It just reinforces my old beliefs that the government is nothing but a bunch of red tape.'
'A symbolic attempt to bring the American people "in touch" with the lofty house on the hill. If having messages scanned, tallied, or instantly deleted with a boiler plate response is important, it could be a little [important to improve communication].'	'It's obvious that my message was received because I received a reply, but I don't know if it was ever read. I'd like to know what they thought of it.'
'… if you were to really use the system, I think you would feel involved. It is faster and the President can receive citizen input on all aspects.'	'I got the impression that my e-mail message was not important and that they didn't have time to answer my questions, so they sent a message back that they send to everyone.'
	'This system does not make me feel involved, but it does give me another channel for possible information. The reply should have some content pertaining to the user's questions.'

While the claim about increasing political efficacy remains unproven, there is evidence supporting the claims that the system and WWW are facilitating the ability of users to contact government officials and agencies, to retrieve information, to conduct online petitioning, to coordinate political activities and to help people locate others with similar interests (Bonchek et al., 1997). Still, the data show that the most prevalent reason for using White House online documents over other sources is the speed of access (32 per cent). Other reasons for this source preference are all below 25 per cent (Bonchek et al., 1997).

One of the current methods for ascertaining how people respond to Web sites is the employment of user studies, usually in small samples with either quantitative, qualitative or both kinds of data (Rich, 1999). Such studies reveal what people like or dislike about this new form of communication. Often the user studies reveal perceptions or attitudes that were not anticipated by the site designers. Sixteen students in a basic communication course were asked to try out the WHCMC system and to describe their reactions to it. Their reactions are listed in Table 7.4.

From this small set of qualitative data (Table 7.4), we can see that these student users of the White House CMC system perceive it as another channel of information and one that can be useful for retrieving information. On the other hand, many of them also perceive an impersonal property to the system and a need for responses to specific message content – what Rafaeli (1988) calls inter-activity in communication. If such views are held by larger numbers of users, there is an indication that WHCMC users are mixed in their views about the system. Positive reactions include perceptions about obtaining information and sending input messages to the White House. Negative reactions include percep-tion of low social presence in the technology. Social presence is a term used in studies and theories of CMC to indicate how much communicators have a sense of interpersonal relationship while using a particular medium. Social presence tends to be a function of a particular medium and how it is used (Short et al., 1976). Obviously, all of the minor empirical observations just described need to be tested with probability-sample and extensive analysis research methods.[7]

Perspectives of Evaluation

The perspectives of evaluation that will be addressed for the WHCMC system concern theories of communication for democracy and theoretical models of democracies. There are three general orientations of evaluation regarding the new media of political communication: optimistic, pessimistic and objective. The optimists hold that political CMC reinvigorates or even creates democracy (Barber, 1984; Groper, 1996; Naisbitt, 1982; Schneider, 1996; Whillock, 1997). Pessimists argue that political CMC simply reinforces or transforms old inequities and injustices into new ones (McChesney, 1996; Schiller, 1996; Webster and Robins, 1989). Alternatively, objectivists hold that there are both positive and negative consequences to the new media and that the contributions to democracy will only follow theory and political will dedicated to democrati-zation of society (Davis and Owen, 1998; Graber, 1996; Hacker, 1996a; Hill and Hughes, 1998; Pavlik, 1998; Rucinski, 1991; van Dijk, 1996).

The assumption or hypothesis that greater acquisition of information results in higher levels of political participation has yet to be tested (Whillock, 1997). Still, WHCMC analysts assume that connectivity and participation are gradual processes which will take years to evolve. They claim that it can be encouraged by the federal government yet moved by private market forces. They also argue that an information infrastructure will benefit all or most Americans in terms of knowledge, political information and democracy in general. Moreover, they assume that the learning and experiencing of high levels of political participation are part of a long-term evolution that will take at least one generation to grow into. In other words, Americans will gradually learn to become more involved with government over time as government becomes more accessible with the NII and WHCMC system. From a scientific point of view, these claims are problem-atic because they push empirical confirmation or falsification far into the future and unspecified points in time. In an e-mail interview with former White House e-mail director Jock Gill, I asked him to comment on the fact that other media were once hailed as ways of enhancing democracy, but seemed to fail with their charge. Gill argued the following (personal mail, November 1996): 'Early stages of diffusion are not very useful for the long term implications. Who had telephones in 1920? TVs in 1950? The Internet in 1994? The interesting data will emerge in 20 or so years.' Gill also argued that the growth in the number of government Web sites is a sign that citizens are becoming more involved with government. While short-term scientific evaluation of the WHCMC system remains problematic, there appears to be some merit in the White House argument about possible long-term changes.

We know that social scientists need to test various assumptions about the linkages between computer networks and citizen involvement. Quite a while back, Gina Garramone, Allan Harris and Gary Pizante (1986) tested citizen motivation to use computer-mediated political communication systems (CMPCS). These researchers note how common it is to assume that interactive media release citizens from the constraints of mass media while never testing the assumption. Their study found that traditional political participation predicts motivation to use computers for political communication for computer owners. Another significant predictor is anticipated satisfaction. The researchers note that '... rather than closing the gap between the politically active and the politically inactive, the CMPCS may widen the gap' (1986: 455). This is a striking finding when found in the middle of a discursive context created by so many Utopian claims about 'teledemocracy' and 'cyberdemocracy'.

Above and beyond the data gathered by the White House CMC analysts, there are many issues which have to be systematically addressed in order to employ CMC as an instrument used to democratize political communication. First, there are access variables such as universal or available service, computer/terminal access, etc. There are also factors of education and training. In addition, citizens who benefit from CMC use are the ones most likely to continue using it. The federal agency, the National Telecommunications and Information Administration (NTIA), has documented, in 1995, 1997 and 1999 that minority group members have been behind Anglo (majority) group members in both computer ownership and online activity. This is true even when controlling for education and income. The NTIA data also indicate that at higher levels of income, people have the resource capabilities that make online political activity more probable for them. US households with an annual income of $75,000 or more, are 20 times as likely to have Internet access as those households at the lowest income levels ('Falling through the net', 1999). As van Dijk shows (Chapter 10), many of the digital divides in Internet usage such as the ethnic digital divide, have worsened in recent years. Doris Graber (1996) argues that the Internet inequalities and divides among rich and poor groups are creating a situation where our polity will become more fragmented. Recently, several online reports have challenged the NTIA studies and have asserted a closure in the ethnic gap. I contacted two of these sources for explanations including methodologies, no replies were received.

The White House CMC planners used a variety of communication concepts in designing the system. Their design was founded on strong arguments about the need to change the broadcast, or top-down nature of previous presidential communication with citizens. However, the communication theory concepts of feedback, interactivity and reciprocity were sparsely employed by the system designers, if they were used at all. These theoretical constructs could be useful in grounding future system development in a theoretical base regarding political communication. Such a conceptualization of political communication could then be brought together with a theory-grounded perspective of democracy and democratic communication.

One might wonder if a strong indictment is in order here since interpersonal communication might not be possible for citizen–government CMC. Perhaps the problems with interactivity as described above abound with all CMC. Will this let the White House off the hook in terms of maintaining a system that is not meeting its strongest challenges? An examination of CMC research and political communication literature indicates that it does not. First of all, we know from the recent studies by Robert Kraut and others (1998) that interpersonal communication is the use of the Internet that appears to be driving other uses. Electronic mail is one use of the Internet found repeatedly as a major activity of Net users. The research of Walther and Burgoon (1992), Park and Floyd (1996) and others regarding CMC and interpersonal communication, indicates that people can form friendships and relationships over the Internet. They can also work on tasks with CMC and on the Internet. Numerous studies regarding organizational communication, distance education, virtual classrooms and computer-mediated interpersonal communication indicate that work and communication can be accomplished by CMC, in the absence of face-to-face contact (Fulk and Steinfield, 1990; Rogers, 1986). With all of this in mind, it is apparent that interactivity and dialogue are possible with CMC, albeit in different forms and structures than found with face-to-face or other communication modalities. Therefore, there is little merit to the suggestion that CMC is inherently problematic as a form of communication in contrast to face-to-face communication.

Political Interactivity and CMC

Traditional mass media-oriented political communication involves channels that provide one-way dissemination of political information such as news and White House press releases. Some observers believe that computer-mediated communication (CMC) offers an alternative to mass communication and its linear flow of information. James Carey (1987) argues that interactivity is necessary to transform consumers into citizens. With this alternative, citizens can arguably be involved with more interaction about policies and issues. Consumers are more likely to respond to messages in routine ways.

Humberto Gonzales (1989) argues that public policies are based upon public argumentation. Feedback, in his view, is not generated solely by receivers of messages. Rather, feedback results from senders of messages stimulating their receivers to provide feedback. This is consistent with the technical meaning of the term feedback as it is used in cybernetics where the term originated (Powers, 1976). Accordingly, effective political communication produces a feedback loop between communicators discussing a political subject. This loop is initiated by the first sender of messages. The concept of feedback, so essential to any valid description of human communication in general, is obviously essential to theoretical discussions of computer-mediated political communication.

In communication theory, the interactivity construct has been developed most by communication scientist Shezaf Rafaeli (1988).[8] He defines interactivity as message interdependence. In any episode of social interaction (communication), there is a degree to which communicators react to statements made by each party. Simple reactions produce what Rafaeli calls message dependence. Message dependence is a situation where the content of one utterance addresses the content of another utterance. An example of this is where an answer is given in relation to a question. With message dependence, statements refer only to preceding utterances. Going further, interdependence of messages is a situation where statements refer back to more of the conversation than immediately preceding utterances. Interactivity is comprised of message interdependence since statements build upon each other and subject matter is developed by the two-way message exchange of the communicators.

Dianne Rucinski (1991) develops the construct of reciprocity to discuss the role of old and new media in serving democracy. Rucinski argues that any improvement of democratic participation or policy making must be preceded by analysis of relevant communication processes. Reciprocity adds to the ideas of feedback and interactivity by signifying the shared knowledge of the interests and perspectives of others engaged in a political communication process or episode. Having knowledge of others' interests and perspectives of situations that form topics of communication, allows communicators to participate in the kind of conciliatory processes necessary to democratic policy formulations (Rucinski, 1991). With a low degree of reciprocity, a communicator knows only his/her own point of view, thus having knowledge of only one political perspective and one set of interests. Conciliatory discourse, which depends on reciprocity, facilitates co-operative political decisions through discussions which respect and consider a diversity of viewpoints (Rucinski, 1991).

If we bring these three communication theory concepts together, we can gain a stronger understanding of how CMC might be used to encourage more democratic communication. Communication about government and with government that involves feedback, message interdependence and reciprocity meets the conditions necessary for the types of communication that have historically contributed to democratic political systems. As these communication theory concepts appear absent in the WHCMC design, interactivity was left at a micro and technical level of user operability and message dependent interactions with the White House. Incoming e-mail messages may be responded to with message responses (message dependence) from appropriate agency representatives. Moreover, feedback is mechanical and reciprocity is scarce.

Laura Gurak (1997) observed the White House responses to what she describes as online activism, in this case, protests against the Clinton proposals for the

Clipper Chip. She found that CMC was useful for activists' efforts at forming a community of protest as well as creating coalitions of groups to form a unified movement of protest. However, she did not observe what we can call interactivity as described above. According to Gurak (1997: 127), White House responses to protestors' questions were too simplistic and did not directly address their concerns: 'The government's posting suggests that officials avoided a true opportunity for dialogue in cyberspace and instead relied on conventional communication methods (the formal-sounding press release) and traditional means of seeking public input (meetings and hearings).' Such observations do not support the White House claims about using CMC to increase responsiveness to citizen concerns and to increase citizen input into government. Still, Gurak (1997) concludes that WHCMC system and other forms of computer-mediated communication are still in their infancy and will be shaped by those who seek power. Accordingly, Gurak (1997: 43) reminds us that the political aspects of CMC are linked to the political aspects of other spheres of power: 'Claims about the Internet, democracy, and the power of the vox populi must be carefully tempered with considerations of the greater social and political forces at work.'

Now that we have discussed standards of interactivity that are derived from communication theory to serve as criteria for evaluating the WHCMC system, we need to add the standards derivable from various theoretical models of democracy.

What Type of Democracy for Electronic Democratization?

Jan van Dijk (1996) argues that there are several types of democracy and that we need to know differences among these types to comprehend varying directions in analyses of digital democracy. In Chapter 3 of this book, he explains a sixth model known as a libertarian model of democracy. Only five of these are reviewed here in order to demonstrate the analytical differences that are necessary for an evaluation of the WHCMC system.

One type of democracy is legalist democracy. This is akin to what is known as liberal democracy as advocated by the political theorists John Locke and Charles de Montesquieu. Like the original ideology of liberalism, liberal democratic thought stresses liberties of individuals, majority rule, free speech and private ownership of property (Ball and Dagger, 1995). Liberal democracy is grounded in the belief that democracy is not a goal in itself, but that democracy should safeguard freedoms and liberties of individuals. It is subscribed to by both liberals and conservatives.

Another model of democracy is the competitive democracy model. This one is strongly committed to representative democracy and views politics as competition between parties and leaders for the support of voters. Through competition, the best leaders are assumed to get elected (van Dijk, 1996). Power is given to the leaders and their experts. It is clearly reinforced by two-party systems in which candidates employ mass media to compete with each other.

Plebiscitary democracy is direct democracy and assumes that political decision making should be given to private and individual voters. It is rule by referendum. Ball and Dagger (1995) describe direct democracy or 'people's democracy' as a system that can fit systems as diverse as that of the ancient Athenians and that of contemporary Communists. Rule in this kind of democracy favours the demos, or common people, but it is permissible to have dictatorship enforce such rule (Ball and Dagger, 1995). This model of democracy assumes that citizens should make decisions by plebiscites.

A fourth model of democracy is pluralist democracy. Organizations and associations of civil society mediate between government and citizens. Democracy is seen as a shifting coalition of minorities rather than the power of majority vote (van Dijk, 1996). Civil society has a role in this model of democracy. The political system is conceptualized as a system of power centres rather than as a pyramid or other hierarchical structure (van Dijk, 1996). Thus, there are shifting coalitions that constitute the largest amount of power, rather than single majority.

A fifth model is participatory democracy. Its central aim is citizenship. It borrows heavily from the political theory of Jean-Jacques Rousseau. Rousseau argued that the will of the people is not shown in measuring the views of individual citizens, but rather in collective discussion and education. It is necessary to educate the citizens as active members of communities. The totality known as the will of the people is created in public discussion. This argument opposes direct democracy and sees it isolating individuals and encouraging manipulation. Public will can be created in discussions and education.

Problems emerge if we try to match CMC system types with models of democracy. More empirical work is necessary before such matching can be confidently relied upon. We must be critical of how democracies are defined and how many actual types of democracies exist. Caution may be in order when we assume that any correspondence between a CMC system and type of democracy is fixed or pre-determined. On the other hand, if a political system names its preferred type of democracy, and we know what the CMC in question is capable of, we can make judgements about how much the system can aid that type of democracy.

The WHCMC system must be evaluated in light of the systems described above, but particularly in relation to participatory democracy because of the fact that numerous White House statements claimed that the system would aid that form of democracy. As shown earlier, the White House repeatedly assured people that the WHCMC system, along with the NII, would help participatory democracy to expand and flourish in the United States. This means that the system should be facilitating collective discussion and public education regarding important political policies.

Evaluation of the WHCMC System
Contributions to Digital Democracy

In light of the White House claims, user data, and theoretical perspectives on democracy and communication, it is now possible to evaluate the WHCMC system for what it has accomplished to date.

It is clear that the system has made government documents easier to retrieve than ever before. This is due directly to the technology of Web pages, browsers and archives. The White House claimed that the WHCMC system would diminish top-down information dissemination and the nature of the Web has made that possible as online explorers can search and navigate through document archives quite easily. Bradley and Frederick (1994) found that the WHCMC system made some documents available that were not found in traditional sources.

The claims regarding the WHCMC system linking people more with their government are true, albeit in a superficial sense. There is greater potential for contact because there are more and faster channels of message sending and receiving. Yet greater contact does not assure improved participation or increased influence. If the WHCMC system is working as it is claimed, we should find changes, even if slow ones, in political efficacy. Between 1992 and 1996, however, the percentage of Americans who agree with the statement, 'People like me don't have any say about what government does', rose from 36 per cent to 44 per cent (Flanigan and Zingale, 1998). This is the highest percentage of problematic political efficacy since 1952. During 1952 and 1996, no more than about 10 per cent of the American population has been actively involved with political party work, donations or meetings (Flanigan and Zingale, 1998). Voting turnout in 1996 was lower than in 1992. In 1956 and 1960, political scientists report that political efficacy was high for 64 per cent of the electorate in the United States; that in 1980, it had sunk to 39 per cent; and by 1996, it was down to 28 per cent (Abrahamson et al., 1999).[9] Clearly one must ponder if digital democracy is having any positive effect if organic democracy continues to decline in the areas of participation and citizen confidence.

While the WHCMC system has provided more connectivity, it is not clear that its claims about increased government responsiveness to citizens can be confirmed. Certainly there is faster routing of messages with e-mail than with paper mail, but we do not know if the former has stronger impact than the latter. If the impact is the same, citizens simply have an alternative channel.

Some White House CMC system analysts suggest that local levels of CMC are more important than the WHCMC for tangible contributions to democracy. This may prove to be true if, as John Keane argues (in Chapter 5), political CMC makes its main contribution by creating numerous political and private spheres which are interrelated and through the spaces themselves and through their connectedness, power is encouraged through various processes of interactivity. Of course, it can also be true in the mundane sense of local issues and problems being easier to address by government officials.

The pattern of use of the White House e-mail system appears consistent with patterns of computer use and CMC user in general. That is, there is a stratification in who uses the White House system despite the fact that it is open for all. The arguments made by analysts of the system that it depends on time and that it must evolve from the bottom up are interesting, but not demonstrable (and not falsifiable). Perhaps most political interactivity, in early stages of innovation at least, will occur with local government CMC systems. At the local levels, it is much more likely that citizens can create micro-CMC public spheres. These spheres, while not capable of social transformation, can provide active centres of political discussion which result in activism and solidarity for certain causes.

For now, we can summarize what the White House accomplished in light of what it claimed it would do with its CMC system. Table 7.5 shows the claims and

TABLE 7.5 *WHCMC claims and accomplishments*

Claimed	Accomplished
Greater connectivity of government and citizens	+
Easier citizen access to government documents	+
More/enhanced democracy in the United States	?
Decreases in political disaffection	−
Less top-down information dissemination	?
Greater citizen participation in government	?

which ones are verifiably (substantiated by empirical data) accomplished. A '+' indicates something which empirical data indicate is accomplished, a '−' indicates an apparent lack of accomplishment, and a '?' indicates that we do not have evidence of such an accomplishment.[10]

The tally above indicates that the WHCMC system added more channels to political communication in the United States, made citizen access to agencies and documents easier, and provided more channels for message input. These are important accomplishments and should not be minimized. However, the changes in democracy that were claimed are not the changes made by the system. The political system in the United States remains as it was before the Clinton administration. It is a representative democracy with most citizens having only minor roles in the governance of the nation. The WHCMC system has contributed to processes that help those who are already involved with political participation.

As noted earlier, the argument by White House analysts that the CMC system has long-term effects that cannot be assessed in the short-term loses it force each year. If we look at political attitudes over time, we see very little difference or significant changes. Polling data still indicate that most Americans have low trust for government officials, politicians, Congress, etc. and that political cynicism in the USA, as in Europe, remains a strong political problem (Tsagarousianou et al., 1998). No changes at this level can be associated with the WHCMC system.

Despite the sharp challenges made on using digital democracy or the Internet to promote democracy or democratization, there is some hope in using this form of communication as a new form of political communication that can be directed toward promoting more democratic communication in general. This will only come about to a significant extent, however, once a scientific and rigorous approach is taken to making political interactivity a key factor in the design of new kinds of citizen–government communication.

Learning Political Participation by Enhancing Political Interactivity

Through routines and practice of social interactions, anyone begins to learn habits and scripts. If citizens have learned to become consumers, it should be possible to help these consumers learn to become citizens. This may be the most important contribution of the Clinton White House CMC system. It may have generated some impetus toward thinking about a new kind of political socialization, one done not only through media or schools, but also by personal searching and interaction within publicly available virtual spaces.

Political participation, in general, is affected by childhood socialization (Flanigan and Zingale, 1994; Savage, 1995), social class (Flanigan and Zingale, 1994), mass media, and control over work that is experienced in one's job and workplace (Deetz, 1992). Political efficacy has been found to be related to socialization. For some working class children, for example, with domineering fathers who do not allow children's input into family decisions, low efficacy can be a learned orientation for political matters in later life (Flanigan and Zingale, 1994). Perhaps political CMC can provide new opportunities and experiences of initiating political input that result in rewarding feedback. Such experimentation might facilitate the kind of learning of political participation that is not found in early socialization. Two critical concepts here are the learning of political behaviour and the long-term nature of socialization and learning.

Jock Gill and other WHCMC analysts may be correct in arguing that the most significant effects of the system are longer-term more than short-term. It is plausible that working with the system will allow citizens to gain more experience with communicating with the federal government. However, what will make those experiences positive and reinforcing, thereby truly related to learning new forms of political participation, are most likely connected to how interactive the system becomes and how political the interactivity becomes in terms of tangible benefits. My arguments about political interactivity hinge around the term 'political'. In other words, I am not talking about simple conversation between citizens or between citizens and leaders, but rather message interdependence that is *political* in nature. As van Dijk argues in Chapter 3 of this book, politics involves relationships among members of society and those relationships are constituted by communication. Gill and the others seem to articulate this concern, but without the theoretical constructs or models necessary to maximize the system's political interactivity. Political interactivity is more than interactivity and interactivity is more than present WHCMC message dependence.

There is a connection between this faith in socialization and what Keane describes with his three layers of spheres. It may be possible to encourage more micro-level communication about political matters in such ways that citizens learn how to organize political actions from channels or sites of political communication. This is what I might have done in my accidental case study that will be discussed shortly.

Assuming an essential importance of political interactivity as multi-directional dialogue within a political system, the construct of political interactivity can be based on a specific application of the interactivity and feedback concepts discussed earlier. From this, a basic model of political interactivity can be formulated.

As shown in the model of political interactivity (Figure 7.1), there are specific lines of interaction and message flow which make up adequate interaction to produce political interactivity. While normal everyday conversation about light topics such as the weather may suffice with simple interacts (one message → responding message) or double interacts (message 1 → message 2 → response to first message), political interactivity requires two additional lines of interaction.

As shown in the model, the first message moves from the citizen to the government (m1). The second message moves from the government back as output from the government and as feedback to the citizen (m2). This feedback connection

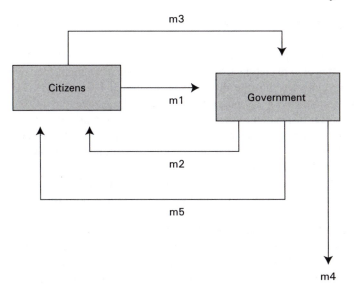

FIGURE 7.1   *A model of basic political interactivity*

from the government to the citizen is a personalized response. It is likely that the quality of the m2 link determines how much further the process of political inter-activity will go. If the quality meets the information needs or expectations of the initiator (citizen), the citizen will most likely evaluate the response as adequate or inadequate and respond to the government message (m3).

The government may react to the second citizen message with either political action (m4) or an explanation of why a particular action cannot be taken (m5). While more messages may be exchanged, this five-step flow of interaction con-stitutes a basic working model of political interactivity from which more complex models can be built. Because it is political, the model shows that communication results in either political action or inaction. Inaction is explained to the person asking for action. This model relates citizen input to government output in a way that truly empowers the citizen and does not simply provide a rhetorical response to the first request, comment or demand. An additional part of this model may be the interchanges (message exchanges) between citizens which occur before one (or a group) sends input to the White House. This is where a coalition or com-munity organizing for political purposes becomes political with its interaction with government. All of the sections or links of this model, of course, are in need of empirical testing.

An Accidental Case Study of Possible Political Interactivity
During work on a phase of this research project, I had an interesting personal experience with political interactivity and the Clinton CMC system. It began with an e-mail message to President Clinton (m1) reporting how my wife, who is a soldier, observed discrimination against female soldiers in the military, specifically in the state of New Mexico. I received confirmation of my e-mail note from the presidential chief of correspondence. Later, in a short time, the director

of the Equal Opportunity Office for a military branch in the Pentagon, phoned me and conversed about the allegations (m2). Letters came later from a colonel and general. After I expressed continuing concern after receiving these letters (m3), another letter of explanation arrived from a colonel at the Pentagon. While I witnessed no evidence that the discrimination ceased, I was impressed with the amount of interactivity that began with one e-mail message to the White House.

Upon closer inspection of the accidental interactivity, however, I realized that nothing more tangible than written excuses were provided to us. The military took no concrete actions against the reported discrimination. In fact, one letter from a general indicated that the discrimination being protested was, in fact, nothing more than what he called 'legal discrimination'. The military respondents did provide reasons as to why they would take no specific actions (m5). While I was not happy with the end results (no m4), I recognized that the government officials did open, albeit in a small way, channels of communication regarding future cases of discrimination and did provide answers to specific questions I had regarding the possibility of constructing a new military base where more women could be employed. From phone calls to letters, I was informed about their evaluations and decisions.

Future interaction could have been continued if I had chosen to continue the feedback loops. I did not, however, and the interactivity soon ceased.[11] It is important to note that, as Gonzales argues, the feedback stopped when the actions of the initiator of communication ceased sending messages. Also, I could have generated more layers of interactivity by starting a group of face-to-face activists, a Web site, etc. to augment the letters and phone calls. Because this was not intended to be a campaign, I ended the feedback loop and interaction at the point that I felt that I had accomplished my goal of drawing attention to the discriminatory practices and getting higher authorities to examine the matter. I also viewed the fact that the military branch in question had been called to task by the White House as a form of political action. Both the Pentagon and the White House were examining the matter.

While this scenario or accidental case study may make it appear that message interdependence or interactivity is already part of the WHCMC system, I need to make three comments about this. First, I have written many e-mail notes to the President and this is the only case where this amount of interaction occurred. All other occasions were cases of either simple replies or message dependence. Secondly, it is important to recognize that the system is capable of accommodating political interactivity at a technical level but the technical level is not enough for widespread social changes. Finally, the interactivity ceased at the point that I gave up the process. This latter observation suggests the possibility that citizen motivation, in addition to government motivation, may be the driving force of political interactivity in this type of communication system.

Toward More Political Interactivity

Davis and Owen (1998) argue that there are four main functions for computer-mediated political communication: accessing information; links between public officials and citizens; forums for political discussions; and public opinion measurement. The first three of these are most relevant here along with the three major concepts of feedback loops, interactivity and reciprocity as well as what John Keane describes as spheres of communication.

As stated earlier, sociological data indicate that both the White House and the World Wide Web cyberspace of political communication continue to be used mainly by those American citizens who already have economic and political power and who are already politically active. It is likely to offer these people new and useful channels, but there is little movement toward empowerment of citizens who do not currently have access to power.[12] White House data show that users of the system browse its contents and do pass on what they find significant to others. Other data, such as that gathered by RAND (Anderson et al., 1995) show that the information rich are increasing their progress into digital democracy at a faster rate than others. Exploratory user data indicate that new users may find the White House CMC system useful for document retrieval more than for personal communication with government officials. New users of The White House Web site find browsing activities useful in terms of discovering sources of information or documents.

In order to conclude that CMC aids democracy, it is necessary to specify how this is done. Communication theory and theories of democratic communication must guide such analyses. At this time, such sophisticated analysis is rare. Instead, we have a morass of Utopian visions of a new Athenian Age of Democracy that emerges from increasing amounts of computer servers, telephone lines, network nodes and fibreoptic backbones. When we communicate, in general, we reduce uncertainties, produce knowledge and form relationships. At the basic level of connectivity, which simply allows social interaction, nothing happens that guarantees democracy. Giving more power to either senders or receivers over how they code or decode messages has no certain effect on power in their relationship. However, increasing political interactivity, which means increasing how much citizens can meaningfully interact with their leaders about issues, with useful feedback about citizen concerns, can move a society in incremental ways toward enhancing democratization.

To accomplish political interactivity as a new political communication project in digital democracy, it may first be necessary to address the barriers to CMC encountered by all citizens of a nation. These barriers are identified earlier by van Dijk as access, opportunities, skills, confidence, etc. Yet there are other obstacles such as uncertainties regarding the efficacy of CMC in interpersonal relationships. New research indicates possible dysfunctional interpersonal communication done with CMC (Kraut et al., 1998). Claims made by social scientists about status equalization with CMC turned out to be either false or exaggerated (Mantovani, 1995). This also occurred with certain claims about the educational benefits of installing computers in schools (Oppenheimer, 1997).

As discussed earlier in reference to learning political participation, it may be possible to encourage more political interactivity by processes of socialization. I wish to acknowledge two possible areas of political empowerment discussed by others. One is the interactive nature of CMC in terms of human–computer/

medium interaction and the other is the power of programming and learning how to change computer program codes. Jacques Vallee (1982) noted that those who learn computer programming always seem to gain power in organizations and societies. More important than this, however, is the fact that previous channels of political communication involving mass media have involved citizens in the role of passive spectators who watch political debates and deliberation. The nature of computers and CMC generally call for greater physical and cognitive involvement if political discussion or deliberation is being attended. Rather than a simulacrum of spectatorship, new formations of CMC can encourage exploration, possible contacts or debate, and the ability to gather and redistribute information. As Kolker (1999) notes, computer involvement involves the learning of skills whereas attending mass media simply involve passive reception.

Through a socialization in political involvement and interactivity by using CMC, it is possible that people will learn how to use e-mail to generate discussions in civil society and contact and discuss issues with government representatives, explore political Web sites to get official and non-official information and arguments about issues, and to create their own repositories (Web sites) for political opinion expression and potential dialogue. These activities alone may seem trivial but taken as a group of involving actions, one can see that citizens who do all of these activities will most likely increase their level of participation in political discussions. Still, this guarantees absolutely nothing about democracy. It can be surmised that the learning of more and more participation behaviours, if they become fulfilling, are likely to entice more people into political involvement which is certainly critical to any democratic political system. Perhaps the most CMC of any sort, at this point in time, can truly accomplish on its own is the enhancement of democracy, rather than the creation or expansion of democracy.

Expectations for social change often accompany the adoption of new communication technologies. As Jones (1995) notes, the White House e-mail system was promoted as a means of connecting citizens to the White House, to make the Presidency more accessible to the people and to increase citizen participation in government. Because the purported intentions and effects of the White House system are long-term in nature, there are three general conclusions that can be argued about its role in democratization. First, it can be argued, as the White House analysts assert, that citizens are becoming more empowered over time and democratization is thus in motion. The second view, which is the converse, is that the whole process mystifies an actual lack of empowerment which is not on the way. An alternative and third view, which I propose, is that the system has initiated important steps toward electronic democratization that are now dependent upon policy guidance in order to genuinely contribute to digital democracy. However, there are critical qualifiers on being optimistic about these steps. First, the initiation of first steps toward democratization does not equal democratization. To some extent, the goals of democratization have been confused with early steps taken toward those goals. This is a conceptual blurring of necessary conditions as sufficient conditions. Secondly, much more work is necessary to supplement these steps, namely greater political interactivity and more concrete steps toward expanding participation and enfranchisement into digital democracy. We will know the system is working as claimed when more people, and people who did not participate in other ways, become involved in democratic political communication and democratic political practices.

When the digital divides begin to close significantly for all social categories, when the organic and digital domains of political communication and politics work closely together for the common good of all Americans and when political interactivity is part of government communication with its citizens, the new technologies of political communication such as the WHCMC system, will be able to contribute to an enhancement of participatory democracy in the United States.

Notes

1 You can presently get this message by sending e-mail to president@white-house.gov

2 Press release from the White House, 30 August, 1993.

3 'The National Information Infrastructure: Agenda for Action', 15 September, 1993. Available at http://www.pub.whitehouse.gov

4 Political Communication Division Pre-Conference, International Communication Association, Washington, DC, 27 May 1993.

5 http://www.info.gov/info/html/customer-service.html

6 It must be noted that the attitude figures reflect feelings about the Web in toto.

7 Nothing can be concluded from such convenience data, especially such a small sample such as this. All that is useful in this description is the simple observation that larger-scale analyses can test the mentioned indications.

8 This concept of interactivity should not be confused with another 'interactivity' concept which refers to human-technology user-friendliness or ease of user control over various technical options.

9 The numbers reported by the researchers are listed for 'white' Americans.

10 By 'evidence', I refer to substantial or significant evidence.

11 One reason for ceasing the interactivity was due to a suspicion my wife and I had that my wife might suffer negative career repercussions if we continued in light of the fact that some of the authorities appeared irritated with the President or his staff inquiring about the issue. I received one angry phone call from a New Mexico military officer who was flushed at the idea of being taken to task by the White House. This particular inter-change was fruitless and cannot be considered political interactivity due to the lack of reciprocity in the officer's discourse.

12 There are at least two opposing views on matters like this. First, one can argue that empowering the empowered is a good thing since those who participate will participate more. The opposing view, and the one I believe most, is that empowerment must not be lopsided in a participatory democracy and that as more and new people are brought into the system of deliberation and decision making, the system becomes more democratic.

References

Anderson, R.H., Bikson, T.K., Law, S.A. and Mitchell, B.M. (eds) (1995) *Universal Access to E-mail: Feasibility and Societal Implications*. Santa Monica, CA: RAND.

Ball, T. and Dagger, R. (1995) *Political Ideologies and the Democratic Ideal*. New York: HarperCollins.

Barber, B. (1984) *Strong Democracy*. Berkeley, CA: University of California Press.

Bonchek, M. (1995) 'Grassroots in cyberspace: using computer networks to facilitate political participation'. Paper presented to the Midwest Political Science Association, April, Chicago.

Bonchek, M. and Gill, J. (1996) 'The internet and retail politics', available on http://www. casti.com/gill/presentations/essays/essay0296.html

Bonchek, M., Hurwitz, R. and Mallery, J. (1997) 'Will the Web democratize or polorize the political process?', *WWW Journal,* 3 (http://www.w3.org).

Bradley, D. and Frederick, J. (1994) 'The Clinton electronic communications project: an experiment in electronic democracy', *Internet Research,* 4: 64–70.

Carey, J.W. (1987) 'The press and public discourse', *The Center Magazine,* March/April: 14.

Chapman, G. (1993) 'Sending a message to the White House', *Technology Review,* July: 16–17.

Davis, R. and Owen, D. (1998) *New Media and American Politics.* New York: Oxford University Press.

Deetz, S. (1992) *Democracy in the Age of Corporate Colonization.* Albany, NY: State University of New York Press.

Diamond, E. and Silverman, R.A. (1997) *White House to Your House: Media and Politics in Virtual America.* Cambridge, MA: MIT Press.

'Electronic communication at the White House' (1994) *Educom Review,* January/February: 16–18.

'Falling through the Net: defining the digital divide' (1999) Available on http://www.ntia.doc.gov/ntiahome/fttn99/contents.html

Flanigan, W.H. and Zingale, N.H. (1994) *Political Behavior of the American Electorate.* Washington, DC: Congressional Quarterly Press.

Flanigan, W.H. and Zingale, N.H. (1998) *Political Behavior of the American Electorate* (9 edn). Washington, DC: Congressional Quarterly Press.

Fulk, J. and Steinfield, C. (eds) (1990) *Organizations and Communication Technology.* Newbury Park, CA: Sage.

Garramone, G.M., Harris, A.C. and Pizante, G. (1986) 'Predictors of motivation to use computer-mediated political communication systems', *Journal of Broadcasting and Electronic Media,* 30: 445–57.

Gladieux, L.E. and Swail, W.S. (1999) *The Virtual University and Educational Opportunity.* Washington, DC: The College Board.

Gonzales, H. (1989) 'Interactivity and feedback in Third World development campaigns', *Critical Studies in Mass Communication,* 6: 295–314.

Graber, D. (1996) 'The "new" media and politics: what does the future hold?', *Political Science and Politics,* 1: 33.

Groper, R. (1996) 'Electronic mail and the reinvigoration of American democracy', *Social Science Computer Review,* 14: 157–68.

Gurak, L. (1997) *Persuasion and Privacy in Cyberspace.* New Haven, CT: Yale University Press.

GVU 5th WWW user Survey (1996a) Available on http://www.cc.gatech.edu/gvu/user_surveys/survey-04-1996/

GVU 6th WWW user Survey (1996b) conducted from 10 Oct.–10 Nov. 1996. Available on http://www.cc.gatech.edu/user_surveys/survey-10-1996/

Hacker, K. (1996a) 'Virtual democracy: a critique of the Clinton administration citizen–White House electronic mail system', in R.E. Denton and R.L. Holloway (eds), *The Clinton Presidency: Images, Issues, and Communication Strategies.* Westport, CT: Praeger. pp. 43–76.

Hacker, K. (1996b) 'Missing links in the evolution of electronic democratization', *Media, Culture & Society,* 18: 213–32.

Hacker, K., Howl, L., Scott, M. and Steiner, R. (1996) 'Uses of computer-mediated political communication in the 1992 presidential campaign: a content analysis of the Bush, Clinton and Perot computer lists', *Communication Research Reports,* 13: 138–46.

Hill, K.A. and Hughes, J.E. (1998) *Cyberpolitics: Citizen Activism in the Age of the Internet.* New York: Rowman & Littlefield.

Jones, S.G. (1995) 'Understanding community in the Information Age', in S.G. Jones (ed.), *Cybersociety: Computer-Mediated Communication and Community*. Thousand Oaks, CA: Sage. pp. 10–35.

Kolker, R. (1999) *Film, Form, and Culture*. Boston: McGraw-Hill.

Kraut, R., Lundmark, V., Patterson, M., Kiesler, S., Mukopadhyay, T. and Scherlis, W. (1998) 'Internet paradox: a social technology that reduces social involvement and psychological well-being?', *American Psychologist*, 53: 1017–31.

Mantovani, G. (1995) *New Communication Environments: From Everyday to Virtual*. London: Taylor & Francis.

Margherio, L., Henry, D. and Montes, S. (1998) *The Emerging Digital Economy*. Washington, DC: United States Department of Commerce.

McChesney, R. (1996) 'Telecon', *In These Times*, July 10: 17.

NII (1995) 'Common ground: fundamental principles for the National Information Infrastructure', National Information Infrastructure Advisory Council release, March.

Oppenheimer, T. (1997) 'The computer delusion', *The Atlantic*, 280: 45–62.

Park, M. and Floyd, K. (1996) 'Making friends in cyberspace', *Journal of Communication*.

Pavlik, J.V. (1998) *New Media Technology*. Boston: Allyn & Bacon.

Powers, W. (1976) *Behavior: The Control of Perception*. New York: Aldinede Gruyter.

Rafaeli, S. (1988) 'Interactivity: from new media to communication', in R.P. Hawkins, J.M. Wiemann and S. Pingree (eds), *Advancing Communication Science: Merging Mass and Interpersonal Processes*. Newbury Park: Sage. pp. 110–34.

'Remarks by the Vice President at the National Press Club Newsmaker luncheon' (1993). National Press Club, Washington, DC, 21 December.

Rich, C. (1999) *Creating Online Media*. New York: McGraw Hill.

Rogers, E. (1986) *Communication Technology*. New York: Free Press.

Rothman, D.H. (1997) 'Inside the White House Web Site', *Yahoo! Internet Life*, 3: 66–71.

Rucinski, D. (1991) 'The centrality of reciprocity to communication and democracy', *Critical Studies in Mass Communication*, 8: 184–94.

Savage, R. (1995) 'Creating the eye of the beholder: candidate images and political socialization', in K. Hacker (ed.), *Candidate Images in Presidential Elections*. Westport, CT: Praeger. pp. 37–49.

Schiller, H. (1996) *Culture, Inc.: The Corporate Takeover of Public Expression*. New York: Oxford University Press.

Schneider, S.M. (1996) 'Creating a democratic public sphere through political discussion', *Social Science Computer Review*, 14: 373–93.

Short, J., Williams, E. and Christie, B. (1976) *The Social Psychology of Telecommunications*. London: John Wiley & Sons.

Tsagarousianou, R., Tambini, D. and Bryan, C. (eds) (1998) *Cyberdemocracy: Technology, Cities and Civic Networks*. London: Routledge.

Vallee, J. (1982) *Network Revolution: Confessions of a Computer Scientist*. Berkeley, CA: And/Or Press.

van Dijk, J. (1996) 'Models of democracy – behind the design and use of new media in politics', *Javnost/The Public*, 3: 43–56.

Walther, J. and Burgoon, J. (1992) 'Relational communication in computer-mediated interaction', *Human Communication Research*, 19: 50–88.

Webster, F. and Robins, K. (1989) 'Towards a cultural history of the Information Society', *Theory and Society*, 18: 323–51.

Whillock, R.K. (1997) 'Cyber-politics', *American Behavioral Scientist*, 40: 1208.

8

Guiding Voters through the Net: the Democracy Network in a California Primary Election

Anita Elberse, Matthew L. Hale and William H. Dutton

Initiatives to encourage digital democracy – sometimes called 'teledemocracy', 'electronic democracy' or 'cyberpolitics' – are wide ranging. They encompass all the various ways in which information and communication technologies can be used to alter relationships between governments and citizens as well as in providing new opportunities for citizens to communicate with one another (Abramson et al., 1988; Becker, 1981; Dutton, 1992). In the 1990s, the public's widespread interest and take-up of the Internet rekindled the debate over electronic democracy (Dutton, 1999: 174–93; Raab et al., 1996; Street, 1997). One promise linked particularly to the Internet and (World Wide) Web to foster more democratic participation has been through its use to stimulate and inform more issue-oriented campaigns (Westen, 1998). However, sharp divisions between teledemocracy proponents and detractors remain over the impact that the Internet and Web will have on campaigns and elections (Hacker, 1996; Solberg, 1996).

Digital Democracy Proponents and their Detractors

On the one hand, many believe that information and communication technologies (ICTs) such as the Internet can enhance democracy by facilitating closer links among citizens as well as between citizens and politicians (Westen, 1998). ICTs could also increase the possibilities for larger-scale debates and more direct forms of democratic participation, through such mechanisms as electronic polling and voting, which might encourage the expanded use of such approaches to direct democracy as the referendum. A related promise is that ICTs could help lower economic barriers created by conventional media, such as with the prohibitive costs associated with TV advertising, and thereby enable more candidates and more issues to reach the public at large. By increasing public access to high-quality information, ICTs could nurture greater interest in politics, and political discourse in general (Becker, 1981; Dutton et al., 1998). One way of increasing the quality of political discourse is by moving discussion away from the current sound bite, image-driven nature of campaigns to campaigns focused on more thoughtful and informed discussions of policy issues, what has been called a move from 'thin' to 'strong democracy' (Barber, 1984). More issue-based political discussion could help voters 'work through' the value choices that are the essence of politics, and reach more considered judgements (Yankelovich, 1991).

On the other hand, concern has also been raised over the potential for ICTs to undermine democratic institutions. For example, it is possible to argue that electronic media will diminish the significance and quality of information in campaigns and elections – updating a criticism frequently levelled at TV (Sabato, 1981). Many early uses of the Web simply broadcast the same information distributed over other media (Musso et al., 2000). Also, ICTs could be used in ways that further distance the public from candidates and erode the quality of debates by encouraging single-issue politics, and only serving actively involved participants. ICTs could therefore reinforce existing patterns of control by helping politicians to more efficiently and frequently gauge and manage public opinion and voting behaviour (Dutton, 1992; Laudon, 1977; McQuail, 1995). A related fear is that ICTs might deepen inequalities in access to information, widening 'knowledge gaps' between information 'haves' and 'have-nots' of an information society (van Dijk, this volume, Chapter 10).

Conceptions of the (Online) Voter: the Netizen

Debate over whether the Internet can be used to stimulate more issue-oriented voter information, and thereby encourage voters to weigh the issues in their choice of candidates, hinges on competing conceptions of the voter, which have been a matter of debate for decades. Are voters 'rational' and what does it mean to behave rationally as a voter in modern democratic societies (see Bennett, 1995; Cukierman, 1991; Downs, 1957; Key, 1966; Kuechler, 1991; O'Keefe and Sheinkopf, 1974)? That is, do citizens weigh the issue positions of candidates in their voting choices?

One view is that the 'responsible' voter should and can make rational choices of candidates if they are well informed on the issue positions of each contender. Key's (1966: 7) seminal work on this question put this clearly in saying: '... voters are not fools. ... in the large the electorate behaves about as rationally and responsibly as we should expect, given the clarity of the alternatives presented to it and the character of the information available to it.' This assumption underpins countless initiatives to improve the quality of issue-oriented information available to voters, from the creation of voter guides to the televising of debates.

There are several alternative views of the voter. One is that voters are 'manageable fools', who can be manipulated by appeals to party, character, region, religion and other buttons that campaign managers can push with predictable results (Key, 1966: 5). Another view is that it is 'rational' for voters to make their choices on the basis of such cues as party affiliation, newspaper endorsements, regional loyalties or liberal-conservative identifications of the candidates. From this perspective, voters are sophisticated enough to use such cues and create a framework for rational choice that avoids the efforts of political campaigns to sway their votes through calculated, issue-oriented appeals.

The thrust of decades of social science research on voting behaviour has supported the view that the position of candidates can make a significant difference in the voting behaviour of the electorate and the outcome of elections (Alverez, 1999: 7–23). But issue voting depends on the 'campaign context' – whether issues are salient and whether the information is available for rational choice (Alverez, 1999). The proliferation of media outlets might supply voters with ample sources of information for making informed choices. Yet many public efforts to provide information to the voter, such as voter guides, are based on a belief that there is more noise than clear signals about the positions of candidates on the issues (Docter and Dutton, 1998).

However, no matter which side of the rational voter debate one takes, the expected effect of lowering the costs of providing and gathering information, such as by lowering barriers of access to information, is to increase the number of voters aware of major issues and to increase the richness of the information gathered (Dutton et al., 1998). Lowering the costs of obtaining information about candidates and issues should enable more issue-oriented voting than otherwise possible.

Digital Democracy in Practice

Since the 1960s, a growing number of initiatives and trial projects centred on digital democracy have been developed in both North America and Europe (Tsagarousianou et al., 1998). Most have focused on providing electronic access to governmental information and institutions. However, some governmental and non-governmental initiatives are aimed at reforming campaigns and elections.

International Initiatives
A well-known example of an early effort to enhance public access to government is the Public Electronic Network (PEN) in Santa Monica, California, which was launched in 1989. This government-sponsored computer network – an 'electronic city hall' – allowed citizens of the city to interact with public officials and with each other. Although initially intended to improve access to city records and officials, the system has become primarily a forum for discussions on a wide range of topics (Docter and Dutton, 1998; Guthrie and Dutton, 1992; O'Sullivan, 1995; Varley, 1991). The City of Santa Monica expressly prohibited the use of PEN for political campaigns and elections (Dutton and Guthrie, 1991). In the late 1990s, a growing number of governments in the US have pursued moves toward electronic service delivery, launching major public sector projects like San Diego County's proposal for creating a 'Virtual Government'.

In Europe, the Digital City projects in Amsterdam, The Netherlands, have received a great deal of attention. These projects, developed in the early 1990s, seek to narrow the gap between politicians and citizens and to increase political participation (Francissen and Brants, 1998), but primarily focus on the provision of various types of public information in electronic forms. Various new ICTs, including the Internet, are used to achieve these goals in similar experiments around the world (Brants et al., 1996; Raab et al., 1996).

Many assume that the conditions for using electronic networks to enhance democracy in the more traditional European political systems are less favourable than in the US (Berra, 1997; Hagen and Jurinic, 1996; Taylor, 1999). For example, some argue that American 'fascination with direct democracy' (Fishkin, 1992) makes the US especially well suited for electronic democracy applications (also see Calabrese and Borchert, 1996). Within the US, California has been identified as the most fertile ground for growing digital democracy initiatives with its ideology of direct citizen participation, which has given rise to such related forms of direct democracy as the referendum (e.g. Barbrook and Cameron, 1996; Westen, 1998).

The Democracy Network (DNet)

California did indeed give birth to The Democracy Network (DNet) – one of the most prominent US initiatives aimed at using the Internet and World Wide Web to support more issue-oriented voting (http://www.dnet.org). DNet is an electronic voter guide geared primarily to the American electorate.[1]

The Center for Governmental Studies (CGS), a non-profit organization, designed DNet as a means for enhancing the quality of information provided about the issues at stake in political campaigns and elections. Its development was in part inspired by the optimism surrounding interactive cable television in the early 1990s. Initial applications were all based on interactive video communication over interactive cable television networks such as Warner's Full Service Network (FSN) outside Orlando, Florida. With the collapse of interactive cable television investments by industry in the mid-1990s, and the closing of Warner's FSN, CGS shifted its attention to the rising media of the time, the Internet and World Wide Web. DNet's Web site was launched during the summer of 1996 (Docter and Dutton, 1998).

DNet developers sought to anticipate the next generation of public affairs television that would eclipse services, such as the Cable-Satellite Public Affairs Network (C-SPAN). It was to be interactive, community-oriented and centred on the TV. With the commercial failure of interactive-TV trials, it shifted to become more anchored on the Internet and Web, but remained focused on fostering more issue-oriented campaigns and more issue-based voting, by providing improved information about the position of all candidates on issues of the campaign.[2]

The Approach of this Study

Our approach to the study of the Internet's role in stimulating issue-oriented political campaigns has been to focus on a case study of DNet and its use in the 1998 California gubernatorial primary elections. DNet was one of a variety of paper and electronic voter guides, such as the 1998 California Primary Election Voter Information Guide/Ballot Pamphlet (http://primary98.ss.ca.gov/voterguide/), yet DNet was the most explicitly focused attempt to stimulate a more informed, issue-oriented debate. Moreover, DNet has been one of the earliest and most successfully implemented efforts to create non-profit, non-partisan, interactive tools for local, state and national political participation (Docter and Dutton, 1998). It has been employed in elections across the US and abroad (CGS, 1998a).

In order to place the study of DNet within a meaningful context, we focused specifically on coverage of the 1998 California Primary Election. Yet even this was too wide ranging to systematically assess. In the five weeks prior to the election, DNet offered California voters position statements and information from candidates for governor, US Senate and attorney general. In addition, DNet provided basic information on all other state-wide candidates, including each candidate's ballot pamphlet statement. DNet also offered official information on all nine state-wide ballot measures, links to local candidates' Web sites and other electronic voter information sources, connections to the media sites covering the elections, an online debate and video candidate statements (CGS, 1998b). We therefore chose our study on the role of DNet in the 1998 California primary on the race for governor.

Case Study Methods

We triangulated on the role of DNet from several vantage points. First, we examined how issues were treated on DNet as compared with television advertising and with the candidates' own Web sites. All three media allow candidates to control content directly, a possibility they do not have in the case of news reports. TV ads are a particularly important point of comparison because of their primacy as a source of information (Atkin and Bowen, 1973; Leary, 1974; Patterson and McClure, 1976; Zhao and Chaffee, 1995).

Only the major contenders for office can afford using television ads, or creating and maintaining their own Web sites in election campaigns. This has been one primary rationale for the development of DNet. While we studied all the gubernatorial campaigns over DNet for the comparisons we draw across TV and the Internet, we focused on the four major candidates, all of whom ran major TV ad campaigns and developed their own Web sites. For these candidates, we compared media in terms of the breadth and depth of issue-oriented discussion, focusing on which issues were discussed in these media outlets, and how candidates treated the issues.

We also interviewed campaign staff, including the campaign managers from three of the four major gubernatorial campaigns.[3] Additional interviews were conducted with other campaign staff, such as 'Web masters', who worked within the campaigns. The primary purpose of these interviews was to provide more qualitative insight into the way in which campaign staff viewed the Internet and, in particular, DNet. This was used to help us understand the reasons behind the ways each campaign used DNet.

Finally, we examined how voters use DNet through an analysis of automatically generated utilization data, particularly server log files.[4] We specifically looked at files for those sections of DNet containing information about the California primary election (http://www.dnet.org/CA/). Furthermore, only usage dealing with the gubernatorial election was studied. The scope of this analysis of usage data was limited to the week immediately prior to the June 1998 election, when voter interest was at its peak.

DNet's Strategies for Improving the Quality of Information

Observation of DNet, interviews with key staff, and reports of the CGS underscore the centrality of several strategies employed to encourage candidates to provide more issue-oriented information to voters. For example, the CGS provided a variety of entry points, so that users could find material in which they were specifically interested.

DNet's site was divided into several sections. Information was provided about voting in general, local elections, ballot measures, campaign finance and media coverage. Visitors (users) were invited to share their views in a chat room. By providing voters with the e-mail address of candidates, visitors were also given a chance to start up a dialogue with candidates.

Also, candidates for governor were asked to post a 5-minute video clip of themselves on the DNet site, which would enable them to go beyond the sound bites of a 30-second commercial. Some candidates decided to use these minutes to air regular television commercials. Others took the opportunity to more extensively introduce themselves. However, some did use this clip to explain their view on issues. Furthermore, DNet had a number of key features designed to encourage candidates to comment on a broader array of issues than might be covered by the traditional mass media and to keep their position statements up to date. In particular the issue grid and 'digital debate' showed how issues could be dealt with on the Internet, and how digital democracy tools could be shaped.

The 'Issue Grid'

DNet's 'issue grid' allowed voters to read each candidate's position on a wide range of issues. Each row of this grid represented an individual candidate for the respective office, in this case governor. Each column represented a particular issue. The cells formed by the intersection of rows and columns identified a candidate's position on the particular issue. A cell was checked if the candidate provided a position statement on the specific issue identified by the respective column. Clicking on the checked boxes led a user to the candidate's statement. If candidates did not provide a statement, a 'no comment' would be displayed in the cell.

The issues were arranged alphabetically in an attempt to treat all issues equally and to avoid editorial decisions by the CGS staff. Candidates could ask for issues to be included in the grid. Other candidates could then submit their opinions on these topics. Namely, a candidate's name would be moved to the top of the candidate list whenever that contender provided new information. Inattention could lead a candidate to move further and further down the issue grid, creating an incentive to address new issues and update their issue positions. Since the issue grid grew to be spread over six screens full of cells, inactive candidates could be in far less visible positions.

Priming the Issue Pump

DNet claimed to give voters the 'first and only online debate featuring all candidates in the Gubernatorial Race' (CGS, 1998a). To accomplish this, DNet staff primed the process by pulling key issue positions of the four major candidates onto the DNet issue grid. The four leading candidates for governor were:

Democrats Al Checchi, a wealthy business leader and former head of Northwest Airlines, Gray Davis, the then incumbent Lieutenant Governor, Jane Harman, a Congresswoman from Southern California, and Republican Dan Lungren, the sitting Attorney General. These were the only candidates given a chance to express their opinions in a traditional televised debate sponsored by the *Los Angeles Times* newspaper. The paper published transcripts on the following day. CGS staff brought these transcripts onto their issue grid and helped to create a critical mass of issue position statements that would encourage others among the 13 candidates for governor to comment on these issues (see Appendix, p. 145).

The Breadth and Depth of Issue-oriented Information on DNet

DNet aimed to broaden the election by allowing all candidates more equal access to the debate than possible over TV and radio. Candidates dubbed marginal by the traditional media theoretically had the same opportunity to participate in DNet activities. Of course, candidates without staff, technological expertise and money may not have had truly equal access, if compared to candidates with well-funded campaigns. Even so, when compared to access to television ads or televised debates, the barriers to entry for minor party candidates were significantly lower for DNet. This was reflected by the fact that 16 of the 17 gubernatorial contenders participated in DNet by submitting position statements on a total of 31 issues (see Appendix, p. 145). For example, CGS staff permitted candidates to call or fax issue-position statements or other material, such as biographical information, to ensure that the lack of Internet access would not destroy a candidate's access to voters over DNet.

Not every candidate participated at the same level. Some provided statements on almost all 31 issues, while others only submitted a few position statements and frequently used the 'no comment' option. For example, one candidate (Pineda) did not participate at all, except for a short introduction provided for by CGS staff. Table 8.1 gives a more detailed overview of the level in which the four major candidates participated in DNet.

Table 8.1 indicates that the four major candidates, particularly Checchi and Davis, submitted a reasonable number of issue statements to the site. However, the major candidates appeared to give priority to their own TV ads and Web sites, using these to feed material to DNet.

For instance, Checchi's opinions on education could be found in all three media outlets. In his television ads, Checchi only merely touched upon the issue. In one ad, a voice-over stated 'Al Checchi will cut state bureaucracy 10 per cent and invest the savings in education'. In another commercial, a voice-over could be heard saying 'Al Checchi – the only candidate to sign the Eastin pledge to raise California school funding to the national average' in an aim to create a distinct profile for Checchi. On his Web site (http://www.alchecchi.com) Checchi discussed the issue in more depth. While in his television ads he rarely talked about proposed action, he devoted an entire section of his Web site to issue positions. In this section he discussed 'Ten big changes for California Education', among

TABLE 8.1   *Issues discussed on the Democracy Network versus candidates' Web sites*

Issue	Checchi		Davis		Harman		Lungren	
	DNet	own site	DNet	own site	DNet	own site	DNet	own site
Abortion				✓		✓		
Accountability of educators	✓	✓	✓	✓	✓	✓	✓	
Agriculture								
Attracting teachers	✓		✓		✓		✓	
Audits								
Auto insurance	✓	✓						
Bilingual education	✓	✓	✓		✓	✓	✓	
Budget surplus	✓		✓		✓	✓	✓	
Corruption								
Crime		✓	✓		✓	✓		✓
Death penalty			✓			✓		
Diversity	✓		✓		✓		✓	
Economic development					✓	✓		✓
Education	✓	✓	✓	✓				✓
Electoral reform						✓		
Environment				✓				
Full-term commitment	✓		✓		✓		✓	
Gay/lesbian rights						✓		
Gun control	✓	✓	✓		✓	✓	✓	
Health	✓	✓	✓			✓		
Housing	✓					✓		✓
Immigration						✓		
Juvenile crime	✓	✓				✓		
Military platform								
Prisons	✓		✓		✓	✓	✓	
Racism	✓							
Responsible investing								
Responsible representation								
Tax relief	✓	✓						
Workers compensation						✓		
Other issues				✓[1]		✓[2]		✓[3]

[1] Including tobacco, protecting the flag, women's rights, veterans, small business, fiscal responsibility and college fees.

[2] Including local government financing, gaming, labour, and women and families.

[3] Including public safety, business and growth, water, transportation and drug use.

other things. Here he dealt with action items in elementary and secondary education: teacher training and standards, school facilities and school safety, textbooks and computers, return to basic skills, bilingual education, universal pre-school, twenty-first century trade schools, local control and charter schools, after-school programmes, long-term planning. A more elaborate discussion of his opinion on bilingual education could also be found on his site. Among his position statements on DNet were comments on 'education' in general, 'accountability of educators', 'attracting teachers' and 'bilingual education'. The latter three comments were his answers taken from the *Los Angeles Times* Forum transcripts by CGS staff. Checchi did not submit any revisions or additions to his comments made in that television programme. Also, Checchi's submitted views on 'education' were identical to those on his own Web site.

Another example is provided by the way Democratic candidate Jane Harman treated health issues. In one of her television commercials, she dealt with patient rights and Health Maintenance Organizations (HMOs) by stating: 'It's an insult when women need permission to see their own gynaecologist. And it's outrageous when people with chronic conditions need permission to see a specialist... As governor, I'll fight for patients' right to choose their own doctor. HMOs must start putting people ahead of insurance company profits'. On her own Web site (http://www.janeharmanforgovernor.com) she provided voters with a more elaborate view. In bullet list format, she discussed various opinions and proposed measurements with regard to the health issue: patients' bill of rights, preventive care, treatment options, tobacco, health research, health insurance. On DNet however, she opted for a 'no comment' box – not submitting a position on the health issue.

The Lure of a Candidate's Own Homepage

All the major primary candidates had their own Internet homepages on the Web, and these influenced the role of DNet in two key ways. First, candidate Web pages, like TV and the newspapers, became another source from which to draw material for the issue grid and candidate biographies. The cannibalization of one media by another is common over time and across media, such as in the early days of cable TV, when cable operators gained critical content by simply relaying over-the-air broadcast stations. Likewise, many newspapers print stories reported first on the Web. In similar ways, candidate homepages became a resource for DNet to create a critical mass of key issue positions, which drew other candidates to the issue grid. In fact, a large part of the issue-oriented information from the four major candidates was derived indirectly from sources, like the *Los Angeles Times*, not from the candidates directly.

We compared issues discussed on DNet with those appearing on candidates' own Web sites and with the *Los Angeles Times* transcripts (Table 8.1), and probed the perceptions of campaign managers. The differences in television and the Web were apparent to at least one campaign manager, who said:

> The fundamental advantage of the Net in communicating to voters is that the other media are quite limited in their capacity to talk about politics. Obviously TV news doesn't cover politics, so you're reduced to 30-second ads created by the campaigns which voters know are self serving ... what the Net offers is basically the ability to make infinite amounts of information available and also because it is so democratic ..., it is empowering to outsiders, notably third parties.

When comparing DNet with candidates' own Web sites it is also apparent that DNet was successful at the margins in fostering a more equitable debate by giving all candidates the possibility to state their positions on certain issues and submit additional issues to be debated. For example, the *Los Angeles Times* transcripts focused on comparing the responses of the major candidates on questions concerning eight issues (accountability of educators, attracting teachers, bilingual education, the budget surplus, diversity, full-term commitment, gun control and prisons). DNet invited all gubernatorial candidates to submit their answers on these same questions. Visitors could view these answers in the 'digital debate' section of the site or in the 'issue grid'.

The majority of position statements were taken from the *Los Angeles Times*. However, three of the four major candidates submitted other issue statements as well. Only the Republican candidate, Dan Lungren, failed to submit any additional statements. Therefore, the use of material from the *Los Angeles Times* seems to have helped generate additional issue statements from the major candidates, and also attract comparable issue-position statements from minor party candidates.[5]

In another way, the candidate homepages actually undermined participation in DNet. Interviews with campaign staff indicated that most campaign managers knew little or nothing about DNet, despite good media coverage and great effort by DNet staff to publicize its existence. A staffer for the Checchi campaign essentially described DNet, yet clearly did not know that it existed. As he put it:

> If we had been approached by someone on the Internet we would certainly have done it. I think it is a great idea. There is not enough of a focus on issues, it is just shocking, there is not a focus on issues. So I think if there were an independent site or issue-orientated site for comparison it would be a great idea.

When the range of position statements on DNet are compared with those on the four major candidates' own Web sites (also see Table 8.1), a mixed situation arises. In general, the candidates' homepages contain a wealth of issue-oriented information. However, candidates often did not submit issue statements available on their own site to DNet.

One example for candidate Harman was discussed above. Several other issues that Checchi, Davis and Harman discussed on their own Web sites were also not submitted to DNet's grid. Sometimes, including Lungren, these candidates gave statements on issues other than the 31 included in the grid. The candidates could have asked for these issues – apparently perceived to be important in their campaigns – to be included in the grid, but they most often did not.

The fact that candidates see their own Web sites to be increasingly important as a campaign tool, such as for organizing, searching for volunteers, soliciting contributions, and registering voters, could be one reason for candidates' desire to strengthen their own sites (see Wasserman, 1998). One campaign manager seems to concur with the importance of each campaign's Web site for activities other than informing voters. He said:

> There are other avenues that help us besides informing the voters, that is part of this, that we probably wouldn't be able to do on a general access site. I doubt we would be

able to put up a finance card [*laughing*] on these [general] sites: 'Please contribute to us by the way'.

In point of fact, DNet did incorporate options for voters to message candidates, such as if they wished to volunteer for an individual's campaign.

In addition to using the Internet as a means for reaching out to voters for contributions and volunteers, the campaign staffers saw the biggest advantage of the Internet as a means for communicating within the campaign organization and not only with voters. All of the campaigns claimed to make wide use of the Internet as a means of contacting the various consultants and field offices. The Checchi campaign even used the Internet as a means for transporting and editing television commercials with great speed. Also, all of the campaigns indicated that the Internet and Web assisted them in various research activities, such as exploring the statements of competing candidates. This focus on using the Internet as a means for internal campaign communication and as a research tool may have blinded the campaigns to the possibilities of using the technology as a mechanism for appealing directly to voters.

In some cases, as the Checchi example demonstrated, position statements were copied from candidates' own Web sites to DNet. This may stem from the fact that in campaigns, time is considered a very precious resource. All of the staffers interviewed indicated that they constantly have to make difficult time allocation decisions. One manager spoke for the others by saying: 'As you know, in a campaign you only have a finite amount of time and you have to pick and choose what you do.' The duplication from the candidates' own sites to DNet and their general lack of interest in introducing new issues may simply be the most expedient resolution of this time allocation problem on the part of the campaign staff. As one campaign staffer thought: 'It didn't make sense to try and replicate pieces of our site everywhere out there. We figured people could just look at our site. Maybe that's something we should have looked at, I don't know.' Nevertheless, we found clear cases in which candidates submitted statements not included on their own sites or in the *Los Angeles Times* debate. In these cases, the issue grid did indeed foster the provision of more issue-oriented information to emerge within the primary election campaign. This is the case, for example, both for Checchi on issues such as housing and racism, and Gray Davis on issues such as crime and health care.

Television Commercials

Undoubtedly, as is obvious from only a cursory view of the campaign, and as examples above help illustrate, DNet offered more in-depth information on more candidates and more campaign issues than offered by television ads. In general, television ads only briefly mention issues important for candidates. The nature of the medium – only a few seconds to communicate a message – makes television ads less suitable for extensive treatment of issues. This was one of the dominant rationales behind the creation of DNet and it remains a valid argument.

This underscores the role played by TV ads within election campaigns, and how this role differs from that played by voter guides in print or on the Internet. In commercials, emphasis is often put on name recognition, association with central issues and slogans and image building, such as the slogan 'Davis. Experience money can't buy' that concluded every Davis ad during this primary.

Television commercials are also often used to attack other candidates' statements and records and to better distinguish a candidate from competitors. Examples of this include: Checchi's ads attacking Davis ('Davis has wasted millions of tax dollars' and 'Davis even charged the taxpayers for his political fund-raising calls'), and Davis' responses ('[Checchi is] a man who killed kindergarten legislation to save a tax break for his airline', and 'a man who fired 4000 people, forced thousands to take pay cuts while paying himself $10 million a year').

There are many examples that support conventional wisdom and the expectations of the CGS staff that the DNet could treat a broader range of issues than commercials. This was reinforced by the fact that campaign staffers viewed television ads and the Internet as two quite different mechanisms for reaching voters. Managers from the Harman and Checchi campaigns, for example, indicated that the Internet was useful, or not, depending on the need to target online voters in a strategic fashion. The Harman manager indicated this with the following;

> I am still a believer that in political campaigns your basic responsibility is to figure out who are your persuadable voters, target swing. If Jane Doe is a target for Jane Harman and she is a suburban mother of two, education, choice, child care, and family leave issues are important to her. How do we get that message to her? Right now the Internet is not a way. She doesn't log on, I think, to figure out which candidate is best for her on those issues. Right now the best way is with television.

Thus, on DNet, candidates were perhaps challenged to participate in debates on a broader range of issues. Unfortunately, the major candidates only made limited use of this possibility. They rarely broadened the debate by introducing statements that voters could not have heard or read before. More often, they used DNet to reinforce messages conveyed over other media as well. Many campaigns failed to look at the voter as rationally driven by the issues, but by more general images of the party candidate's image, such as one manager noted:

> It [the race] is going to come down to potentially who the voters like better, character and personality, who is the funnier guy, a nicer guy, who is the more down to earth kind of guy that you can trust and all that kind of stuff. I think the pictures help and commercials although quick sound bites flashes. It (commercials) shows what kind of person that they are.

However, DNet gave minor candidates a chance to enter the debate, and gain attention for their viewpoints. In that sense, DNet created a more level playing field for all candidates. It also managed to compile a great amount of issue-oriented information.

Usage of DNet Site

The content of TV ads and Web pages is only one side of the coin. The other involves whether and how readers, viewers and Netizens see and use this content. Therefore, we examined the extent to which DNet visitors explored candidates' viewpoints and issue positions. An analysis of server log files, here generated for

TABLE 8.2   *DNet visits, pages and hits running up to primary*[a]

Date	Visits	Pages	Hits
Wednesday 27 May	517	1609	1635
Thursday 28 May	526	1719	1730
Friday 29 May	467	1455	1461
Saturday 30 May	346	1157	1163
Sunday 31 May	581	2454	2460
Monday 1 June	1170	5714	5730
Tuesday 2 June	1838	6796	6800
Total	5445	20,904	20,979

[a] Visits are defined as a series of hits, not separated by more than 20 minutes, while a page is a download of either a file with the extension 'htm', 'html' or 'cgi'. A hit is download of any file type, including 'gif' and 'jpg' files.

the week leading up to the primary (27 May until 2 June), revealed much about DNet usage by visitors who are presumably potential voters. One piece of evidence can be found in the daily number of 'visits', which are counted as a series of 'hits' that are not separated by more than 20 minutes. Another indicator is the number of 'pages' viewed, which is defined as a download of a file with either the extension 'htm', html' or 'cgi'. A 'hit' is a download of any file type, including a 'gif' or 'jpg' file. One Web page, for example, can be composed of a large number of 'gif' and 'jpeg' files (see Table 8.2).

Usage of DNet steadily increased in the last days before and on the day of the primary elections. The number of visits increased from 517 on Wednesday 27 May to 1170 on Monday 1 June and 1838 on election day. This could suggest that DNet was especially useful for voters who did not have time to closely follow media coverage of the Primary Election in the weeks prior to 2 June. The fact that usage of the pages containing issue-oriented information increased during this week may indicate that users are particularly interested in issues as the election draws near. Another cause for the trend could well be the increasing media attention for the elections. Media attention for a certain subject usually results in an increase in Internet traffic on sites related to that subject. The fact that several sites covering the Primary Election and some candidates' own Web sites also featured a link to DNet, probably reinforced this trend.

In total, 3431 unique visitors were identified in the week running from 27 May until 2 June. These numbers are comparable, certainly not low, with usage of other sites with information about elections or political campaigns (Wasserman, 1998). Moreover, it should be taken into account that DNet is a fairly new initiative on a medium that, despite an incredible growth in recent years, still has a marginal reach compared with more traditional mass media. However, this limited number of visitors does imply that DNet's role in the political arena is at the margins. The perception that Internet sites like DNet have a limited reach was a significant factor noted by campaign staff for not participating in DNet.

Daily and hourly averages for hits, pages, visitors and pages/visitors displayed a relatively even distribution of use throughout the workday and evening hours. This could be an indication of the fact that the site was accessed from locations both at work and home.

We were unable to gather information about the characteristics of DNet users. However, it is likely (on the basis of other studies) that DNet users are those most interested in the primary elections and politics in general, and therefore most likely to use other media as well (Bimber, 1998; Guthrie et al., 1990). The providers of DNet are reluctant to survey their own users in light of their concerns over their privacy and limited time. The only information that the log files provide is that the users originated from different domains, most notably 'com' (US commercial), 'net' (network), 'edu' (US educational) and 'us' (US general) domains. Among the first group are many America Online (AOL) subscribers.

Despite a lack of documented information about the characteristics of DNet users, there was a general expectation about campaign and CGS staff that the users were likely to be important constituencies. The most common example cited by our interviewees was the widespread perception that journalists and campaign staff used DNet and the Internet more generally to research the candidates. Moreover, there was a general expectation that computer owners and AOL subscribers represented important segments of opinion leaders.

A key strategy of DNet has been to position their guide so that it would be visible to Internet users. AOL provided a link to DNet on its site – the site that many AOL subscribers view whenever they log into their AOL account – and DNet staff value this placement as one key mechanism for reaching potential voters. However, the log files did not reveal the site where visitors originated from, only the domain they logged in at, so it is not certain how many users were funnelled to DNet by AOL or other gatekeepers.

The uncertainty surrounding the identity of users has an impact on the way campaigns thought about the use of the Internet. For example, this has contributed to campaign staff seeing the Internet as of less utility to the campaign, because they did not view it as valuable for targeting specific 'swing' voters.

Patterns for Using the Issue Grid

Whether and how users navigated through the issue grid are important to assessing the limits of its utility. The log files enabled us to gauge the frequency with which users looked at specific pages of issue-oriented information. The size of the issue grid (32 columns, comprised of 31 issues and 1 general introduction) required that it be spread over 7 separate pages or screens of information.

The issue grid attracted more viewers than other features on DNet, with the number of grid pages viewed being relatively high compared to other parts of the site. For instance, users viewed the California Index page – the page that provided users an overview of all information with regard to the California Primary Election available on the site – a total of 1238 times during the week; one third of the total for the first page of the grid. For many visitors the grid thus seemed the heart of DNet.

However, our analysis found that many visitors only looked at the first couple of pages of the grid. The first page was viewed 3465 times compared to 329 times for page 6 (9 per cent of the total for the first page), and 193 times for page 7 (6 per cent of the total for the first page). Thus, there were relatively few visitors that even scanned or browsed through the complete grid, even though issues were listed alphabetically, rather than in order of importance.[6]

The issue grid did not force all viewers to take the candidates in order. Although the four major candidates were not displayed at the top of the candidate list, issue statements provided by these candidates (Checchi, Davis, Harman and Lungren) were viewed more often than statements provided by other candidates. It seems that name recognition, the popularity of the candidates and media attention therefore also played a role. Only a few other candidates' pages, usually those located near the top of the issue grid, appeared in the top 25 of pages viewed by users.

The Digital Debate

In the same manner an overview can be made of the pages concerning the digital debate that were accessed most frequently. As noted above, DNet opened up the *Los Angeles Times* Forum by allowing all gubernatorial candidates to participate. The questions were listed on one page, and candidates' answers were listed on a total of 8 pages (one for each of the questions posed). The same results emerge. First, the order in which questions or issues were discussed on the site influenced viewing. The first debate questions were viewed most frequently. This linear reading of Web pages from 'beginning to end', despite the possibilities that hypertext creates, is consistent with findings in other studies of how people read hypertext (Douglas, 1993). Secondly, the opinions of the four major candidates (Checchi, Davis, Harman and Lungren) were viewed more frequently than those of other candidates. Only a few minority candidates' opinions appeared among the top 25 of pages viewed.

Summary and Discussion: Developing a Virtuous Cycle of Utilization

The aim of this study was to provide lessons from early uses of an innovative electronic voter guide designed to better inform voters about the full range of issues and candidates. We chose to conduct a case study of DNet in the 1998 California gubernatorial primary, which enabled us to triangulate on our questions through direct observation, interviews with developers and campaign staff, analysis of usage statistics, and comparisons with other media, including TV, newspapers and candidate Web sites.

This case study reinforces the view that DNet does not provide a quick technical fix to problems of campaign financing, and the limited role that issues can sometimes play in voting decisions. However, at the margins, the Internet can, as DNet has demonstrated, make a difference in the coverage of candidates and issues in political campaigns and elections. DNet did contribute to the provision of a broader and more in-depth discussion of the issues than available over the mass media, if in part because the Internet can build upon the content provided through other media. The nature of the medium and the design of DNet contributed to this outcome.

DNet gave candidates outside the mainstream, those with limited means to reach the public in other ways, a chance to be included in the debate and to make voters aware of their ideas. It thus created a relatively more level playing field for all candidates. It also compiled a useful array of issue-oriented information of value to campaign staff, journalists and other political information-seekers. Nevertheless, the limited participation by the major candidates and the vast majority of voters shows that DNet has far to go to reach its long-term objectives. Its novelty and limited use by Californians in the 1998 primary allowed major candidates to focus on their own Web sites, and on more traditional media campaigns, that staff knew how to use to target specific groups of voters.

However, there are reasons for optimism about the prospects of DNet and similar applications of the Internet. First, the public's use of this network increased dramatically as election day approached. Usage in the 1998 general election in California was much higher than in the primary. Secondly, DNet, in particular, has gained the support of important backers and gatekeepers on the Web, such as AOL, and in real-life politics, such as the League of Women Voters. Finally, CGS staff have learned from early experiences, and have embarked on efforts to redesign features of their Web site, including aspects of their issue grid, to fit their increasingly sophisticated conceptions of their users. These developments – with time – could expand the nation-wide reach of providers like CGS and increase utilization. If this happens, a small number of electronic voter guides could gain a critical mass of users that will prime a virtuous cycle for encouraging major as well as minor candidates to follow and support a more issue-oriented debate on the Web. The new question might become: will the new information providers increase their editorial role and functionality in ways that will achieve this critical mass, but also make the Internet converge toward more conventional mass media?

Appendix

Gubernatorial candidates and issues in the 1998 California Primary Election

Candidates		
Bloomfield H.H.	Harman J.	Palitz M.
Checci A.	Jensen P.	Peron D.
Crawford J.D.	Johnson N.E.	Pineda Jr. C.
Davis G.	Kubby S.W.	Rivera E.M.
Feinland M.	La Riva G.E.	Williams J.
Hamburg D.	Lungren D.	

Issues		
Abortion	Diversity	Immigration
Accountability of educators	Economic development	Juvenile crime
Agriculture	Education	Military platform
Attracting teachers	Electoral reform	
Audits	Environment	Prisons
Auto insurance	Full-term commitment	Racism
Bilingual education	Gay/lesbian rights	Responsible investing
Budget surplus	Gun control	Responsible representation
Corruption	Health	
Crime	Housing	Tax relief
Death penalty		Workers compensation

Notes

This manuscript is a revised and expanded version of a manuscript submitted for publication in *Communications of the ACM* (Dutton et al., 1999).

1   Similar electronic guides for voters include Minnesota E-Democracy (http://www.e-democracy.org).

2   Docter and Dutton (1998) provide a more detailed discussion of the motivations and aims behind the development and design of DNet.

3   These included the managers of the Checchi, Harman and Lungren campaigns, Gray Davis' campaign manager was unavailable for interviews in part because he was busy running the general election campaign.

4   These log files were analysed in two ways. First, server statistics such as hits, pages viewed, visits and visitors were obtained by using 'SurfReport' software. Secondly, more detailed information about users' navigating behaviour was gained by analysing raw log files, generated for different times and days included in the sample period, and for visitors originating from different domains.

5   Personal interview with A. Madaras, Project Manager and Producer, The Democracy Network, Center for Government Studies, Sept. 1998.

6   The low number of times pages were viewed can be explained by the fact that only those answers that users viewed after clicking on a certain candidate were recorded. They also had the option to scroll down the page to view candidates' answers on a certain question, but because that did not require clicking, that could not be recorded in the log files.

References

Abramson, J.B., Arterton, C. and Orren, G.R. (1988) *The Electronic Commonwealth*. Cambridge, MA: Harvard University Press.

Alverez, R.M. (1999) *Information and Elections*. Ann Arbor: University of Michigan Press.

Atkin, C.K. and Bowen, L. (1973) 'Quality versus quantity in televised political ads', *Public Opinion Quarterly*, 37(2): 209–24.

Barber, B.R. (1984) *Strong Democracy: Participatory Politics in a New Age*. Los Angeles, CA: University of California Press.

Barbrook, R. and Cameron, A. (1996) 'The Californian ideology'. Paper presented at the 9th Colloquium on Communication and Culture, Piran, Slovenia, April.

Becker, T. (1981) 'Teledemocracy', *Futurist* (December) 7(6): 6–9.

Bennett, S.E. (1995) 'Comparing Americans' political information in 1988 and 1992', *Journal of Politics*, 57(2): 521–32.

Berra, M. (1997) 'Le reti civiche fra comunita e mercato' ('Civic networks linking community and market'), *Quaderni di Sociologia*, 41(13): 5–32.

Bimber, B. (1998) 'Toward an empirical map of political participation on the internet'. Paper presented at the 1998 Annual Meeting of the American Political Science Association, Boston, MA, September.

Brants, K., Huizenga, M. and Van Meerten, R. (1996) 'The new canals of Amsterdam: an exercise in local electronic democracy', *Media, Culture and Society*, 18(2): 233–47.

Calabrese, A. and Borchert, M. (1996) 'Prospects for electronic democracy in the United States: rethinking communication and social policy', *Media, Culture and Society*, 18(2): 249–68.

The Center for Governmental Studies (1998a) 'The democracy network', Los Angeles, CA, June. Available on http://www.dnet.org

The Center for Governmental Studies (1998b) 'The democracy network wins in California: a report from the primary election', Los Angeles, CA, June.

Cukierman, A. (1991) 'Asymmetric information and the electoral momentum of public opinion polls', *Public Choice*, 70(2): 181–213.

Docter, S. and Dutton, W.H. (1998) 'The First Amendment online: Santa Monica's Public Electronic Network', in R. Tsagarousianou, D. Tambini and C. Bryan (eds), *Cyberdemocracy: Technology, Cities, and Civic Networks*. London and New York: Routledge. pp. 125–51.

Douglas, J. (1993) 'Social impacts: the framing of hypertext: revolutionary for whom?', *Social Science Computer Review*, 11(4): 417–29.

Downs, A. (1957) *An Economic Theory of Democracy*. New York: Harper & Row.

Dutton, W.H. (1992) 'Political science research on teledemocracy', *Social Science Computer Review*, 10(4): 505–22.

Dutton, W.H. (1999) *Society on the Line: Information Politics in the Digital Age*. Oxford: Oxford University Press.

Dutton, W. and Guthrie, K. (1991) 'An ecology of games: the political construction of Santa Monica's Public Electronic Network', *Informatization and the Public Sector*, 1(4): 1–24.

Dutton, W.H., Westen, T., Madaras, A. and Weare, C. (1998) 'Designing digital democracy: a field experiment with an Internet initiative aimed at fostering issue-oriented campaigns and elections'. Proposal submitted to the National Science Foundation, 29 January.

Dutton, W.H., Elberse, A. and Hale, M. (1999) 'A casestudy of a Netizen's guide to elections', *Communications of the ACM*, 42(12): 49–54.

Fishkin, J.S. (1992) 'Beyond teledemocracy: America on the line', *Responsive Community*, 2(3): 13–19.

Francissen, L. and Brants, K. (1998) 'Virtually going places: square-hopping in Amsterdam's Digital City', in R. Tsagarousianou, D. Tambini and C. Bryan (eds), *Cyberdemocracy: Technology, Cities, and Civic Networks*. London and New York: Routledge. pp. 18–40.

Guthrie, K.K. and Dutton, W.H. (1992) 'The politics of citizen access technology', *Policy Studies Journal*, 20: 574–97.

Guthrie, K., Schmitz, J., Ryu, D., Harris, J., Rogers, E. and Dutton, W. (1990) 'Communication technology and democratic participation: PENners in Santa Monica'. Paper presented at the Association for Computer Machinery (ACM) Conference on Computers and the Quality of Life, Washington, DC, September.

Hacker, K.L. (ed.) (1995) *Candidate Images in Presidential Elections*. Westport, CT: Greenwood Publishing Group.

Hacker, K.L. (1996) 'Missing links in the evolution of electronic democratization', *Media, Culture and Society*, 18(2): 213–32.

Hagen, M. and Jurinic, M. (1996) 'Americki koncepti elektronicke demokracije i njihovo znacenje za njemacku politiku' ('American concepts of electronic democracy and their implications for German politics'), *Medijska Istrazivanja*, 2(1): 47–70.

Key, V.O., Jr. (1966) *The Responsible Electorate: Rationality in Presidential Voting 1936–1960*. New York: Vintage.

Kuechler, M. (1991) 'Issues and voting in the European elections 1989', *European Journal of Political Research*, 19(1): 81–103.

Laudon, K.C. (1977) *Communications Technology and Democratic Participation*. New York and London: Praeger.

Leary, M.L. (1974) *Phantom Politics: Campaigning in California*. Washington, DC: Public Affairs Press.

McQuail, D. (1995) 'New roles for new times?', *Media Studies Journal*, 9(3): 11–19.

Musso, J., Weare, C. and Hale, M. (2000) 'Designing web technologies for local governance reform: good management or good democracy?', *Political Communication*, 17(1): 1–19.

O'Keefe, M. and Sheinkopf, K.G. (1974) 'The voter decides: candidate image or campaign issue?', *Journal of Broadcasting*, 18(4): 403–12.

O'Sullivan, P.B. (1995) 'Computer networks and political participation: Santa Monica's teledemocracy project', *Journal of Applied Communication Research*, 23(2): 93–107.

Patterson, T.E. and McClure, R.D. (1976) 'Television and the less-interested voter: the costs of an informed electorate', *Annals of the American Academy of Political and Social Science*, 425: 88–97.

Raab, C., Bellamy, C., Taylor, J., Dutton, W.H. and Peltu, M. (1996) 'The information polity: electronic democracy, privacy, and surveillance', in W.H. Dutton (ed.), *Information and Communication Technologies – Visions and Realities*. New York and Oxford: Oxford University Press. pp. 283–99.

Sabato, L.J. (1981) *The Rise of Political Consultants*. New York: Basic Books.

Solberg, J. (1996) 'Disconnected: haves and have nots in the information age', *Library Journal*, 121(14): 200–20.

Street, J. (1997) 'Remote control? Politics, technology, and electronic democracy', *European Journal of Communication*, 12(1): 27–42.

Taylor, J. (1999) 'The information polity', in W.H. Dutton (ed.), *Information and Communication Technologies – Visions and Realities*. New York and Oxford: Oxford University Press. pp. 197–8.

Tsagarousianou, R., Tambini, D. and Bryan, C. (eds) (1998) *Cyberdemocracy: Technology, Cities, and Civic Networks*. London and New York: Routledge.

Varley, P. (1991) 'Electronic democracy', *Technology Review*, 94(8): 42–51.

Wasserman, E. (1998) 'Washington's new strategists spin the web', *CNN Interactive,* June. Available on http://wwwcnn.com/TECH/computing/9806/10/netspin.idg

Westen, T. (1998) 'Can technology save democracy?', *National Civic Review*, 87(1): 47–56.

Yankelovich, D. (1991) *Coming to Public Judgement: Making Democracy Work in a Complex World*. Syracuse, NY: Syracuse University.

Zhao, X. and Chaffee, S.H. (1995) 'Campaign advertisements versus television news as sources of political issue information', *Public Opinion Quarterly*, 59(1): 41–65.

9

The Promise and Practice of Public Debate in Cyberspace

Nicholas Jankowski and Martine van Selm

Widespread introduction of the Internet has been accompanied by hope for a revival of citizen interest and involvement in the democratic process. This hope was the basis for an explosion of initiatives in the second half of the 1990s making reference to 'virtual' democracy, teledemocracy, digital democracy, electronic democracy and similar notions.[1] Further, governmental bodies were – and still are – busily constructing Webster and experimenting with various ways to involve citizens in policy discussions via public debates held in cyberspace.[2]

Although much of this hope can be traced to the hype commonly associated with the introduction of almost any new medium, such 'guilt by association' does not qualify as serious argument with which to support, refute or revise the claims. Rather, empirically-based investigations are needed of such public debates in order to test the claims. It is too early in the history of digital democracy, however, for many such investigations to have been conducted and reported. A few of the presently available studies are reviewed here as illustrations of the research that may eventually provide the kind of scientifically grounded basis for assessing their value. In this chapter findings from three such studies are presented: a year-long investigation of a Usenet discussion, an experiment with specially developed Internet software for supporting public discussions and decision making, and a debate between senior citizens and political candidates on the eve of a national election.

In order to provide a conceptual backdrop for these studies, the 'promise' of cyberspace regarding citizen participation in the political process is considered. Here, some of the literature is briefly reviewed as well as recent tracts promoting the features of virtual discussions for political participation.

It would be unwise to formulate sweeping conclusions based on three modest empirical studies; it would be equally inappropriate to conclude this chapter without suggesting areas worthy of further empirical scrutiny and critical assessment regarding public debates in cyberspace. That such debates will transpire is certain;

that the design of such debates transpires in the light of systematic study of these pioneering initiatives is the ultimate objective of this contribution.

A Typology of Promises

The claims made for digital democracy predate the Internet by several decades and can be traced to the development of earlier communication conduits, particularly radio and television. Television, in its early years, was proclaimed as the long-awaited tool for enlightening the 'masses' (see Kellner, 1990); radio was envisioned as an instrument for achieving emancipatory objectives and facilitating political mobilization (Enzensberger, 1970). Later, with the introduction of cable delivery systems and experimentation with community television, the 'promise' took on a local orientation, but generally with the same aspirations: to contribute to the awareness and engagement of citizens in community action and development (e.g., Jankowski, 1988). And then, with technological innovations like the two-way television experiment *Qube* in Columbus, OH, the 'promise' shifted towards the possibility of direct democracy through instant polling of the population on any issue of the day (Arterton, 1987).

Rheingold (1995) has perhaps popularized the societal possibilities of electronic networks more than any other author. In his now-classic tract on virtual communities he philosophizes on the impact these networks may have for the functioning of politics. He suggests they may allow users to challenge the conventional hierarchies of these systems and thereby reinvigorate citizen involvement in the political process. This development, he contends, may allow the dominant role played by traditional mass media to be circumvented.

Similar Utopian proclamations have been made, albeit in modified form, by American politicians such as Al Gore and Newt Gingrich, and European commissions such as found in the report by Bangemann and colleagues (1994). Although emphasis by these figures is generally placed on improving access to information through its availability on the Information Highway, Gingrich is noted for advancing electronic versions of the classic town hall meeting, and suggesting input from diverse geographic locations to national government committee sessions.

Such claims have been echoed, if not endorsed, by various scholarly commentators. Brants, Huizenga and Van Meerten (1996: 236), for example, suggest that electronic networks have 'the potential to develop into the means of democracy'. They suggest that it may become possible for citizens to select information more accurately and for politicians to direct this information at more narrowly defined target audiences. Once again, increasing the amount and access to information is seen as one of the potential values of electronic networks regarding the reinforcement of democracy. Beyond information, however, electronic networks may also reduce the gap between public discourse and provisions for involvement in decision making (Brants et al., 1996: 243).

In a study of involvement by academic professionals in electronic forums, Rojo and Ragsdale (1997) identify a number of characteristics of Internet newsgroups and discussion lists that relate to some of the 'promises' of digital democracy. One of the positive characteristics cited is development of a shared pool of information for participants. The information contributed to the site becomes a collective 'public good' available to all, independent of the labour or contribution of a particular person. The authors also signal less positive aspects of electronic forums such as the required investment of time and potential risk to reputation that may result from association. They also note the 'free rider' or 'lurker' syndrome common to many newsgroups and discussion lists: that many people passively attend or subscribe to these services, but few actively contribute.

An extensive overview of initiatives with digital democracy has been compiled by Tsagarousianou, Tambini and Bryan in 1998. These authors suggest that digital democracy initiatives may increase the efficiency and ease in accessing information, improve polling of citizens and providing feedback mechanisms, and contribute to a climate favourable to collective political action. Further, these initiatives may facilitate formation of interest-oriented groups and encourage formulation of ideas by citizens. In addition, the 'middle men' – journalists, political parties and politicians – may become less influential in the process of political debate and decision making. Finally, digital democracy is thought to generate services targeted at specific groups, and to contribute to solving key problems associated with representative democracy, e.g. proportional representation, agenda setting, territorial basis of constituencies.

These points are presented in the form of an ordered list and suggest more structure than deserved. There is little reason to assume more value or importance is attributed to the first claim in the list than to the last. Moreover, there appears to be overlap in some of the illustrations cited under different claims. Such matters are common problems with initial typologies and should not be construed as fundamental criticisms. Furthermore, one of the authors of the edited volume (Tsagarousianou, 1999) has since continued the search for a suitable overview of the claims of digital democracy. In her more compact typology, Tsagarousianou suggests three core claims:

- obtaining information;
- engaging in deliberation;
- participating in decision making.

In this unordered list, obtaining information is directly related to the issue regarding which members of society can – and cannot – have access to information made available via electronic networks. Stated in question form, 'are citizens able to interact within the system or is the latter inflexible and therefore characterized by limited access and interactivity?' (Tsagarousiano, 1999: 195).

The point 'deliberation' as noted above is associated with the public sphere and its relation to citizen involvement in a democratic state. Tsagarousianou does not restrict this point to the Habermasian formulation of a single public sphere, but to a multitude of such opportunities for representation and negotiation. According to Tsagarousianou (1999: 195–6), 'new technologies clearly have the potential to sustain such spaces as they enable both deliberation (citizen to citizen communication) and "hearing" (citizen to authorities communication).'

The third and last point, participating in decision making, is said to have two manifestations: through involvement in institutionalized channels such as elections and referenda, and through collective actions occurring outside the vested political order. Tsagarousianou believes the second type, collective actions, may have more promise regarding digital democracy. Here, as with the second point, interactivity is said to be the most important factor for achievement of the potential.

This typology constitutes, in our opinion, the essence of activities related to the democratic process; the related political activities can, in contrast to the way Tsagarousianou presents them, be considered ordered and cumulative in nature. Unhampered access to information relevant to a particular political issue is a pre-requisite for engaging in rational public debate, and such debate is a desired pre-liminary phase prior to political action – be it in an institutionalized form such as voting or in a form organized outside the conventional political structures such as mass demonstrations. The central question, then, is in what manner and to what degree can electronic networks contribute to this political process? More speci-fically, what is the place of virtual public debates in the political process? It is much too premature to consider answering such questions or to conducting an overall assessment of initiatives regarding digital democracy, but initial steps in that direction can be made through examination of initiatives which have been subjected to empirical study, making use of the three-point typology of promises introduced above. In the following section, an illustrative review is provided of three such studies: a Usenet discussion group, an experiment with teledemocracy via an Internet site, and a political debate with electoral candidates 'assembled' on an Internet site established for senior citizens. These three illustrations of empiri-cal study indicate the contours of and need for further research to assess the claims made in favour of digital democracy; some of these contours and needs are sketched in the final section of this chapter.

Usenet Discussion Groups as Venues for Public Debate

Steven Schneider (1996, 1997) has carried out an extensive empirical investiga-tion of computer-mediated communication related to aspects of democracy on a Usenet newsgroup dealing with the issue of abortion. Schneider measured the presence of four core dimensions of the concept public sphere in postings to the newsgroup *talk.abortion*. He investigated the newsgroup for a year (April 1994– March 1995), a period in which nearly 46,000 messages were placed by almost 3000 authors.

Schneider takes the work of Habermas (1974, 1989) as point of departure and differentiates the so-called idealized from the liberal vision of the public sphere. Based on an interpretation of the relation of public sphere to participatory demo-cratic theory, Schneider identifies four dimensions he considers important for development of an idealized version of public sphere. The first dimension is called *equality* and involves removal of barriers impeding involvement in the public sphere. Equality presupposes access to the necessary equipment for any type of substantive involvement, as well as competence in basic communicative skills. This dimension is related to the status of participants and implies a horizontal framework for discourse.

The second dimension, *diversity*, involves the range of topics under consideration. This dimension goes beyond mere opportunity to discuss issues and stresses inclusion of opinions across the spectrum of a particular subject on the public agenda. The third dimension, *reciprocity*, is concerned with gaining awareness of the perspectives of others and is quite similar to what others (e.g. Hanssen et al., 1996; Rafaeli, 1988; Williams et al., 1988) term interactivity in the communication process. Finally, the fourth dimension is the *quality* of the discourse and can be considered, according to Schneider, as a measure of the ability of contributors to remain engaged with the topic at hand, and was operationalized in this study as the proportion of messages concerned with abortion.

Schneider operationalized each of these dimensions in such a manner that a series of quantitative tests could be conducted on the 46,000 postings to the Usenet newsgroup. The sheer volume of postings subject to analysis necessitated a quantitative, automated methodology. Elaboration of the methodological procedures followed in the study goes beyond the scope of this chapter; here, only the main conclusions are summarized.

Overall, contributions to the newsgroup were found to be diverse and reciprocal, but were lacking in Schneider's formulation of equality and quality. The range of conversational patterns was measured as an indicator of the dimension diversity. Schneider found that the number of postings fluctuated considerably during the course of the year of study. Also, much fluctuation was seen regarding the number of participants who would enter and exit at any particular time. Still, there was both a consistent group of regular contributors as well as a subset of authors which was constantly changing, and Schneider thus concludes that the range of participants in the newsgroup was highly diverse.

In order to collect indications of reciprocity, Schneider applied citation analysis procedures as developed in bibliometric studies. Along all seven groups of contributors, ranging from the 'very frequent' to the 'one-time' authors, it appeared that all groups of authors interrelated with sizeable numbers of other contributors. Schneider (1997: 94) calculated that an average contributor interacted with around 35 other authors. His conclusion was that this dimension was particularly prominent on the newsgroup.

As for the dimension equality, the newsgroup displayed a characteristic common to most newsgroups – unrestricted opportunities to post messages and engage in discussion with other contributors – and in this sense it reflected the equality dimension. Nevertheless, the distribution of contributions from participants was highly skewed. Of the 3000-odd contributors, about 150 (0.05 per cent) persons were responsible for more than 40 per cent of the 46,000 postings. Measured slightly differently, some 5 per cent of the contributors to the newsgroup authored almost 80 per cent of the articles. This relation between authors and postings is graphically represented in a Lorenz curve[3] which relates the percentage of total messages per author while ranking the authors in terms of frequency of messages; see Figure 9.1. Regarding the dimension quality, the most frequent contributors to the debate were, in fact, those least likely to post

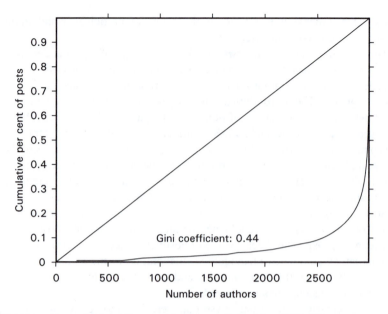

FIGURE 9.1   *Concentration of ownership (Source: Schneider, 1997: 83)*

messages 'on topic', i.e., related to the issue abortion. Schneider (1997: 105) suggests this finding strongly exacerbates the inequality noted above among contributors to the debate.

Schneider's general conclusion is that newsgroups have much potential for contributing to the idealized version of the public sphere. Although two of the dimensions of public sphere did not measure positively in this study, Schneider believes that this form of computer-mediated communication is preferable over alternatives employing moderated CMC discussions. Such editorial control might reduce the range of topics to those deemed suitable by the editorial gatekeeper.

The Achilles' heel in Schneider's study is the disputable manner in which the four concepts have been operationalized. In particular, the quantitative exercise to measure the quality of a debate is suspect, and one of the efforts to replicate Schneider's work (Heilbron, 1999) has added a qualitative interpretative analysis of newsgroup texts to the data collection in an effort to compensate for this deficiency. Further, the analysis is exclusively text-oriented; possible elaboration or interpretation from the persons involved in the newsgroup discussion is absent from the overview.

As for the three central 'promises' of digital democracy outlined earlier, this study seems to imply an abundance of information made available, given the volume of postings. And, given the absolute number of contributors – 46,000 – it also appears as if access to the debate was open and relatively easily arranged. It would be difficult, however, to claim that deliberation took place in the sense of extensive exchanges between contributors. Schneider's efforts to measure this aspect suggest a relatively small number of such exchanges meeting the requirements of an interactive communication process. Finally, involvement in decision making is the most difficult to assess. At best, the newsgroup provided contributors with the opportunity for developing and enacting collective actions. No evidence is presented as to whether such action emerged during the course of the period studied.

Experiment with Teledemocracy

An Internet debate explicitly related to many of the traditional components of electoral politics took place in the Netherlands in 1996. In November of that year a month-long experiment was held with Internet software designed to support public discussions, opinion polling and voting. It focused around regional land use policy, a topic with high standing on the political agenda of the province in which the debate was organized.

The developers of the software had made arrangements with the regional government and with a large number of social and cultural organizations to test the software and a specially designed model for political debate. For practical reasons, the number of persons invited to participate was limited to 100. The research that accompanied the initiative was concerned with determining the characteristics and levels of involvement of the participants, their experiences with and assessment of the debate, and the nature and quality of the discussion conducted.[4] Here, only a brief sketch is given of the central findings as related to the three-point typology of promises sketched above.

It is important to note that participants were not selected in such a manner so as to ensure they were representative for residents of the geographical region. On the contrary, persons predisposed to the topic of discussion, land use policy, and those with interest and experience in Internet-based discussions were more likely to take part. In fact, this last reason – interest in virtual debates – may have been the overriding motivation of a large number of persons in registering for this experiment. By the start of the experiment 87 persons had completed the required electronic registration form – considerably less than the number which the organizers had anticipated.

The persons registered to take part in the experiment ranged in age from 15 to 74 years, 40 being the average age. The group was overwhelmingly male dominated; only two women registered for the event. Almost half had completed a university degree and more than 90 per cent were employed. Nearly two-thirds lived in an urban area of the region, most with a partner and children. The participants owned their own homes and were born and raised in the region. In summary, this profile suggests that the persons who registered to participate in the teledemocracy experiment were well-educated males employed and living for a long time within the province. Apart from the gender bias, the group could be considered a reflection of the established and settled sector of the population with long-term 'roots' in the region.

As for the information made available on the site, there was more than any single participant would want to consume on the topic of regional planning. The regional newspaper opened its archives, organizations and action groups posted statements and documentation, and the provincial government placed policy documents on the site. Regarding the point 'obtaining information' formulated earlier in the typology of promises, then, it seems as if much was made available to the group involved in the experiment.

Individuals and representatives of organizations were able to contribute statements and reactions to other postings during the four-week period. The number of contributions to one discussion, however, far surpassed all others: a discussion initiated by a political representative within the provincial government responsible for land use policy. Nearly three times as many contributions were made to that discussion as to all others. Another way to examine participation is by comparing the total number of contributions from individuals with the number of reactions each of these individuals received to his or her contributions. Once again, the political representative from the regional government had a higher average number of reactions per contribution than any other participant during the debate. These findings indicate that the discussion revolved around the political representative and much less around any individual citizen or organizational representative. This aspect has serious implications for the equality claim often made for Internet-based debates: there was a clustering of debate activity around the participant most obviously representing political power. Taken together with the fact that only a small handful of participants were responsible for most of the contributions, this suggests that a small elite mainly conducted the debate. About half of all the persons registered to participate were responsible for the 298 contributions, and most of these persons made no more than a single contribution during the debate. In fact, 15 persons were responsible for three-quarters of all contributions to the debate. Essentially the same elitist character was found as in the much larger Usenet study that was described earlier. It may be, then, that online discussions are quite similar to real-life discussions when it comes to participation being confined to a small minority.

One of the most important intentions of the experiment was that the results of the debate would contribute in some manner to formulation of regional land use policy – the decision-making point in the typology of promises presented earlier. This aspect was perhaps the most problematic – and unfulfilled – aspect of the entire experiment. One reason for this was that the debate was initiated outside the division of the provincial government responsible for land use policy; the government officials from this department consequently played a very limited role during the debate. Moreover, there was from the very beginning uncertainty as to how the debate might contribute to policy formation. In fact, land use policy had already reached an advanced stage of completion and it was consequently unclear what role there might even be for 'interesting ideas' emerging from the public debate.

Political Debate on *Seniorweb.nl*

A public debate related to the 1998 national elections in the Netherlands was organized on a Web site especially designed for senior citizens, *Seniorweb.nl*. This Web sites had been operational for some time prior to the debate, and is a 'virtual' place where elderly Internet users can 'meet', gather information and participate in moderated discussions about various topics. Older adults have been considered the most resistant group in adopting new technologies. A survey conducted among US citizens aged 55 and older suggests that this stereotype no longer holds; this age group has begun to make use of computers in substantial numbers.[5] Also in Europe a growing number of seniors are making use of computers and Internet services (Gilligan et al., 1998). European, national and local initiatives have been undertaken to create virtual spaces specifically for older adults.[6] In addition, barriers for older adults in assessing the information society have been specified, and recommendations for policy, aimed at the further inclusion of older adults are being formulated (Campbell et al., 1999).

Seniorweb.nl decided to host an electronic debate prior to the national elections scheduled for May 1998. Well-known political candidates were asked to join a forum discussion, and representatives of organizations for the elderly were invited to participate in the editorial board. The debate was moderated by an independent host and centred on four themes considered relevant to the lives of senior citizens: health care; crime; participation in politics; employment and income. The debate had an open character and was accessible by all visitors to *Seniorweb.nl*; registration was not required. This particular debate was different from many earlier debates in that the topics discussed did not centre on a local issue, nor was it the case that the participants lived within a specific geographical locality. The participants were interested in discussing political issues, and could be considered a so-called community of interest. From the point of view of candidates participating in the debate, it constituted one of the many campaign activities designed to increase contact with potential electoral supporters.

One objective of this study was to investigate whether and how the three promises of digital democracy described earlier shaped this particular political debate. As an indication of the first promise, the issue of who had access to the debate was examined. The second promise, engaging in deliberation, can be examined in various ways. Regarding this debate, focus was placed on the manner in which deliberation transpired: the extent to which interaction between participants was made possible in the discussion, and on the style of conversing employed by the participants during the debate. The third promise, decision making, was addressed by illustrating some participants' evaluation of the relationship between the debate's content and real-life political decisions. These evaluations came to the fore in responses to questions posed in an online questionnaire and in face-to-face interviews held with senior participants.

In order to address the issue of access, the *Seniorweb.nl* site was designed for older Internet users. Not surprisingly, the participants in the debate deviated with respect to age from the stereotypical affluent young male surfer in cyberspace, as their age ranged from 50 to 77. The site appeared to be successful in its objective to trigger participation of the not so 'average' Internet users. This could imply that the creation of specific spaces on the Internet for specific groups of users is valuable in order to support access to these non-typical users. Most of the senior participants had more than two years experience with various Internet services; around 60 per cent spent between two and five hours weekly logged onto the Internet.

Examination was made of the number and direction of contributions posted by three groups of participants: individual senior citizens, representatives of

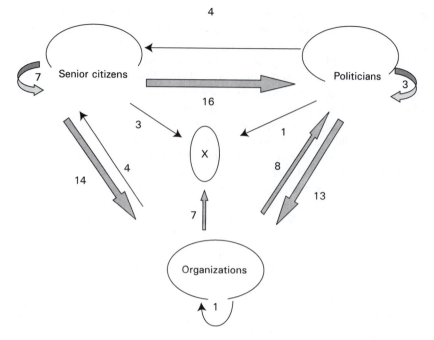

X = undirected contributions; total = 83

FIGURE 9.2   *Number and direction of participants' contributions (absolute figures)*

organizations and national political candidates. The number and direction of contributions by participants are reflected in Figure 9.2. The arrows pointing at the 'X' in the middle of the figure indicate messages not addressed to anyone in particular. Elsewhere, the figure indicates the relative number of messages between the three groups of participants. The politicians and representatives were each responsible for a quarter of the contributions, while senior citizens posted the other half of the contributions. Many of the senior citizens posted only a single message; only three posted more than two contributions. This skewedness was characteristic of the overall debate: 7 of the 31 participants were responsible for more than half of all contributions.

As is shown in Figure 9.2, the postings made by the senior citizens were directed at the organizational representatives and the political candidates. The politicians and organizations directed most of their postings towards each other; only a few of their postings were addressed at the senior citizens. The senior citizens were the most active group of participants, but received the least number of reactions to their postings. Participants from organizations, in contrast, concentrated on communicating with the political candidates, whereas politicians did so with the organizational representatives. There was, in fact, a one-way stream of messages from individual senior participants to the candidates.

How did the senior citizens perceive this imbalance in the debate? In the online questionnaire and the face-to-face interviews the senior participants were asked to comment on their assessment of the interaction between the participants.

Both satisfaction and disappointment concerning the level of interaction were expressed. Nearly a quarter of the respondents mentioned the interactive process as a positive aspect of the debate, while another quarter suggested that the level of interactivity in the debate could be improved. Some respondents expressed disappointment about the unwillingness of the candidates to answer questions posed by the elderly participants:

> I received only one real answer in which no reference was made to what I really meant in my comments. I definitely expected more of it [the debate].

> The most important [aspect of the debate] was that I could contact candidates directly. This makes you feel that your opinion is heard, although nobody responded to my contribution, which was a pity.

> This medium [the Internet] is over-estimated. People are free to respond, but also free not to. There were no reactions to my critical remarks....In fact, it was only a small group of in-crowd persons who participated in the debate.

In order to assess the quality of the deliberation, the style of conversing employed by the participants was examined. A content analysis was conducted on postings to one of the discussions. A coding scheme was developed in which categories indicating formality (e.g. 'Dear Mr Jansen' versus 'Hi Simon'), emotionality (e.g. use of capitals, exclamation marks), and emphasis (e.g. use of quotations, familiar sayings). Contributions from the senior participants and political candidates were compared on these aspects.

The senior citizens employed conventional openings in their postings more often than the political candidates did. In the event an opening was employed, both groups tended to use formal language. The senior participants also employed enumerations, quotations and sayings more often than the political candidates. One explanation for these differences may be that the topics discussed were more central to the lives of the senior citizens than to the candidates. Another explanation may be that the senior citizens were more familiar with the Internet than the candidates, and thereby followed general newsgroup conventions. The specific characteristics of communicating in an electronic debate were commented upon in the online questionnaire and the face-to face interviews.

> Well, I was personally addressed by [a candidate]. In his opening words he wrote 'My best Hubert/Dear Hubert', even though I don't know him personally. I wasn't really bothered, but it surprised me. I think this familiar way of speaking or addressing someone is a characteristic of the medium.

The participants seemed aware of the opportunity this form of debate offers to carefully compose contributions and to discuss in a structured manner.

> I edited my contributions several times. It's actually nice to read and change your contributions before sending them off.

> This medium makes you discuss to-the-point. I like an electronic debate more because it is better structured. Real-life discussions always 'run out of hand' and are dominated by a few persons. Here you can express exactly what you mean; you feel freer. This means that more opinions can came to the fore.

Although the electronic debate also appeared to be dominated by a few, the participants appreciated the debate for its structure and for the possibility to formulate and react at their own tempo. This characteristic of electronic debate may be of particular importance for older Internet users, as with age the ability to formulate prompt reactions in general decreases (e.g. Salthouse, 1991).

Of considerable importance, however, remains the issue of power, which relates to the third point in the typology of promises of digital democracy. To what extent and in what manner do citizens influence political decision-making processes by participating in electronic debates? In this particular debate, the possible consequences for 'real-life' politics were not considered. There were, however, a few references to this issue spontaneously made by participants:

> This debate has shown what a tremendous medium the Internet is in expressing opinions. On the other hand, we should not be too optimistic about our influence. Politicians normally forget immediately any suggestions given by citizens.

> I liked the debate because it gave you the feeling of having some say in the overall political discussion.

This debate on *Seniorweb.nl* manifested, as compared with other Internet-based public debates, at best a modest level of participant involvement. In the first place discussions consisted of a limited number of reactions, and there were many single postings without response. Secondly, the senior citizens directed many of their contributions to the political candidates, but received less response than they would have liked. A third indication of the modest level of involvement is that a small number of participants were responsible for more than half of the contributions. The senior citizens perceived the imbalance between the number of their own postings versus the number of reactions as a negative aspect of the debate. On the other hand, the possibility of formulating arguments carefully and discussing in a structured manner, as provided by this and other electronic debates, was seen as valuable. In addition, some senior participants believed their level of political influence was enhanced through the debate.

Conclusions

The three empirical studies presented examine versions of digital democracy and consider public debate as a baseline for political engagement. The studies differ in their relation to traditional politics and the electoral process, and in the specific concepts emphasized and investigated. The 'typology of promises' initially formulated by Tsagarousianou (1999) reflects the core claims of digital democracy: obtaining information, engaging in deliberation, and participation in decision making. We examined the evidence for these promises in a Usenet discussion, an experiment with teledemocracy, and in a political debate held on an Internet site.

The Usenet discussion reflected a skewed distribution of contributions from participants, and was considered lacking in equality of involvement among the participants. The same kind of inequality also characterized the discussions monitored in the other two studies. In the experiment with teledemocracy contributions clustered around a political representative. In the Internet-based electoral debate, most postings were similarly addressed to the political candidates. In this debate, inequality also was evident in the manner participants addressed each other. Whereas the senior citizens often addressed political candidates by means of a formal salutation, the candidates rarely used such formal expressions. This suggests that differences in status in real life were also present in the virtual debate. In summary, all three of the empirical studies presented failed to support the equality claim often made for Internet-based debates.

Another important issue here, is access to the necessary equipment for involvement in a debate, as well as proficiency in the communicative and technical skills demanded of the hardware. This aspect was not investigated in depth in any of the three studies, but participants in the teledemocracy experiment seemed to resemble the stereotypical affluent young male 'surfer in cyberspace'. As stated, the *Seniorweb.nl* site was specifically created for senior participants and succeeded in attracting participants who deviated with respect to age from this stereotype.

In analysis of the Usenet debate, quality of deliberation in the typology of promises was defined as the degree to which the debate displayed characteristics of a rational-critical argument, as proposed in Habermas' idealized vision of the public sphere. This study did not strongly display this dimension because of the limited number of phrases in postings related to a base list of words associated with the central topic under discussion. In the teledemocracy experiment and *Seniorweb.nl* debate, this dimension was examined differently: emphasis was placed on participants' experiences and assessment of the debate. This participants in the *Seniorweb.nl* debate were mixed in their assessments. On the one hand, they evaluated the experience positively because of its textual character which provided time for carefully constructing postings, and the participatory character of the debate which provided participants with a kind of 'political voice'. On the other hand, participants criticized the overall lack of quality in the debate, and complained about the disappointing number of responses from political candidates to their postings.

The third promise in the typology, participating in decision making, refers to a yet unresolved issue regarding the relation of virtual political debates to those held in real life, and to their relation with further political action (see Fernback and Thompson, 1995). A central question dominating such initiatives is: in what manner and to what extent can initiatives with digital democracy influence the real-life political process? It may be that such initiatives can not only contribute to an increase in citizen involvement, but also to a reformulation of what is considered part of the democratic process. Virtual debates may lend more legitimacy to the principles of participatory, or 'strong' (Barber, 1984) democracy in which communication is seen as the core component of an on-going democracy process. From this view, various 'bottom-up' conceptualizations of democracy have been developed and may provide a sense of personal empowerment for participants, which results in political action.[7]

Further Research

The empirical studies presented in this chapter suggest a number of areas for further investigation. A central concern remains acquiring access to the forums of electronically mediated public debates. This concern relates to both the hardware and the software on which initiatives of teledemocracy depend, as well as the technological and communicative skills necessary to make use of the technology (see Jankowski, 1995). Policy initiatives related to this aspect have already been identified as objects of study (e.g. Cuilenburg, 1999; Cuilenburg and Verhoest, 1998), and this work should be expanded to include empirical investigations as well. In particular, attention should be paid to how access can be increased for those groups in society traditionally denied or deprived access – the economically poor, minorities and women – again making use of various studies already completed in this area (e.g. Ebo, 1998; Pfister, 1999).

Secondly, more research is necessary on the way control and procedural mechanisms imposed on virtual debates influence the degree of citizen involvement. In the studies presented here, the role of moderators was not highlighted even though both the teledemocracy experiment and the *Seniorweb.nl* debate incorporated this function.[8] Much research done in the context of Group Decision Rooms and other Group Decision Support Systems has been concerned with the role of moderators and anonymity of participants (see, e.g. Postmes, 1997); these findings and the strategies developed in this environment should be considered in the arena of digital democracy.

A third area for further research has to do with the similarities and differences between characteristics of contributions to electronically mediated debates and those made during real-life debates. Participants in the *Seniorweb.nl* debate commented on typical characteristics of electronic debates (no face-to-face contact, disjuncture of time and place) both positively and negatively. In future studies, such evaluations should be systematically compared with characteristics of real-life debates. In other settings such comparisons between real-life and virtual communication have been made (e.g. Althaus, 1997; Kraut et al., 1998; Parks and Floyd, 1996) and could serve to guide this investigation in this arena.

Finally, more research on the relation of virtual debates to real-life debates and subsequent political action remains necessary in order to develop an understanding of the consequences of Internet-based public debates may have for the public sphere and, more generally, for political life. For example, there may be a similar feeling of group association experienced by the 'lurkers' passively attending to virtual debates as there often is among the 'silent majority' attending to real-life discussions. It may also be the case that the degree of involvement changes for different types of individuals, depending on which of these environments the debate takes place, the virtual or the 'real'. The speculative statements now formulated on these matters could be transformed into empirically-grounded expressions with the aid of a research programme concentrating on such initiatives for digital democracy.

Notes

1   Unravelling this terminology would be a valuable exercise; in this respect, Hagen (1997) has proposed a useful typology for his over-arching term electronic democracy: teledemocracy, cyberdemocracy and electronic democratization. Briefly, teledemocracy is associated with forms of electronic polling and voting. Digital democracy is a more general term encompassing other activities usually associated with the democratic process.

2   Connell (1996) describes some of the early government initiatives at site-building in the UK, and Boussen (1997) examines the organizational considerations in developing a Web site at a Dutch government ministry. For other examples see the following Web site: http://www.gotzespace.dk/gol-democracy/

3   The Lorenz curve is a technique for summarizing the concentration of data. In the case of the Usenet newsgroup study, it depicts the percentage of total postings attributed to an individual to the newsgroup, with the authors ranked in order of the frequency of their postings. The Gini coefficient, noted in Figure 9.1, is a summary measure of concentration; the value shown in this figure suggests a high level of concentration (Schneider, 1997: 80).

4   Elaboration of the research design and other findings may be found in the project report and subsequent publications (Jankowski et al., 1997; Leeuwis et al., 1997).

5   See further: http://www.seniornet.org/research/survey2.html

6   Examples of such sites are: http://www.eurolinkage.org/euro, http://www.euroag. org, http://www.ThirdAge.com

7   There are other 'bottom-up' formulations in fields as diverse as community development and action (Alinsky, 1969; Beck, 1974) and organization communication (Evers and Putte, 1995). Initiatives have also been undertaken to incorporate this perspective into new definitions of politics.

8   The Usenet abortion debate was unmoderated.

References

Alinsky, S. (1969) *Reveille for Radicals*. New York: Vintage Books.

Althaus, S.L. (1997) 'Computer mediated communication in the university classroom: an experiment with on-line discussions', *Communication-Education*, 46(3): 158–74.

Arterton, F.C. (1987) *Teledemocracy: Can Technology Protect Democracy?*. Newbury Park, CA: Sage.

Bangemann, M. et al. (1994) 'Europe and the global information society: recommendations to the European Council'. http://www.cec.lu/en/comm/20c/bange.html

Barber, B.R. (1984) *Strong Democracy: Participatory Politics for a New Age*. Berkeley, CA: University of California Press.

Beck, W. (1974) *Democratie in de wijken: Een onderzoek naar buurtacties in Nederland*. (Democracy in Neighborhoods: A Study of Neighborhood Actions in the Netherlands). Amsterdam: Van Gennep.

Boussen, H. (1997) 'De digitale verkeersplein van Verkeer en Waterstaat' ('The digital traffic square of the Ministry of Transport'). Master's thesis, University of Nijmegen, Department of Communication.

Brants, K., Huizenga, M. and Van Meerten, R. (1996) 'The new canals of Amsterdam: an exercise in local electronic democracy', *Media, Culture and Society*, 18: 233–47.

Campbell, R., Dries, J. and Gilligan, R. (1999) *Inclusion of Older People in the Information Society: Policies and Initiatives in Europe at EU and National Level and in the USA*. Dusseldorf: European Institute for the Media.

Connell, I. (1996) 'Cyberspace: the continuation of political education by other means', *Javnost/The Public*, 3(1): 87–102.

Cuilenburg, J. van (1999) 'Access and diversity in communications and information. Some remarks on communications policy in the Information Age', *New Media & Society*, 1(2): 183–207.

Cuilenburg, J. van and Verhoest, P. (1998) 'Free and equal access to communications: in search of policy models for converging communications systems', *Telecommunications Policy*, 22: 171–81.

Ebo, B. (ed.) (1998) *Cyberghetto or Cybertopia: Race, Class, and Gender on the Internet*. Westport, CT: Praeger.

Enzensberger, H.M. (1970) 'Constituents of a theory of the media', *New Left Review*, 64: 13–36.

Evers, W. and Putte, M. van (1995) 'Organisationele openbaarheid. Interne communicatie vanuit communicatiewetenschappelijk perspectief' ('Public sphere in organizations. Internal communication from the perspective of communication science'), in E. Hollander, C. van der Linden and P. Rutten (eds), *Communication Culture and Community*. Houten, The Netherlands: Bohn Stafleu Van Loghum. pp. 307–20.

Fernback, J. and Thompson, B. (1995) 'Virtual communities: abort, retry, failure?' http://www.com/user/hir/texts/VCcivil.html

Gilligan, R., Campbell, R. and Dries, J. (1998) *The Current Barriers for Older People in Assessing the Information Society*. Dusseldorf: European Institute for the Media.

Habermas, J. (1974) *Communication and the Evolution of Society*. Boston: Unwin Hyman.

Habermas, J. (1989) *The Structural Transformation of the Public Sphere. An Inquiry into a Category of Bourgeois Society*. Cambridge: Polity Press.

Hagen, M. (1997) 'A typology of electronic democracy'. http://www.uni-giessen.de/fb03/vinci/labore/netz/hag_en.htm

Hanssen, L., Jankowski, N.W. and Etienne, R. (1996) 'Interactivity from the perspective of communication studies', in N.W. Jankowski and L. Hanssen (eds), *The Contours of Multimedia; Recent Technological, Theoretical and Empirical Developments*. London: John Libbey Media. pp. 61–73.

Heilbron, B. (1999) 'Internet als openbaarheid. Vier diªmensies van de publieke sfeer binnen drie Nederlandse nieuwsgroepen' ('Internet as public sphere. Four dimensions of the public sphere within three Dutch newsgroups'). Master's thesis, University of Nijmegen.

Jankowski, N. (1995) 'Reflections on the origins and meanings of media access', *The Public/Javnost*, 2(4): 7–19.

Jankowski, N.W. (1988) 'Community television in Amsterdam; access to, participation in and use of the "Lokale Omroep Bijlmermeer"'. PhD dissertation, University of Amsterdam.

Jankowski, N., Leeuwis, C., Martin, P., Noordhof, M. and Rossum, J. van (1997) 'Teledemocracy in the province: an experiment with public debate and opinion polling Internet-based software'. Paper presented at Media and Politics conference, Brussels, 27 Feb.–1 March.

Kellner, D. (1990) *Television and the Crisis of Democracy*. Boulder, CO: Westview Press.

Kraut, R., Lundmark, V., Patterson, M., Kiesler, S., Mukopadhyay, T. and Scherlis, W. (1998) 'Internet paradox. A social technology that reduces social involvement and psychological well-being?', *American Psychologist*, 53(9): 1017–31.

Leeuwis, C., Jankowski, N., Martin, P., Noordhof, M. and Rossum, J. van (1997) *Besliswijzer beproefd. Een onderzoek naar teledemocratie in de provincie* (*Testing Besliswijzer. A Study of Teledemocracy in the Province*). Amsterdam: Instituut voor Publiek en Politiek.

Parks, M.R. and Floyd, K. (1996) 'Making friends in cyberspace', *Journal of Communication*, 46(1): 80–97.

Pfister, R. (1999) 'Africa's right to information: a review of past developments and future prospects', *Social Science Computer Review*, 17(1): 88–106.

Postmes, T. (1997) 'Social influence in computer-mediated groups'. PhD dissertation, University of Amsterdam.

Rafaeli, S. (1988) 'Interactivity from new media to communication', in R. Hawkins, J.M. Wieman and S. Pingree (eds), *Advancing Communication Science: Merging Mass and Interpersonal Processes. Sage Annual Review of Communication Research 16*. Newbury Park: Sage. pp. 110–34.

Rheingold, H. (1995) *The Virtual Community: Homesteading on the Electronic Frontier*. London: Minerva.

Rojo, A. and Rogsdale, R.G. (1997) 'Participation in electric forums: implications for the design and implementation of collaborative distributed multi media', *Telematics and Informatics*, 14: 83–96.

Salthouse, T.A. (1991) *Theeoretical Perspectives on Cognitive Aging*. Hillsdale, NJ: Lawrence Erlbaum.

Schneider, S. (1996) 'A case study of abortion conversation on the Internet', *Social Science Computer Review*, 14(4): 373–93.

Schneider, S. (1997) 'Expanding the public sphere through computer-mediated communication: political discussion about abortion in a Usenet newsgroup'. PhD dissertation, MIT, Cambridge, MA. http://www.sunyit.edu/!steve/

Tsagarousianou, R. (1999) 'Electronic democracy: rhetoric and reality', *Communications; The European Journal of Communication Research*, 24(2): 189–208.

Tsagarousianou, R., Tambini, D. and Bryan, C. (eds) (1998) *Cyberdemocracy: Technology, Cities, and Civic networks*. London: Routledge.

Williams, F., Rice, R. and Rogers, E. (1988) *Research Methods and the New Media*. New York: Free Press.

10

Widening Information Gaps and Policies of Prevention

Jan van Dijk

One of the most hotly debated issues of the information society is the divide of the so-called 'information haves' and 'have-nots'. What is most striking in this discussion is the simplification of the subject which actually is very complicated. It is a matter of information inequality – to be defined here as the inequality in the possession and the usage of sources of information and communication in a particular society. In this contribution it appears that information inequality is a subject matter with many aspects and that some of them may grow while others decline in importance. Anyway, a dichotomy of homogeneous groups of information rich and poor, with a wide gap in between, is shown to be a false image of a two-tiered society. It is far too simple as contemporary society actually is not characterized by homogeneous groups but by a very complex differentiation. This also goes for the distribution of resources and uses of information and communication. It will be claimed that the potential divide between information rich and poor would have to be seen as the stretching of a continually differentiating spectrum of positions taken by people anyway.

The potential increase of information inequality is crucial for the prospects of digital democracy. For its advocates promise just the opposite. The advent of ICT would improve the opportunities of participation in political processes removing barriers of place and time and offering new channels for the exchange of political information and discussion. For many writers on the subject ICT is a technology of freedom with lots of new chances for democracy in societies and organizations (e.g. Pool, 1983). However, when it is observed that access to the new media increasingly is unequal at the present stage of their adoption, as it is done in this chapter, this promise would not be fulfilled. Instead, the prospect of digital democracy would be in serious trouble.

The notion of increasing differences between information rich and poor is very old actually. This notion has appeared with every arrival of a new medium in history. In contemporary society, it was reinvented by Tichenor et al. in their thesis of the so-called knowledge gap. Their description of this gap is summarized in the following sentence: 'As the infusion of mass media information into a social system increases, segments of the population with higher socio-economic status tend to acquire this information at a faster rate than the lower status segments, so that the gap in knowledge between these segments tends to increase rather than decrease' (Tichenor et al., 1970: 159). Two notes should be added to this thesis. First, it is about increasing differences, not about the first appearance of them. Secondly, the gap widens as (mass media) information is distributed in society, not because access is denied to some people. However, the thesis of the knowledge gap was not supported by sufficient empirical evidence in a large number of research projects conducted during the 1970s. Some data appeared to support it, others did not. See Gaziano (1983) for a summary.

In the 1980s comparable theses were made following the advent of computers and the perspective of the information society. Now the supposed differences were called an information gap. While the thesis of a knowledge gap was only about information supplied by the mass media and about differences in cognition and information processing, the information gap theses were much broader. They have dealt first of all with conditions of access, that is to say the differences in social and economic position and the usage opportunities of different kinds of information technology users. Particularly they were about the possession of computers and the skill to master them. These characteristics were seen as conditions of access to the information society and abilities to use the information gathered and processed with ICT. The usage itself was barely investigated.

In the 1990s it has become clear that usage patterns are of prime importance. In this chapter it will be argued that inequality of access to ICT appears in at least four successive stages presenting themselves as barriers or hurdles to people who want to use information and communication technology in one way or another. A problem is that the commonsense concept *access* (to technology) is freely used and badly operationalized. Actually it is a multifaceted concept, as will be shown in the course of describing four types of access in this chapter. Access to ICT not only means possession of the necessary computers, software and connections, but also basic skills of using them and actual usage of these resources. It will be claimed that acquiring significant usage opportunities is the most important type of access and ultimately the most difficult hurdle to clear in getting access to computers, networks, the information society, digital political participation and so forth. It means that if inequalities of access can be shown to exist among people, the growth of a usage gap will have the most lasting effect. Although one can imagine that the large majority of the Western populations will possess a computer and a network connection within a few decades, and is able to operate this equipment, it is still to be expected that people will do increasingly different things with these media. One of these things is a different level and nature of political participation.

First of all, we have to give sufficient evidence of not only an existing but also an increasing gap in types of access between different kinds of people. We can look at their age, education, income, sex, ethnicity and country or region of origin. This has to be done because knowledge gaps, information gaps and usage gaps have always existed among people, at least since the invention of writing and perhaps even since the first primitive division of labour. And they are very likely to remain in advanced societies. What would be striking is the growth of these gaps in using particular media in a given society, in this case the media of ICT in contemporary Western society. Moreover, it has to be made plausible that the growth of these differences is no temporary phenomenon only appearing with the introduction of a new technology, as we have seen in the first years of the radio, the TV, the telephone and the video-recorder. After some time, sometimes short (radio and television) and sometimes long (the telephone), these media were adopted by the majority of the Western populations and used in relatively equal ways.

We will supply all the evidence we can get to describe the present situation of information (in)equality in the perspective of the potential user of ICT. Successive barriers of entry and use will be analysed and presented as a series of hurdles to cross by a potential user. It will be specified what these barriers or hurdles mean for political information processing and political participation. Then the data will be explained presenting a number of backgrounds of current information inequality. In section four the situation will be evaluated. What is wrong with increasing differences in the usage of ICT in a multiform and differentiating society anyway? Are they a risk or a chance for democracy in such a society? Finally, a number of general policies with regard to contemporary information inequality and political participation will be suggested.

Four Hurdles of Access to the Information Society

1 Lack of Basic Skills and 'Computer Fear'

The first hurdle looming up for a user willing to use electrical devices in general and computers in particular is a matter of routines and psychology. For a large number of people, first of all the old and illiterate ones, the command of these devices is found to be difficult. First attempts might have produced negative experiences. One should not underestimate the number of these people. In 1996 a general survey was made for the so-called digital skills of the Dutch population (Doets and Huisman, 1997). The Netherlands belongs to the European countries most advanced in using ICT. Still the results must be shocking to people daily talking about the splendid opportunities of the Internet, multimedia and the information super highway. Among the Dutch population between 18 and 70 years old a large proportion did not master, or very poorly mastered the following actions on the electronic equipment they possessed or had access to in 1996: playing a CD (33 per cent), using Teletext on TV (23 per cent), playing a video-recorder, programming a video-recorder (62 per cent), paying with a PIN-card (23 per cent), buying a train ticket from a vending-machine (61 per cent). A small majority of the Dutch population (52 per cent) claimed to be able to command a PC in 1996, but the following of its applications were not, or very poorly mastered by the users: word processing (54 per cent), using spreadsheets (85 per cent), transferring money (93 per cent), playing computer games (81 per cent), sending messages of e-mail (89 per cent), searching for information on the Internet (92 per cent).

Large differences of mastering these actions and applications appeared between the young and the old and between people with high and low education. However, almost every respondent found it difficult to programme a video-recorder and serve the just-called PC-applications. Most important is the fact that the majority of the people interviewed called the lack of these skills a 'personal shortcoming': one finds them important, but is not able to practise them in a satisfactory way. Not being able to command a PC was experienced as a large personal shortcoming by 26 per cent of the Dutch below 50 years of age and more than 40 per cent of the people above 50. Sixty-two percent of the respondents agreed to the proposition that if you cannot use electronic equipment and cards you will eventually become marginalized in society. However, 28 per cent of the Dutch population, 66 per cent of its low educated, 41 per cent of its unemployed and 54 per cent of the part of its old people aged 64–70 have a negative attitude to the 'digitalization' of society (1997: 26–8).

Neglecting the objective level of difficulty of these applications and the lack of present experience with them for a moment – they will be considered below – one has to admit that subjective and emotional factors are a prime cause of the lack of these basic 'digital' skills. The feeling of personal shortcoming (leading to insecurity), the fear of being excluded and the negative attitude towards 'digitalization' of people most lacking these skills give rise to 'computer fear' or 'button fear'. The operations mentioned are said to be difficult and people are afraid to start mastering them.

What does this first hurdle mean to the prospects of digital democracy? It means that for a large part of the Western population the first condition of digital democracy (inclusion) is not fulfilled yet. It entails that the use of ICT in politics does not make it easier for these people to participate in political and other social affairs. The promise of removing limits of time, place and insufficient channels or opportunities for political information and discussion may be better fulfilled for sick, disabled, remotely living and busy people, but for people lacking any digital skills conditions get worse. A hurdle is added instead of removed. This will surely happen when analogous media are prematurely replaced by digital media. For those managing to use digital means another potential effect is a restriction to relatively simple modes of participation like voting and polling, modes sometimes disparagingly called 'push button democracy'.

2   No Access to Computers and Networks

Some people might suppose that clearing this first hurdle is just a matter of time. It concerns people with old age and low education in the first place. The ageing of the 'digital generation', the dying of the old generations, the penetration of computers in society, rising educational levels with many more computer courses would solve this problem all by themselves. This assumption would be partly incorrect. Moreover, it would be ethically unacceptable. The survey mentioned above reveals that a majority of the Dutch population *below* 50 in 1996 experienced personal shortcomings commanding a PC and 60 per cent of people above 50. Still many elderly people wanted to learn to command a PC (29 per cent of people aged 57–63 and 20 per cent of those aged 64–70). With these kind of figures in mind it would be ethically unacceptable to abandon the elderly for participation in the information society in which they have to live for so many years to come yet. The people concerned are not simply 'want-nots', as claimed by people belittling the problem of the 'have-nots' and information inequality in general.

Now, suppose that the people experiencing personal shortcomings manage to get across the first threshold and are ready to use computers and networks like the Internet. Then they would meet the evident hurdle of not possessing a computer and a network connection or not having access to them at work or at school. The discussion about this hurdle dominates public opinion about the accessibility of the new media. It is the most common meaning of access. From every investigation of the social composition of computer and network users it becomes evident that the differences are large and permanent among most social categories. So it seems justified to call them gaps. The vast majority of users are male, relatively young, well-trained, having a high or medium-sized income and are originating from an affluent Western country, most often even an advanced region of it (Cyberatlas, 1996–99; GVU Centre, 1994–99; Nielsen Media/CommerceNet, 1995; Nielsen Media Research, 1996–99; and the Dutch survey described above). A large longitudinal survey among American households showed that most of these gaps have widened between 1989 and 1993 (see Anderson et al., 1995 and Figure 10.1 drawn from US census surveys US-Census Bureau 1984–97). Access to computers and networks is rising in absolute figures among all social categories. However, the young, the well-trained, the relatively rich and the people from affluent Western countries and regions *are increasing their advantage* to the old, the less-educated, the relatively poor and the people from poor countries and regions (Western and non-Western). See the gaps of income, education and age in Figure 10.1.

This was the situation at the beginning of the 1990s in the US. After 1993 people with low income and education and of older age have caught up somewhat, primarily in the US (see the biannual surveys of the GVU Centre, 1994–99 and Figure 10.1). One of the reasons for this is that the absolute number of people with no high income or education and above 35 years of age is bigger and has a higher growth potential. However, this does not mean that the (relative) gap is closing. The rate of adoption of the new media still is much higher among the rich, the well-educated and the younger generations than among their counterparts. There is only one exception: the gap of access to computers and networks between males and females is narrowing (Anderson et al., 1995; GVU Centre, 1994–99), be it much more in the US than in Europe (GVU Centre, 1997–99). See Figure 10.2 for the general trend.

At this point, many economists and media experts will note that this is a normal pattern in the adoption of new media, like those for the introduction of the telephone, the radio, the television and the VCR. Some people are much faster in adopting new technologies than others and, in fact, pay for further development. In that case, the adoption of computers and networks will have just left the phase of the 'pioneers' and the 'early adopters' and will be now taking its first bend upwards in the well-known S-curve. Indeed, such a curve may occur in this case as well. But when it does, it remains to be seen whether this curve will rise as fast and as high as has been observed in the diffusion of the radio, the television and the VCR. The adoption pattern of the telephone, a comparable medium linked in

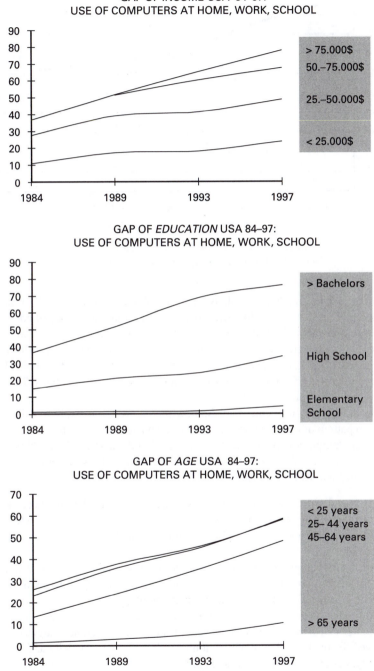

FIGURE 10.1 *Gaps of Income, Education and Age in using computers, USA 1984–97. (Source: US-Census Bureau, 1984, 1989, 1993, 1997)*

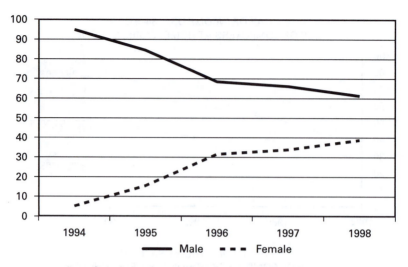

FIGURE 10.2   *Gap of gender in the use of the Internet world-wide*
(Source: 1st–10th GVU (Georgia University) WWW User Surveys)

networks, seems much more likely. The telephone needed over 70 years to become more or less generally diffused as a medium in the developed countries. And even now, about half of the world population does not have access to a telephone, and in the rich Western countries about one-quarter or one-fifth of the low-income households in particular cities or regions still has no telephone. Even in the motherland of contemporary communications, the United States, 7 million homes had no telephone in 1995.

It would be fair to assume that the new media are more likely to follow the adoption pattern of the telephone than that of television. If this is true, it is not very likely that computer networks will reach a level of diffusion of 80 or 90 per cent within the next decades, even in the most developed countries. Several arguments can be put forward for this view:

- all expenditures taken together the new media are considerably more expensive than the old ones, among other reasons because they are obsolete much faster and because new peripheral equipment and software are continually needed;
- with the development of multimedia the need of audio-visual hardware and software is increasing; however, they are the most costly in terms of equipment, bandwidth and intellectual property rights;
- old media do not disappear; new media are adopted beside the old ones in a pattern of accumulation; however, in the total household budget the part saved for media and communication reveals not much elasticity and extensibility, certainly not for the low incomes;
- the general diffusion of old media like the television and the telephone emerged in a period of strong economic growth, massification and levelling of incomes in the Western world; the new media are introduced in a period

of a relative slackening of economic growth, individualization, social and cultural differentiation, increasing income differences and the rise of so-called modern poverty in Western countries;

- the diffusion of these old media was supported by a policy of universal service and public service, mainly supported by the state; the spread of new media, including the construction of information superhighways, is almost completely left to the market with the inevitable result that commercial motives are getting more important and universal and public services are getting under pressure.

Nevertheless, as computers and networks become indispensable to living and working in modern society, it seems likely that within 25 years a large majority of the Western and some Eastern-Asian populations will possess computers and networks in their homes and have access to them at work, at school or at public buildings. Computers and their networks are supplied in ever more simple and cheap versions: besides game and home computers we now get palmtop and network computers. The Internet becomes available on all kinds of platforms, including cable and satellite. However, even when the elementary condition of access to new media equipment will be fulfilled within two or three decades, questions with regard to the access*ibility* for users in practice remain (see hurdle three below).

First we have to claim that the second hurdle makes the prospects of digital democracy as a viable way to practise politics for everyone even worse. The crucial fact is that well-known correlates of relatively low political participation in the Western democracies, that is low-education, low-income, low-occupation, female sex and (most often) minority ethnic origin relate as well with low access to computers and networks (see earlier in this chapter). To say it bluntly, those already practising a relatively high level of political participation and possessing a large number of media and other channels of communication get yet other means at their disposal. Those revealing low levels of political participation remain excluded as before. Compared to people with high rates of connection to the new media and with high political participation they are in fact losing ground. There is only one important exception: the older generations, usually the most faithful people in voting and other engagements in official politics, have less access to ICT than the younger generations. However, many young people use ICT for either apolitical purposes or other ways of online political activity than supporting institutional politics (see GVU, 7th WWW survey, April 1997 for differences of online and offline political activity between young and old people).

3 Insufficient User-Friendliness

Until recent times personal computers and even more computer networks, were notoriously unfriendly in their operations. With the advent of new graphical and audio-visual interfaces and operation systems the situation has improved. Still, it is all but rosy as one can gather from the data of lacking elementary skills supplied above, to be partly explained by the insufficient user-friendliness of hardware, software and operating instructions. Among the most popular electronic equipment this qualification is the most valid for are video-recorders and personal computers. In Holland 14 per cent of the population wanted to have a computer in 1996, but did not purchase it because the operation was perceived to be too difficult; 23 per cent of people possessing PCs did not use it at all for the same reason (Doets and Huisman, 1997: 37).

A broader interpretation of user-friendliness is the usage style offered. Some say that the usage style offered with the new media is not attractive to many women, low educated people and particular ethnic minorities (van Dijk, 1991, 1994; van Zoonen, 1994). This style would not meet the needs and practice of seeking information of these categories. Not much has been proved yet on this score. But according to a conception of technology as human effort it would be no surprise that the design of new media techniques leaves the traces of the social-cultural characteristics of its producers: predominantly male, well-educated, English speaking and being members of the ethnic majority in a particular country.

User-friendliness and user styles are relevant as well for the practice of digital democracy. Most experiments in digital democracy require rather high levels of intellectual and technical skill. It is not easy for an ordinary citizen to look for political information in a search engine on the Internet or to follow or contribute to one of its many discussion groups. To say nothing of the participation in all kinds of advanced individual or group decision support systems invented to help people in decisions of voting or opinion formation in social and political affairs. Moreover, the usage style offered in all these applications most often reveals the intellectual skills and ways of thinking of their inventors that might not be attractive to everyone.

However, insufficient user-friendliness and unattractiveness of the usage style offered might not even be the most important reasons for the lacking elementary skills described above. The user-friendliness and usage style of the new media and their political applications can be improved and made more popular relatively easy, and this will certainly be done by the ICT industry for evident commercial reasons. Even more important seems to be lacking *experience* with PC applications which in turn is caused by lacking and unequally distributed *usage opportunities*. It will be claimed that this fourth hurdle is the most difficult to pass.

4   Insufficient and Unevenly Distributed Usage Opportunities

In practice, word processing turns out to be by far the most important application of PCs. It is followed at a great distance by the other applications mentioned earlier, which in 1998 were only used by an average of 10 to 20 per cent of the Western populations (the Internet, electronic mail and the like). An exception is the use of computer games as this is very common among young people. To the average user, however, the PC is nothing but an enhanced typewriter. It is well-known that this multifunctional device is utilized far below its capacity. Applications other than word processing, computer games and, recently, reference and education using CD-Roms, are with minor exceptions used only by professionals for work and education. Household applications are still lagging behind. Many home computers, purchased through subsidies for PC ownership by students and employees or bought for the benefit of the children, are left unused in the study or the attic.

In the meantime the usage opportunities for professional applications at work or at school are increasing rapidly. This is so to such an extent that many users have the impression of not being able to catch up anymore. A new version or update is already available before the old one is mastered. However, this is a reality for about 20 or 30 per cent of some Western populations. Those who have nothing to do with computers in education or occupation are probably not going to use them at their own initiative. The only exception is that of parents of children attending school, who are among the most important purchasers of home computers: they have the opportunity to learn to master a computer, often with the help of their children.

A first indication of a usage gap is the fact that increased home PC and Internet access does not result in increased use. An Arbitron study revealed that the home penetration of PCs in the US rose from 29 per cent in 1995 to 54 per cent in 1999. However, the percentage of PC owners who actually used their PC fell from 90 per cent in 1995 to 53 per cent in 1999. The same goes for Internet access – 38 per cent of American households reported to have a Web subscription, while only 24 per cent actually used the Web (Arbitron New Media, 1999). Further analysis of the domestic use of computers shows well-educated people making far more use of applications in work, private business and education. The favourite applications of people with low education and the youth are amusement and/or computer games, followed by education (Nielsen Media Research, 1996, 1998). Here a usage gap appears. The important thing is that it is likely to grow, instead of decline, with the larger distribution of computers among the population. If this turns out to be true, the difference between advanced and simple uses will increase. The same pattern might appear with different kinds or levels of political participation. In this case relatively low levels or simple kinds of political participation would be practised and attained by some classes of ICT users, while high levels and complicated kinds would be reached by other classes. Then it may be projected that the existing unequal distribution of the following kinds and levels of political participation among the populations of the Western democracies as it is portrayed in Table 10.1 will be *reinforced* by the use of ICT in politics.

The projection entails that the mass of citizens using means of ICT in politics would stick to the first three kinds and levels of participation in Table 10.1, even more than before the introduction of ICT. This practice is called 'push button democracy' sometimes and it closely corresponds to the marketing model of the future information superhighway (see Chapter 2). Still, these people are participating in one way or another, as at the one end of the whole spectrum of electronic political activity we will find the excluded, who do not even vote or poll electronically. At the other end of the spectrum we will be confronted with the politically active elite using advanced electronic means to improve their say in social and political affairs or to take part in political discussions. Perhaps they even become a member of an electronic or traditional political organization and stand as a candidate. (See the kinds of political participation at the bottom of Table 10.1.) They would shape the Internet model of the future information

TABLE 10.1 *Kinds and levels of political participation*

	LOW	
OWN INITIATIVE AND ACTION REQUIRED	• responding to an opinion poll • signing a petition • voting • having a say in a political or social affair • contributing to a mass political discussion • active membership of a political organization • running as a candidate for a seat or office	SKILLS REQUIRED
	HIGH	

superhighway (see Chapter 3). Of course, this rather dark prediction has to be tested in time series of a large number of years as the present data are still scarce and they have a short time span.

Let's draw a first partial conclusion. It cannot be ruled out, and in fact it is likely, that in the long-term the first three hurdles of access to the network society will be crossed by the majority of populations in the developed countries. However, in saying this, one has to acknowledge that a considerable minority will continue to be excluded. At the time of writing an average of 10 per cent of the adult, non-handicapped population in the developed countries is still a real illiterate or a functional illiterate (United Nations, 1998). The number of 'digital illiterates' will probably remain much higher for some time. Primary skills will gradually increase and 'computer fear' will diminish. In time the ownership of and access to computers and networks may reach the majority of the population. Great improvements can still be made in respect of the user-friendliness of hardware, software and manuals, and the user style offered can be made more appealing. However, all this does not rule out an increase of differences in usage. How can this be explained? Why should a technology, so much suited for the spread of information in society and into the world, in practice lead to more private appropriation and greater inequality in the usage of it?

Backgrounds of Increasing Information Inequality

This contradiction is perceivable in a large number of problems of the information society which appear to be difficult to solve. Take the protection of the right of intellectual and material property in the context of ICT (authors rights, copyright, safety of payment) and the right of privacy. The difficulty of these protections in digital environments is both an expression of the societalization of information and the desire to keep it in our own hands. The tendency of societalization is technologically supported by the ease of distribution, registration and copying by digital media. However, in current (Western) societies there are a number of strong counter-tendencies supporting the opposite way, that is private appropriation. The first tendency is a social-cultural one. It is a combination of processes of differentiation and individualization in (post)modern society. ICT supports these processes because its most important medium, the computer, pre-eminently is a device to be served by individuals, although it is also able to connect individuals in groups and communities by means of networks. Social-cultural differentiation is also supported by computers and networks because their uniform digital substructure helps to produce and spread all kinds of cultural arte-facts in every quality and quantity desired. So, increasing information inequality might just be an aspect of general social-cultural differentiation and choice opportunities in society. However, there is more, if we look at a second tendency which is a part of current social-economic development. It is the rising material inequality and differences of incomes perceivable in all Western countries to some degree since the beginning of the 1980s. This tendency causes increasing unequal divisions of material resources and in extreme cases even an exclusion or marginalization of segments of the lower social classes living on welfare or minimum wages. The means of information and communication are a part of these resources. In this case increasing information inequality might be a conse-quence of rising relative costs of information and communication in general and the goods and services of ICT in particular, while the household budget is shrink-ing or remains the same.

The third tendency is a political one. It serves to tolerate rising material inequalities. It is the policy of privatization and stimulation of the free market economy in most countries. It is leading to the commercialization of formerly public information supply and communication facilities and the surge of private education. Inevitably it expands the opportunities of information inequality. For instance, a consequence might be that people with low income and low education will use the cheap and simple content on the Internet, while people with high income and high education will benefit from its expensive and advanced content, just like these groups presently do in the use of commercial broadcasting.

Finally, we have to mention the continually diverging areas of application of ICT. This technological tendency originates from the multifunctional capacities of computers. The most important property of these devices is that they are (re)programmable for extremely diverging activities. One can use computers not only for very advanced and difficult applications, but also for familiar and simple affairs. Computers are used for complex economic and political decisions and for high-level education. They are also used, most often even the same computers, for relatively simple actions like paying and receiving money, ordering products, typ-ing letters and playing games. The multifunctionality of ICT is much more extended than the functionalities of old media like the press, broadcasting and the telephone. The press and broadcasting only have information contents of a dif-ferent kind and level. The telephone allows all kinds of interpersonal communica-tion. The extended multifunctionality of ICT is a neutral property in its own right, but in particular circumstances it offers many more opportunities than less func-tional media and techniques to expand existing information inequalities.

Such a combination of circumstances is the key to an understanding of present information inequality. When the four tendencies described above come together and interweave, as they do in the current era, they produce a force which easily induces greater information inequality and is very difficult to prevent when this would be desired.

An Evaluation of Present Information Inequality

What is wrong with increasing differences among people anyway? Some might perceive a tone of concern and threat in this text. It seems like it would be the prime purpose of the author to help everyone, without exception, to have access to a computer and use it to the maximum as soon as possible. Of course, the fact that large parts of the population experience personal shortcomings not having a computer or being able to command a computer or other electronic equipment, would be a sufficient reason for wanting to make up for these shortcomings. Still, this is not the prime motivation and concern expressed in this text. To say it bluntly, using a computer or another new medium does not necessarily make one more happy. It is not even sure that it gives one a better position in society, certainly not when simple entertainment and repetitive work of data entry prevail. The consideration here is primarily strategic. It is based on a support of the most important values of civil society since the French revolution (freedom, equality and solidarity) and a sober scientific analysis of structural information inequalities growing in network society (Castells, 1996, 1998; Schiller, 1996; van Dijk, 1991, 1994, 1997). The network society is an expression for a society shaped by more or less diffuse social networks increasingly supported and supplanted by media networks gradually replacing the so-called mass society of dense gatherings of people with primarily face-to-face interactions (van Dijk, 1999). In network society the positions people take in media networks will be decisive for their influence in taking decisions on all kinds of social affairs. To have access to this media, in all the senses described above, is absolutely vital for the participation in this society. However, it appears to be that the present use of ICT is much more to the benefit of the existing information elite, as it is to the rest of society. There is even a risk of social and communicative exclusion of groups already marginal in society. Once again this is no simple dichotomy, as in fact between these two sides of society, the elite and the marginal, the whole spectrum of positions, taken by the majority of the Western populations, is being stretched. This goes for positions on the labour market, in education, in social-cultural life and in political participation (see Anderson et al., 1995). The same goes for the dichotomy observed by Castells (1996) in the usage of communication networks. On the one end he describes the development of a fairly homogeneous, globally operating elite using their networks and other media to appropriate, transmit and control capital and information without limits of time and place. At the other end all kinds of subordinate groups, much more tied to time and place, are filling these resources and networks with labour, data and increasingly heterogeneous cultural expressions without having any hold on the market, technology and the world outside (Castells, 1996: 469).

The assumption behind this analysis is certainly not that information inequality is a new phenomenon. As has been said, this type of inequality has existed ever since the invention of writing, at least. It is very likely to remain. Perhaps we will even have to accept the fact that information inequality will increase in the network society. It might be an inescapable side-effect of social and cultural differentiation. However, we have to be very careful not to let structural or basic inequalities arise within a society and between societies. This would certainly undermine political, social and cultural democracy and strip formal civil rights from their actual substance. Structural inequality would appear when on the one hand, an 'information elite' strengthens its position, while on the other hand those groups already living on the margins of society become excluded from communications in society because these are practised in media they do not possess or control. The differences become structural when the positions people occupy in networks and other media determine whether they have any influence on decisions made in several fields of society. In this case every political, social and cultural democracy would become hollow and citizen rights would be emptied of their substances. In fact we would get first-, second- and third-class citizens and digital democracy would turn from a hopeful dream into a terrible nightmare.

The Prevention of Structural Information Inequality

So, it is possible to *mitigate* information inequality, but it is necessary to *prevent* structural inequality. Both require effective social and information policies. First of all, they are a matter of making the right strategic choices among the conditions determining whether people are included or excluded in the information society. For this purpose one can devise more general and more specific policies. These policies are not only a matter for governments and public administrations, but for the organizations of civil society and socially responsible private corporations as well. First the general policies. The most important action to be taken is the realization, in one way or another, of a minimum of provisions of information and communication for every citizen, if not every inhabitant of a particular country. The question is which information and facilities of communication everyone should have in an information society.

Basic Resources
In the first place it is a matter of giving access to the following basic resources of information and communication elaborating policies of extension of universal service and modernization of public service in an information society characterized by economic privatization and technological convergence. The question is which information and facilities of communication everyone should have in an information society.

1 *Basic private and public communication connections,* to be able to participate in society and social life generally. Until now this function has been realised to a large degree by the telephone and printed mail (requiring universal access) along with face-to-face communications. In the new media environment the existing universal access in telephony has to be extended to electronic mail and audio-visual channels of broadcasting in a short or medium-term (Anderson et al., 1995; Information Society Forum, 1999). For the present practice of digital democracy it means that no representativeness, legitimacy or decisiveness can

be attached to the results of its applications as long as there are not sufficient connections at home or at proximate public buildings.

2 *Public information and communication* for a citizen who is supposed to know the law and able to participate in a democratic society. In the new media environment the traditional means of the government and the public administration have to be extended to electronic sources. As citizens have the duty to know the law and the right to inspection of official documents adopted by parliaments, councils, etc., all documents containing laws and regulations or decisions of official bodies and sources of information used for these decisions – paid out of tax money! – have to be supplied in electronic shape for free or very low prices: the price of real extra costs of electronic supply as a maximum. Moreover, citizens must be given the opportunity to react to them along electronic channels (communication). In public broadcasting it has to be safeguarded that all citizens keep access to a diversity of sources and feedback channels putting in mind the trends towards narrowcasting and pay-TV.

3 *Health communication and information,* for evident vital reasons, for example emergency services.

4 *Educational information and communication* as a logical consequence of compulsory education.

Basic Skills

Besides these resources basic skills of dealing with them are essential. The transformation of these resources in meaningful usage opportunities is an important capacity to acquire as well. Of course, one has to be able to command hardware and software to achieve this. Still, it is not the most important skill in this case. This is the capacity to search, select and process information from the fast growing supply of information and media. This capacity is perhaps the most unequally distributed one among Western populations. Yet, it is decisive for the potential to live and work in the information society. School subjects of information and communication in general or media education will only partly satisfy the need for this potential. Much more important than these fairly marginal subjects are the main school subjects of mathematics and language. They will have to be partly transformed into courses of data processing and of searching, selecting and processing information respectively. In the language courses much more attention should be given to the language of images and to audio-visual contents.

More specific policies for the prevention of information inequality should confront the four hurdles described in the most direct way. Let's mention the policies required briefly.

Basic skills in the command of electronic equipment, computers in particular, are acquired first of all in everyday uses and in education. The integration of learning computer skills in education, first of all in the obligatory subjects, in adult education and in the mastery of equipment at home are the best ways forward. In the context of the home people can also learn from each other. The young and better-trained may teach their older and lesser-trained household members in practice. A common use of the same equipment by house-mates might be helpful against the current inclination to use them alone. However, most important is the disappearance of the technical image of digital devices. This might happen when more user-friendly digital equipment is integrated in everyday activities.

The *possession of and the access to computers and networks* can be supported by the distribution of the four resources of public infrastructure called above. The extension of universal service and the modernization of the offerings of public administration, broadcasting and other public information services in general will motivate all people in need of these services. It will improve their chances to purchase themselves the hardware and software needed. Ultimately, this has to happen in every household. The supply of provisions in public buildings is only a second-best solution, although it offers better opportunities to guide starting computer users.

For the remainder, possession of and access to equipment are a matter of general income policies. These are much more popular in Europe than in the US. Yet, both of them have some policy for welfare, poverty and minimum wages. However, the basic subsistence level deemed necessary in these policies is running behind all kinds of developments in modern society. The increasing part of average household expenditures for communication and media is not taken into account at all. It follows that some European countries with relatively high levels of social welfare feel urged to provide the people living on welfare and the unemployed with supplementary benefits of telephone connections, daily newspapers and even computers with Internet connections (an experiment in Amsterdam in 1997).

User-Friendliness and a More Equal Distribution of Usage Opportunities

The *user-friendliness* of hardware, software and operating instructions can improve considerably yet. For commercial reasons the industry concerned will certainly do this. However, this does not mean that the users and their organizations (user groups, consumer organizations and trade unions) will be engaged in the design. This ideal – for many concerned – has barely been put into practice. It means, for instance, that users get the chance, in one way or another, to 'negotiate' about designs offered and to learn what fits to their daily practice (Leeuwis, 1996). Unfortunately, it is still common practice that suppliers reason too much from the capacities of their own technical and economic supply and too less from the needs and contexts of users. It follows that the usage styles offered remain unattractive to exactly those parts of the population with the lowest access to the new media.

Finally, the lack of meaningful usage opportunities might also disappear with increasing user-friendliness and the penetration of new media in households, schools and working places. When this happens, the chances of an unequal distribution of these opportunities grow accordingly. This cannot be prevented, and it does not have to be prevented. What matters most is the removal of stiffening structures systematically sticking particular parts of the population to some applications, in this case some kind and level of political participation, while other parts get the chance to choose every application. For example, this would happen when the lower social classes will *only* use the new media for cashing and paying electronic money, teleshopping or entertainment at home and simple data entry or an execution of other computer tasks at work. In politics they might practise kinds of participation requiring the least skills and effort or initiative (answering opinion polls or voting). In the meantime the higher social classes would primarily use the new media for the interpretation and utilization of data in advanced applications, for taking decisions at work and for supplementary professional work and educational multimedia programmes at home. In politics they might be the absolutely dominant participants in electronic discussions, decision support systems and the active contribution of ideas, issues and candidates. Such divisions are extremely difficult to prevent. They are deeply entrenched in our societies and ways of practising politics. The biggest mistake made by many advocates of digital democracy is the presumption that the technical features of the new media (breaking particular limits of time, place and physical necessity) will solve fundamental problems of citizen participation in politics in their own right. These problems have deep social, cultural and mental roots. They can not even be solved by specific information and communication policies alone. Much broader and generally supported policies would be needed. They would have to deal with lifelong learning, mobility on the job, schemes of job rotation, policies for employment and for the emancipation of women and ethnic minorities, to mention only the most important ones. With regard to politics it would mean the development of sufficiently attractive means of both traditional and digital democracy. They should not require too much skill and effort for an average citizen. Simultaneously, they should not yield too much to the audio-visual ways of popularizing politics by means of (electronic) games, contests, talk shows and commercials. Challenging structural information inequality in politics and society has to be an integral part of these general policies first of all.

References

Anderson, R., Bikson, T., Law, S.-A. and Mitchell, B. (eds) (1995) *Universal Access to E-mail: Feasability and Societal Implications*. Santa Monica, CA: RAND; http://www.rand.org/publications/MR/MR650

Arbitron New Media (1999) 'PC home ownership doubles while home usage stagnates reveals pathfinder study', http://www.arbitron.com/article4.htm

Castells, M. (1996) *The Information Age: Economy, Society and Culture Vol I: The Rise of the Network Society*. Cambridge, MA/Oxford, UK: Blackwell.

Castells, M. (1998) *The Information Age: Economy, Society and Culture Vol III: End of Millennium*. Cambridge, MA/Oxford, UK: Blackwell.

CommerceNet/Nielsen Internet Demographics (1996–99) 'Recontact study March/April 1996', http://www.commerce.net/work/pilot/nielsen_96/exec.html

Cyberatlas (1996–99) 'Internet demographics, usage patterns', http://www.cyberatlas.com/demographics.html

Doets, C. and Huisman, T. (1997) *Digital Skills, The State of the Art in the Netherlands*. 's-Hertogenbosch: CINOP; http://www.cinop.nl (English summary)

Gaziano, C. (1983) 'The knowledge gap: an analytical review of media effects', *Communication Research*, 10: 447–86.

GVU Centre (1994–99) 1st–10th WWW User Surveys, Georgia University. http://www.gvu.gatech.edu/user_surveys/

Information Society Forum (1999) 'Report 1997; working group 3, universal service and consumer protection', Luxembourg: Office for Official Publications of the European Communities.

Leeuwis, C. (1996) 'Communication technologies for information-based services', in N. Jankowski and L. Hanssen (eds), *The Contours of Multimedia*. Luton: University of Luton Press/John Libbey Media.

Nielsen Media Research (1996, 1999) 'Home technology report 1996 and 1998', New York: Nielsen Media Research Interactive Services; http://www.nielsenmedia.com/news

Pool, I. de Sola (1983) *Technologies of Freedom*. Harvard, MA: Belknap Press.

Schiller, H. (1996) *Information Inequality. The Deepening Social Crisis in America*. New York/London: Routledge.

Tichenor, P.J., Donohue, G. and Olien, C. (1970) 'Mass media flow and differential growth in knowledge', *Public Opinion Quarterly*, 34: 159–70.

United Nations (1998) *Human Development Report 1998*. UN Development Programme. New York: Oxford University Press.

van Dijk, J. (1991, 1994, 1997) *De Netwerkmaatschappij: Sociale aspecten van nieuwe media*, 1st, 2nd, 3rd edns. Houten: Both Stafleu van Loghum.

van Dijk, J. (1997a) *Nieuwe Media en Politiek, Informatie- en communicatietechnologie voor politici, ambtenaren en burgers* (*New Media and Politics, ICT for Politicians, Citizens and Civil Servants*). Houten/Diegem: Bohn Stafleu van Loghum.

van Dijk, J. (1997b) 'The reality of virtual communities', *Trends in Communication 1997/1, New Media Developments*: 39–61.

van Dijk, J. (1999) *The Network Society, Social Aspects of New Media*. London/Thousand Oaks/New Delhi: Sage.

van Zoonen, L. (1994) *Feminist Media Studies* (Media, Culture and Society Series). London/Thousand Oaks/New Delhi: Sage.

11

Public Policies for Digital Democracy

Michel Catinat and Thierry Vedel

Devising a public policy for a digital democracy may sound surprising. Traditionally, the idea of democracy implies a limitation of state's powers and evokes more a bottom-up process, in which individuals initiate action, than public intervention. Secondly, the development of information superhighways has illustrated a shift in telecommunications policies and marked a retreat of the state. In all industrialized countries, the implementation of the information infrastructure is market-led and should primarily depend on private initiatives. Finally, the Internet, to which the notion of digital democracy is intimately linked, may appear as an inherently democratic medium because of its structure and of the principles on which it functions.

This chapter argues that, in order to open the way to a digital democracy, public action is necessary. The marketplace is not always the best mechanism to ensure the basic values associated to the notion of digital democracy (such as freedom of communication, equal access to information infrastructure). Moreover, technological changes are ambivalent and may lead to different kinds of information society, more or less democratic. Democratic quality will largely depend on how information and communication technologies (ICTs) are applied, and consequently on how public authorities are able to frame their usage.

Yet, if public authorities have an important role to play in the shaping of a digital democracy, this role does not necessarily have to acquire the same forms that have prevailed in the past. Besides their traditional functions of regulators, operators and sponsors, public authorities are to invent new policy styles, more flexible and decentralized, to stimulate a bottom-up emergence of digital democracy.

What is Digital Democracy about?

The Notion of Digital Democracy

The exchange and free movement of information has always been a key element in democracy.[1] As democracy means a political system in which people make the basic decisions on crucial matters of public policy, the citizens in a democracy, as the ultimate decision makers, need full or at least a lot of information to make intelligent political choices. Democracy therefore requires freedom of communication which serves several purposes. First, it helps citizens to get an understanding of situations on which they have to make decisions. It has also a deliberative function by allowing citizens to discuss public issues. Finally, it has a critical function: the media play a role of people's watchdog and ensure criticism and evaluation of the established powers. Commonly, democracy has often a subsidiary meaning connected with the concept of equality. A democratic system is one which provides citizens with equal opportunities.

Although the notion of democracy is reasonably clear, it tends to be obscured by the diversity of forms it takes. Today, after the collapse of people's democracies in Eastern Europe, the dominant form of democracy is liberal democracy, in which the power of the government is limited and individual freedoms are protected. These freedoms (of speech, of association, etc.) are regarded as key elements and necessary conditions to democracy without which democracy could not exist at all. Additionally, besides freedom and equality, many other values are often associated to the idea of democracy. Democracy tends to be an ideal system which guarantees individual's autonomy, promotes cultural diversity, protects minority groups, and ensures social justice.

As a result, the notion of digital democracy can be defined in different ways. In a neutral way, it can be defined as encompassing all the uses of information and communication technology (ICT) which might affect and change the functioning of a democracy – and more especially the fundamental operations of expressing opinions, debating, voting, making decisions. In a normative perspective, digital democracy can be defined as a political system in which the use of ICT ensures democratic values.

ICT might have two kinds of impact on democratic systems. They can be used to correct failures or imperfections of the current political system, in order to increase their democratic quality without fundamentally changing their structures. Digital democracy is then a continuation of representative, liberal democracy, but with a greater participation of citizens in public affairs, a wider access of social forces to public debates, a better accountability of governments. Digital democracy may also be understood as a new age of democracy which will replace the representative democracy and establish a form of direct democracy. From this perspective, the roles of parliaments, political parties, medias and, more generally of all mediating structures and organizations, would be deeply challenged. Public debates would take place within fora which would trigger citizenship and allow for direct participation of people in public affairs through new procedures. New relationships among citizens, and between citizens and governments, would be established.

The Case for Public Intervention

Whereas freedom of communication[2] has always been considered as a key element to democracy, it has always been hampered by a number of difficulties and biases:

– since the provision and dissemination of information entail material and human costs, freedom of communication depends on the financial capacities of people that are not equally spread over the society. Access to information is inequitably distributed according to income;

- the marketplace is often seen as the best mechanism to ensure freedom of communication, but it often leads to the dominance of information by large corporations;
- information in its raw form does not necessarily enhance democracy, and is often useless to those who do not know how to evaluate and value it. Information needs to be placed in context. Information rights must be complemented by knowledge rights which sustain the public's access to the widest possible range of interpretation, debate and explanation;
- information is never neutral; it embodies national or social culture and the free flow of information may lead to cultural domination or homogenization.

In order to tackle these difficulties, public authorities have historically taken actions through media or communication policies. As the information society is changing the means through which information is carried, these policies have to be adapted.

Another argument for public intervention is linked to the fact that the implementation of digital democracy will be dependent on the political environment in which it takes place and on the balance of powers among various social actors. ICT may be used in different ways. They can lead to a surveillance society (Lyon, 1994), reinforce the interests of the most powerful actors, and reproduce the existing inequality in resources. They can also be used to promote more active participation. Digital democracy could lead to a strong democracy, e.g. a society organized along egalitarian and participatory lines in which people are directly and effectively able to take the decisions that shape their lives (Barber, 1984). It could also lead to a thin or weak democracy in which political participation is limited to periodic elections, influence on important decisions is only indirect, and the public debate is not fully accessible to all. For this reason, public policies regarding the development of information superhighways are extremely important: they condition the possible uses of ICT and their impact on political systems; they also express the general will of the society regarding its future and specific social concerns. As in the past for other media and communication services, the emergence of the information society will be the outcome of the interplay among all social forces – business, civil society and government. Public authorities have a unique role to play. Firms can certainly develop some services that serve democratic purposes, but they will only do so for profitable services. Democracy is not in general a profit-making undertaking and should not let the sole marketplace or the Internet determine the range of desirable democratic applications. Moreover, in their quest for profit, firms can be tempted to develop services which limit or even threaten democracy.[3] The dynamics of civil society alone are also insufficient to reach a digital democracy. Threat to democratic values can originate from social groups. On different occassions ICT have been used by neo-Nazi groups to diffuse their ideas. ICT might allow some well-organized minority groups to exert political domination, for instance by manipulating public forums.

To sum it up, public action is needed to develop a digital democracy for two major reasons: first, to complement private action and promote applications which are essential to democracy but might not be provided by the marketplace; secondly, to ensure the respect of democratic values and avoid, limit or fight against any practices detrimental to democracy which can stem from commercial or political interests alike. In addition, public authorities have specific obligations regarding their own structures and functioning. As a central actor in political systems, they have to take part in the advent of digital democracy by modernizing their relationship to citizens and enhancing their operating modes.

Policy Issues Related to Digital Democracy

While state action for digital democracy raises many problems and issues,[4] some of them seem to be more crucial to the extent that they condition any subsequent development of digital democracy. They include:

– access to infrastructure and to information services. If some categories of the population are durably excluded, the possibility of building digital democracy is jeopardized;
– protection of privacy. Harm of it might affect individual's autonomy and acceptance of digital democracy;
– access to public information. It serves as a test to evaluate the commitment of the state to establish digital democracy. Public authorities process a large amount of information, and often data associated with the exercise of citizenship. If they are unable or unwilling to guarantee a full access to public information, there is little chance that digital democracy occurs.

Equal Access to Information Infrastructure

While the number of Internet users is growing rapidly, surveys show that access to the Internet is not equal neither geographically, nor socially and demographically (see the previous chapter in this book). The Internet is primarily developing in industrialized countries, although at different paces. Amongst industrialized countries, access to the Internet is not equal and varies according to social groups.

Internet users tend to be highly educated, and well off; they are predominantly male (in a ratio ranging from 2:3 to 9:10 depending on surveys). Infrastructural, financial and cultural obstacles still prevent large amounts of people accessing the Internet. In some countries, including large parts of South America and Africa, communication infrastructures are underdeveloped or even non-existent. The cost of equipment and communications also plays a role. While the price of PCs has dramatically dropped down over the last 5 years and is now similar to the price of TV sets (from about 600 Euros), PCs are still too expensive for broad parts of the population. Browsing the Internet includes local telecommunication costs, which, in the absence of flat rates in most of the European countries, represent a high part of the cost of Internet usage. Telecommunication liberalization has up to now had little impact on local telecommunication tariffs, but this could be a question of time. Too high costs of Internet access have resulted in different forms of dissatisfaction, including strikes of usage. More importantly, Internet penetration is slowed down by cultural factors. Although PCs are now user-friendly in comparison to previous generations and the Web has made the use of the Internet much easier, browsing and processing information services remain a difficult task for most people. It requires basic skills – to start with the ability to read,[5] not to mention more sophisticated ones – such as the ability to deal with hyper-text or to do keywords search.

Such a situation could be considered as temporary. One could expect that in the long-term, technical progress, productivity gains, and competition altogether will lead to improved, totally new man-machine interfaces, and cheap rates. Moreover, future generations of users, who will have grown up and been educated in a digital environment, will likely be more comfortable with the Internet. From this perspective, public authorities might be inclined not to take any specific measures to enlarge citizens' access to the Internet, besides loosening regulations and strengthening competition. Universal access to the information society would be a question of time, not a public policy issue. Just as the penetration of TV took several decades to finally reach every household, in the same way, the Internet would finally reach every household.

Yet, this point of view can be challenged for two reasons. Competition can certainly lower financial and material obstacles, but it is doubtful that the marketplace will overcome cultural inequalities vis-à-vis information services. Free or cheap access to the Internet is not sufficient to guarantee equal access to the Internet and therefore public action is needed notably to improve skills of people (van Dijk, 1997). Secondly, current inequalities might be particularly difficult to deal with. The gap between information rich and information poor, between haves and have-nots, could become structural. The first users of information services could enjoy decisive advantages over the latter users and build up a permanent domination of them.[6] Public action is then necessary so as to give every citizen the same opportunities and assets.

Privacy

Invasion of privacy has long been recognized as one of the major political issues raised by ICT development. Kevin Robins and Frank Webster suggested that ICT – particularly in the form of an integrated electronic grid – could permit a massive extension and transformation of Panoptic principles (as described by Bentham and later on by Foucault – see Gandy, 1993). With the information revolution, the social totality would come to function as a hierarchical and disciplinary machine for surveillance (Robins and Webster, 1988). Privacy invasion is contrary to the very idea of democracy. Democracy supposes a limitation of state powers and a protection of individual freedoms. If the state is able to control and monitor citizens, this might have a 'chilling' effect on expression (Raab, 1997). The perspective of a digital democracy creates new risks to anonymity and privacy. The development of online governmental services opens possibilities of intrusion by third parties in the personal information held by public administrations. Bureaucracies may also be led to exchange files about individuals. Digital democracy, rather than transparency of public action, could result in a tighter social control.

The fear of a surveillance society is not new but the Internet makes it much more acute (Lyon, 1994). Every time users log on to a Web site, they expose themselves and their computers to data-mining: information about their favourite sites; their contributions to newsgroups; the orders they made through specialized electronic-commerce sites can be collected, sorted out, and compiled with other databases. Besides search engines (to which users communicate the topics they are interested in), different techniques exist to collect personal data. Some of them imply an implicit consent from users: by filling in a questionnaire and allowing their personal data to be monitored, users are granted free access to the Internet or to enhanced information services. Other techniques – such as cookies or chips included in microprocessors – are implemented without the knowledge and agreement of users.

Several problems arise from the collection of personal data through the Internet and other ICT. First, users are not always aware of this practice and are not asked whether they accept to reveal pieces of their privacy. Secondly, users do not always know for what purpose and who will use their personal data. Data collected by a given operator are often sold to a third party. Finally, the commercialization of personal data raises an equity problem: while some users will be rich enough to afford to pay for enhanced information services, others will have to accept information-monitoring to access the same services (Reingold, 1993). Information-rich and information-poor will not have the same right to privacy.

Protection against privacy invasion can be left to self-regulation or to the marketplace. It can be argued that, if citizens are concerned about their privacy, they will primarily use services protecting privacy. In addition, a number of technical tools can be implemented by users to protect their communication and information. Providers can adopt codes of conduct. However, it is also necessary that some principles and standards are embodied in laws and regulations and made mandatory. If not, there is a risk that a market-driven or a self-regulation approach will ration the right to privacy according to personal income or knowledge.

Access to Information and Content Issues

In a digital democracy, access to information cannot be limited to technical or economic issues, but should also focus on the kind of information and content which is necessary to promote digital citizenship. Ideally, a digital democracy should provide diversity of content and quality information with high cultural value, notions which are not easy to define. However, it is generally agreed that citizens should at least have full access to public data which inform them about their governments.

In the past, the right of access to public data has often been restricted for two reasons. Politically, the philosophy of representative democracy makes the government accountable to the parliament alone, and not directly to the citizens. In addition, governments were not willing to disclose information about their internal functioning. As a result, when a right of access to public data was recognized it was often limited to documents involving requesters directly and personally and exemptions to the right of access in order to protect the interest of the state were established. The dissemination of public data was also, and more simply, hampered by material factors. It was costly and resource-consuming to make public data available. However, the development of Xerox copying allowed more active dissemination policies in the 1970s and the 1980s, exactly when many

European countries adopted laws widening or establishing rights of access to public data. Public administrations also became aware that a commercial demand for some public data existed and they could sell them.

The development of the Internet is structurally changing policies regarding the access to public information in a number of ways. It makes the distribution of public information materially much easier and less costly. The Internet, and more generally the concept of the information society, introduce in the political system new values such as transparency. However, change in public data policies has also been spurred by other factors. Representative democracy in its traditional form is increasingly challenged, and citizens demand more participation in public affairs, including new forms of accountability and control of governments. Secondly, in a context of public budgets cutting, governments started using electronic devices more intensively as a means to reduce costs and to make money.

The protection of intellectual property rights (IPR) is another delicate issue for which public authorities can play a crucial role. Two conflicting interests between right owners and users clash with each other, but need to be reconciled in order to ensure smooth democratic activities. On the one side, creativity and innovation must not only develop freely, but also be protected, notably when commercial issues are at stake. The sophisticated legislation which has been implemented for decades in the European Union and the USA to protect creators and innovators must now be adapted to a digital environment. On the other side, creation and innovation are a collective asset for society; their broad diffusion triggers new activities and enriches the cultural and technical heritage of democracy. Access to creation and innovation has thus to be fairly facilitated (as it has been in the past when legal exemptions to copyrights were granted to allow free of charge access for schools, libraries, research centres or journalists).

The advent of the information age – and in particular the availability of new tools allowing computers to reproduce works and deliver them to users with rapidity, easiness, quality and low cost – is raising new challenges to public authorities. The way the current balance between owners of rights and users will evolve is extremely difficult to foresee. The easiness of circumventing intellectual rights as soon as the content is digital and the capability to escape national laws by taking advantage of the global nature of networks lead some observers to argue that digital democracy will be progressively free of any digital intellectual property rights. However, new technologies, in particular the so-called 'trusted systems', are being developed and would allow right owners to control access to their digital work automatically, selectively and quite efficiently (Catinat, 1998). Which trends will dominate is currently unclear. For public authorities, the challenge is to preserve a fair balance of interests, and for the legislator to escape the risk that technology prevails over legislation and policy objectives.

Forms of Public Authorities' Action

The public action to promote a digital democracy can be pursued through a variety of means: regulation, support (subsidies, training, education), direct intervention and finally catalysing effort.

TABLE 11.1 *Policy issues related to digital democracy and possible forms of public action*

	Regulation	**Sponsoring**	**Operator**
Access to infrastructure	Universal service policies.	Plans to equip schools. Free access in public places. Subsidies to equipment.	Local authorities as IAP. Free access in public places (libraries, etc)
Access to information	Right of access. Definition of essential public data.	Training, education. Communication vouchers.	On-line provision of public data. public kiosks.
Freedom of expression	Constitutional Laws.	Subsidies to associations. Training.	Free hosting. provision of services aimed at public debate.
Privacy	Protection of privacy codes. Obligation of consent.	Support to civil liberties associations.	Anonymizer.[29]
Content diversity	Cross-ownership restrictions, quotas.	Subsidies to specific information providers.	Public service providers offering specific contents.

Public Authorities as Regulator

While for the countries that met at the G7 ministerial conference on the information society in Brussels in February 1995, the emergence of the information society is basically a market-driven phenomenon, it nevertheless requires from governments a new regulatory environment and the implementation of safeguards. Schematically different cases have to be dealt with. First, regulatory and legal frameworks have to be adapted to the new digital context because they were designed at a time when activities mainly concerned physical products. Secondly, the use of ICT magnifies issues and makes them drastically more sensitive. Such is the case of privacy because of the ease of gathering, processing and exploiting personal data commercially. The need for new relations between public authorities and the citizens is another example where ICT allows for interactivity and citizens' empowerment. Finally, entirely new issues emerge and have to be tackled through new rules: liability of Internet service providers relative to illegal or harmful content provisionally copied in their computers ('caching') has for example to be clarified. The action plans for regulatory and legal adaptation are burdensome in most OECD countries. However, they are quite similar in terms of agenda and objectives and deal with the same issues.

Universal service   Universal service regulation is important for the development of digital democracy in that it may guarantee and ease the access to information infrastructure. In the European Union, up to the 1990s, universal service had no genuine legal statute. However, with the progressively increasing penetration of telephony service, most member states required their national monopoly to provide voice telephony to anybody requesting it whatever his location. In the USA, prior to the 1996 Telecom Act, the situation was very similar. The universal service concept was inherited from the past and likened to access to the local phone service at reasonable rates. Its definition resulted from practice more than legal obligation and it was implemented 'through a patchwork quilt of implicit and explicit subsidies', as stated by the FCC itself.[8]

When the European Telecommunication Council decided in November 1995 to completely open up to competition European telecommunication markets from 1 January 1998 onwards, the provision of universal service was regarded as a necessary safeguard for the full telecommunication liberalization.[9] This decision to balance market forces and social concerns was based on two main acknowledgements: first, the market forces alone could not ensure provision of basic telecommunication services to everyone from everywhere; secondly, and more fundamentally, the lack of universal service would create unacceptable discrimination amongst the European citizens in an emerging information society where access to information is becoming an essential condition of life. For the Council of European Ministers, universal service was a way to permit 'access to a defined minimum service of specified quality to all users everywhere and, in the light of specific national conditions, at an affordable price'. Politically, universal service has been regarded as an effective means to avoid a 'two-tier-society' where some 'haves' would have been able to fully profit from the opportunities created by the information society and some 'have-nots' would have been unable, unwilling or excluded from access to the new possibilities.

In the USA, the same political thrust has been given to universal service. For the Clinton administration, market forces are indeed the key driver. But they are nevertheless to be tempered by safeguards, in particular, by the provision of universal service that is considered as a prerequisite to any liberalization decision. This statement has raised no controversy in the USA hitherto. The first report of the NII Task Force entitled 'The National Information Infrastructure: Agenda for Action', which launched the NII policy implementation in late 1993, made it clear that the provision of universal service was one out of nine basic principles guiding the NII policy: 'Extend the universal service concept to ensure that information resources are available to all at affordable prices'. The Telecom Act promulgated in 1996 has taken into account this political willingness to guarantee universal service. In its section 254(b), it establishes principles on which the US policy should be based to preserve and advance universal service on the basis of seven principles including quality and affordability, access to advanced services, specific measures for rural, insular and high-cost areas as well as schools, health care and libraries.

Both in the EU and in the USA, the definition of the concept of universal has raised a debate in which two positions conflicted: either to adopt a broad, forward-looking definition, but with the risk of ending up with users paying for services they don't use and deterring entry of competitors because of too demanding requirements; or to adopt a limited, traditional definition with the consequence of failing to provide services necessary to live in the information society. On both sides of the Atlantic, solution was to agree on an evolving concept, starting with a narrow concept to be broadened progressively with technological progress and changes in needs and expectations of citizens. Both in the EU and the USA, the concept of universal service is therefore intended to deeply change in nature and scope, as the information society is developing.

Universal service should not only ensure access from anywhere to voice telephony as previously, but it should also ensure access to telecommunication and information services by anybody at an affordable price. 'By anybody at an affordable price' makes all the difference: anybody, whatever his/her abilities or disabilities, and whatever his/her social and economic situation, should be able to afford it.

This evolving definition, although wise and pragmatic, raises its own problems. The private actors subject to universal service obligations need a certain degree of certainty and temporal stability against which they will make their investment decisions. Consequently and paradoxically, the risk of a supposedly evolving concept is likely to result in a particularly low evolution of the concept. More importantly, it can be considered that this exceptional and unique opportunity of telecommunication liberalization to trigger access of everybody to advanced services has been wasted.

Indeed, the current implementation of the universal service concept fell short of declared political objectives. Its scope failed to be as forward-looking and innovative as expected. At the European level, the Voice Telephony Directive (adopted by the European Parliament and the Council in December 1995) has only made binding for universal service obligations what was explicitly done previously in most of the European Union: the provisions of voice telephony service via a fixed connection, operator assistance, public payphones, and emergency and directory enquiry. There is neither explicit requirement on affordability, nor obligation on bandwidth or on adequate services for certain groups of customers at the European level, for example text-phones for the deaf. In the USA by comparison, the universal service concept is broader. It comprises voice grade access to the public switched network, emergency services, operator services and directory assistance as in the EU, but also touch-tone services, the so-called 'lifeline and link up' services, namely reductions of phone and connection charges for qualified low-income consumers, as well as universal service support for eligible schools, libraries and rural health care providers. However there is actually no general obligation to provide universal service, except for the incumbent regional telecommunication operators[10] but incentives through different types of explicit or implicit budgetary support and conditions to be respected for eligibility to universal service support.

Fortunately markets concretized what politicians wanted to do by enlarging the universal service legally. Most of the improvement has resulted from market forces: the decrease in rates from tougher competition has raised penetration, quality and diversity of telecommunication services. Liberalization has therefore been an efficient tool for broadening the provision of universal service for voice telephony services and, through it, for a lot of other services such as fax services and Internet access. However, the situation although improved is not satisfactory. Many services, in particular the access to the Internet or e-mail services, remain not affordable to everybody. The appraisal has thus to be mitigated: in the current exceptional situation of awareness about the potentialities of the information society, time was ripe for an ambitious definition of universal service. This opportunity was not fully seized.

Competition and pluralism   Liberalization of telecommunication in recent years was considered to be an effective means to improve access to information by every citizen. In spite of their goals, the liberalization of telecommunication markets followed different paths in Europe and in the USA. In Europe, it was a long and continuous process started in 1984, whereas, in the USA, it was a discontinuous process punctuated with two major turning points: the AT&T divestiture in 1984, then the Telecom Act in February 1996. The European approach to liberalization also significantly differs from the American one for historical reasons. In Europe, the initial situation was characterized by the juxtaposition of technically different national networks, whereas the American market was integrated by the previous dominance of AT&T. Europe had to integrate to create competition; the US had to disintegrate to strengthen competition. For this reason, the European approach has always struck a balance between liberalization and harmonization. European telecommunication liberalization has been accompanied by standardization policy to ensure interoperability, mutual recognition to create the internal market, and rules for access to networks in order to promote competition (the so-called Open Network Provision).

Whatever the methods, market liberalization has generally resulted in a downward pressure on telecommunication rates, increase in the number of operators and service providers, diversity and strengthened quality of services. In its fourth report on the implementation of telecommunication liberalization in November 1998, the Commission expressed a great deal of satisfaction: 'the bulk of the European rules has been taken over into national law and is being applied effectively in the member states, with tangible benefits for the whole European economy.' The new national frameworks for licensing appear to be functioning well. The total number of authorized telecom operators in the EU is now impressive: only six months after the deadline of 1 January 1998, there were 218 operators with authorization to provide national public voice telephony, 284 to provide international voice services and 526 to offer local network services in the European Union.[11] Tariffs have started to fall sometimes sharply in some countries, generally in the previously less liberalized countries. But the average decrease sometimes hides a tariff rebalancing towards the costs structure. Consequently whereas long distance tariffs generally fell down, local call tariffs increased. In the perspective of digital democracy, liberalization mainly benefited long distance call users, namely the companies and the richest consumers and inversely was detrimental or neutral to most of the consumers, in particular the poorest ones. Furthermore the cost of accessing the Internet remained high in Europe in comparison with the USA preventing a lot of citizens accessing Internet-based services. Concerns still remained in the European Union. The Commission has not only to scrupulously scrutinize national transposition of the liberalization directives and, whenever required, to continue to initiate formal infringement procedures against member states but also to go further in its telecommunication policy in such a way as to achieve an overall and significant decrease in telecommunication tariffs. In a way, implementation of telecommunication liberalization, although progressing steadily and in a relatively smooth way in Europe, has to go further. By contrast, the implementation in the USA is more chaotic and less engaged in particular with regard to interconnection rules, but this does not mean lack of competition in the USA. On the contrary – this is the chance and the paradox of the USA – operators behave competitively, offer low-price, high-quality services and invest, even if competition is not tough as in the case of the local loops.

In the European Union, competition policy has been a tool to consolidate and strengthen competition in the telecommunication and the media markets. Competition policy has been used to clear large strategic alliances involving incumbents, such as GlobalOne or Unisource, conditional to commitments by national governments to speed up the opening up of their domestic markets. In the media sector, competition policy has aimed at preserving access to open markets as the best means to ensure pluralism. The European Commission had to prohibit mergers which might have resulted in dominant positions and deterred new entry. For example, different joint ventures involving Bertelsmann, Kirch and Deutsche Telekom have been blocked because they would have made competition difficult on the German pay-TV market, which in turn might have been detrimental to cultural diversity.

Privacy   Protection of privacy is a constitutional principle or a legal right in most OECD countries. With the advent of the information society and the ease of copying, transferring and exploiting personal data as soon as they are digital, most governments started adapting their provisions for privacy protection. Such adaptation stands high in the political agenda of most OECD countries and guidelines have been issued to make coherent national initiatives. In February 1995 during their meeting in Brussels, the G7 countries highlighted that protecting privacy and personal data plays an essential role in strengthening citizens' trust in the information society and thereby should encourage them to appropriate the new tools and online services.

In October 1995, the European Community enacted a directive on the protection of personal data.[12] Its objectives were twofold: ensuring the free movement of personal data within the European internal market through common rules and secondly guaranteeing a high degree of privacy protection in the whole European Union (see Gasparinetti, 1999). The Directive lays down the basic individual rights: the right to know where the personal data originated, who will use them and for which objectives; the right of access to those data; the right to have inaccurate data rectified; the right to withhold permission to use the data in certain circumstances; and the right of appeal in case of unlawful use. In the case of sensitive data, such as an individual's ethnic or racial origin, political or religious beliefs, trade union membership, health or sexuality, personal data can only be processed with the explicit consent of the individual. Exceptions are possible (e.g. for medical or scientific research, or public security reasons), however alternative safeguards have to be established. Those who collect, hold or transmit personal data should do so only for specified, explicit and legitimate purposes, and the data held only if it is relevant, accurate and up to date. All member states are required to establish an independent supervisory authority to monitor data processing and to function as ombudsman for citizens' complaints about misuse of personal data. The European Union's comprehensive privacy legislation became effective on 25 October 1998.

To avoid circumvention, the directive in Article 25 includes provisions on transfers of data to third countries. This article gave rise to misinterpretation in particular in the USA where the industrial interested parties backed by the American administration described the directive as interfering with their own American regulation on privacy. Actually the European Union has never attempted to dictate to third countries what they have to do, but only to protect its own citizens against misuse of personal data when they are transferred abroad.

In a certain way, the European initiative has highlighted the paradox of the American situation as to privacy. In the USA, there is a long tradition of enforcing privacy rights through legislation as in the European member states. But the USA, for some decades, has taken a sectorial approach as opposed to an omnibus approach: they have legislated whenever new issues or new technologies emerged, for instance for credit reports, video records or cable subscriber records. Although the number of privacy related Acts is impressive, there still exists an incredible deficiency in the legal arsenal of the USA: neither medical nor insurance records are protected for example. American skimpiness of privacy is becoming of great concern for the general public, and whereas many countries are moving to reinforce privacy standards and laws, the American administration lobbied by industry stands on its self-regulatory approaches. It seems that such an approach does not receive much support from users. A recent Harris poll found that 53 per cent of Americans think that 'Government should pass laws for how personal information can be collected and used on the Internet' against 19 per cent believing that 'Government should let groups develop privacy standards but not take any action unless real problems arise'. Distrust of the general public about self-regulation for privacy protection results from the enormous commercial interests of industry: potential benefits of processing and selling personal data are so high that self-regulation may not strike the right balance between industry and users. Even if there is a sharp increase in the percentage of commercial sites displaying some types of warning about collection of personal information in the USA (according to recent surveys, about 66 per cent in May 1999 against only 14 per cent the year before), warning consumers is not enough and most sites' practices leave much to be desired. In fact, only 1 in 10 sites offering privacy policies follow guidelines for issues like consumers' choice about the data being collected and consumer access to such information.

The US Department of Commerce has devoted a lot of effort to tackle both the European and domestic concerns about privacy. The proposal is to 'self-regulate with teeth' through the so-called safe harbour principles. A safe harbour is a qualification for US companies that voluntarily adhere to a list of privacy principles such as information to individuals, opt-out choice, security, data integrity, access by individuals to their personal data and enforcement mechanisms. The list of principles prepared by the Department of Commerce has been established in such a way as to meet the privacy protection required by the European Directive and to boost confidence in the USA.

The final acceptance or refusal of the safe harbour principles will be totally independent of the self-regulatory approach by the USA. The European directive in Article 26 also allows for adequate safeguards provided by the company itself. The result of transatlantic negotiations will rely on whether the privacy protection in the USA is high enough to meet the European standards.

Access to public data   Laws regulating the access to public information deal in general with four aspects:[13]

The right of access which gives citizens the possibility to request public documents. This right can be general, meaning that citizens are in principle allowed to request any public document like in Sweden which has the oldest access law in the world (1766). However, this right is often restricted to specific documents and/or limited by various exemptions. In France, only documents directly concerning the requester (for example a report preparing a decision about the requester) can be obtained. In Italy and Spain, a legal interest in the requested information is required. In the Netherlands, it is not possible to get documents giving confidential information on third parties and there are provisions protecting the decision-making process. Very often also, there are exemptions to the right of access, and secrecy provisions, when the interest of state or defence matters are involved.

The obligation of publicity which defines the documents that public administrations are required to publish independently of citizens' requests. Additional regulations can define the means through which the publicity of documents might or should be achieved, including the obligation of electronic dissemination. In most European countries, there is no legal obligation of publicity and dissemination depends on governmental policies. In many European countries, however, pending regulations will compel public administrations to open Web sites. In France, a forthcoming law will define essential public data which must be provided online.

Pricing policies. Documents can be provided free of charge (for example, in France when documents are accessed in situ or in Sweden up to 9 pages). More often, documents are given away at the price of copying or dissemination costs, as in the USA. However, when commercial use of public documents is intended, high charges can apply.

Commercialization policies rule the possibility and conditions of commercial use of public data. In most European countries, there is no general law regarding the commercial exploitation of public sector information and provisions are defined on a case-by-case basis. There are many examples of public/private co-operation especially in the domain of statistics. In some countries, private companies are given a monopoly under a concession regime to commercialize public data. This practice has raised competition issues and is often challenged before national courts or the European Court of Justice.

Intellectual property rights   As far as intellectual property rights are concerned, the first priority of industrialized countries in recent years has been to update their legislation, which was designed for most of them decades ago when the support of ideas to be protected was physical (books for example). The guidelines for legal adaptation have been given by the World Intellectual Property Organization in December 1996 when two new treaties were signed: the 'WIPO Copyright Treaty' and the 'WIPO Treaty on Performances and Phonograms', which clarified the international protection regime and adapted it to the digital world. Their ratification is now achieved in the USA with the enactment of the 'Digital Millenium Copyright Act' in October 1998. In the European Union, this is still underway; the European Commission forwarded a proposal in December 1997 which, if adopted, would extend copyright legislation to cover all forms of reproductions of work by broadcasters, phonogram and film producers, authors and artists. The draft directive is being discussed in the European Parliament in mid-1999. Whatever the delay, legislative adaptation will be achieved in the coming months, and will have to be transposed to national laws.

But the right owners have regarded this adaptation as a unique opportunity to question the current balance with the user rights. In the perspective of digital democracy, a drift is occurring towards stricter protection of intellectual property rights and against further exemptions for specific uses. In the USA, the 'fair use' clause was instituted by law in respect of the Constitution itself in order to strike a valuable balance between the power given to the owners to limit diffusion of ideas and the public interest to access them. Libraries, educational and research institutions, news reporting and criticism are legally authorized to reproduce and distribute copies of protected works for the general interest. However, exemptions over time became increasingly difficult to be accepted by courts and actually the fair use clause is more and more loosely applied. This evolution is likely to be aggravated by the new technologies and the tools offered to owners, such as the so-called trusted systems, technical applications which would allow them to individually and selectively separate authorized users from non-authorized ones. A legislator, whatever his/her political willingness, may be neutralized by technologies. Up to now neither in Europe nor in the USA, has any signal occurred, politically or legally, to deal with this evolution and to fairly protect use and diffusion of ideas when the collective interest requests it.

Public Authorities as Operator
Since the beginning of the 1980s, telecommunication markets have been progressively liberalized in many countries. The process of liberalization accelerated from the mid-1990s when many governments became aware that the 'Information Society' would require as cheap as possible access to information. About 70 countries have signed the telecommunication agreement in the framework of the WTO in February 1997 and committed to open up their telecommunication markets to competition. For the EU and the USA, this achievement is a paramount success. The challenge was to obtain a level playing field in telecommunication markets and consequently to avoid the situation where any difference in national regulation could deter their telecommunication operators from entering global telecommunication markets.

Subsequent to telecommunication market liberalization, most governments, in particular in the EU, decided to privatize their public telecom operators bearing in mind that their state-owned statute was no more politically consistent with and economically effective in markets opened up to competition. The states of those countries definitely drew the curtain on the role they had played for several decades.[14] In the emerging information society, they would not act any longer as network operators. Market forces and private actors would drive investments in network infrastructure and provision of telecommunication services. Public telecommunication services have given up to private services with the view that the latter would better meet demand from citizens and companies with regard to price, quality and diversity. However, this does not mean that public authorities have no operating role to play in a digital democracy. First, their infrastructure provision role although different will continue through regulation, for instance by defining interconnection rules, promoting standardization and stimulating investment in infrastructure. Secondly, their role as information service provider should be reinforced. As public authorities hold a considerable amount of data which can be used to make citizens better informed, they have to organize the dissemination of these on fair principles.

Providing public information has an important political dimension: it will bring public administration closer to the citizen. The relationship between the citizens and the public sector has been witnessing significant change for some years. The information and communication technologies provide the public sector with new tools to facilitate access to public information and extend online delivery of public services. As public administrations started experimenting with new usage of ICT, both citizens and businesses became more demanding and requested more direct and faster response to their needs, namely enhanced transparency and greater efficiency of public administrations. Technology only played a facilitator role; the key drivers were new requirements for improved democracy and cost savings for taxpayers. For the politicians who have been structurally suffering from an increasing distrust by their constituents in most of the industrialized countries, online administration or even digital government was regarded as a panacea to regain trust, a way to appear forward-looking and boost confidence. This change is part of a general movement towards greater participation and direct empowerment of citizens in democracy. Such change has been triggered in the USA by free speech advocacy and all those American associations whose goal is the strict enforcement of the first amendment.

For a long time, the USA has been ahead in developing a digital administration. They have a long tradition of active public sector information policy. Since 1966 with the enactment of the Freedom of Information Act (FOIA), then in 1996 with the Electronic Freedom of Information Act (EFOIA), access to public information including electronic access is guaranteed to American citizens. The USA has even strongly encouraged the private sector to exploit public sector information commercially through legislation, low pricing[15] and lack of any copyright on government information at the federal level. This long-standing US policy was supported by an appropriate internal policy to ensure its efficient implementation. The Office of Management and Budget effectively administered this policy and controlled how the federal agencies were providing electronic access to public information.[16] Training of officials with an emphasis on stressing their duty to make government information available has been implemented in the whole American public sector.

Since the beginning of the National Information Infrastructure Initiative, the Clinton administration was eager to modernize means of access to public information. An outstandingly high number of public Web pages were created very rapidly to help citizens to be informed of public and political life as well as to retrieve public information. The White House, the House of Representatives, the Senate and most of the agencies and administration departments applied to themselves what the government advised the private sector to do, namely to use the information and communications technologies extensively to improve their performance.

The US policy went much beyond access to public information. Online public procurement was actively developed. Additionally, the Internal Revenue Service, the American Tax Agency, launched an ambitious programme aimed at tripling the number of taxpayers who would file in their tax forms electronically by 2007. Currently about 20 per cent of American taxpayers do it electronically.

As far as new relationships between the citizens and their administration are concerned, the USA is a laboratory and a prefiguration of public governance in the future information society.

In the EU, the current situation in member states regarding legislation and policy on access to public sector information is very heterogeneous and the potentialities offered by the information and communications technologies might still further magnify the existing differences.[17] In the past few years, the relationship of citizens with the public sector has given rise to increasing attention. There has been a bundle of reasons which altogether have driven political awareness. Pressure came both from the European institutions and the citizens themselves. The European Monetary Union forced consolidation of national budgets and called for increased efficiency of administrations through their usage of ICT, which in turn offers so many new ways of interaction with the citizens. The new Treaty of the European Community conferred to 'any citizen of the Union, and any natural or legal person residing or having its registered office in a Member State, a right of access to Commission, Council and European Parliament documents'.[18] The European citizens questioned in the framework of the Eurobarometer inquiry (March 1999) expressed their priority interest for using information society services. The highest interest (47.8 per cent) was given to electronic contacts with (municipal) administrations, in particular the possibility to access and download administrative documents thus avoiding the need for physical movements. Interestingly, only a few people asked for online contacts with politicians: direct electronic democracy is neither an operational nor a credible concept in the near future for the European citizens.

The G7 government online project[19] provides a snapshot of plans and activities undertaken in the G7 countries and was devoted to the development of electronic contacts between administrations and citizens, in particular the provision of online administrative forms. The number of national initiatives is impressive in this latter domain, but there is still a long way to go: in the case of administrative forms, there are many thousands of forms just for dealings between citizens or business and their public administration in any single G7 country. Making them accessible online is both a way of streamlining the current situation inherited from decades of red tape, and a means to improve the quality of relations between administrations and their administrees. Worth mentioning is the European programme 'Interchange of Data between Administration' (IDA) which for many years contributes to providing national administrations in the European Union with basic telematic infrastructures and thus with the tools necessary to deliver online services to the citizens.

Another way for public authorities to take part in the development of a digital democracy as operator is to host, free of charge, Web pages of individuals on their computers. By providing such facilities (possibly complemented by technical assistance), they can encourage citizens to discuss political issues and be actively involved in social exchange. Other initiatives consist of establishing platforms or kiosks where citizens can access reliable information, directories and guides, public interest forums and newsgroups, and where they may be redirected by links to useful independent sites (Bardoel and Frissen, 1999). In the USA, the government information system implemented by the state of Minnesota gives a good illustration of such a policy. These kiosks contribute to solving one of the key problems of the information society, namely the abundance of data. It is complicated and lengthy to get pertinent and trusted information among the thousands of Web sites now available on the Internet. This galaxy tends to fragment the public sphere in niches and does not allow a nation-wide public debate which requires a common frame. A further step – which seems only feasible in Europe – would be an application of the notion of public broadcasters to the Internet. As public intervention in broadcasting is considered legitimate in Europe in order to achieve cultural goals, the development of public service providers could be imagined.[20]

Although assistance to help citizens find their way in the complex digital world and enable them to fulfil their social communication needs can be considered a public service, some groups or economic actors oppose this approach. They consider, in line with the usual carrier traditions,[21] that content matters should not be the responsibility of public authorities and should be left entirely to the private sector.

Public Authorities as Sponsor

In order to enlarge access of citizens to the Internet, public authorities have undertaken different actions. For several years, plans to equip schools and universities have been launched in many countries, either through public funding or with the support of private companies. In the USA, following the High Performance Computer Act in 1991, the NII policy challenged the industry to connect all classrooms to the Internet by the year 2000 and $2 billion have been allocated in order to deliver the information society to American teachers and students.[22] In Canada, the SchoolNet project set up in 1993 has aimed at connecting the majority of the country's 16,000 schools to the Internet. In the UK, the government has pledged £700 million to assist schools in purchasing hardware and software and an additional £200 million to train teachers with the objective of creating a 'national grid for learning'. The objectives of these plans are twofold: providing free access, thus dropping financial and material barriers to the information infrastructure; reaching a large portion of youth without almost any exception, since schooling is mandatory in most countries.

In parallel to plans for equipment, public authorities have implemented other actions to provide free access to the Internet, especially at the local level. These include:

Free access to the Internet in public libraries, city halls, youth or sports centres, etc. which has become common in many countries. In France, some cities have even subsidised Web cafés, operated by private associations or individuals. However, the strategy of supplying access to the Internet in public places has raised some concerns. First, it comes up against the controversial issue of harmful and illegal content, which are available on the Internet. Should the access to Web sites be fully open, or restricted to selected services? In the USA, public libraries have blocked access to some Web sites, a decision which was immediately challenged in courts by local citizens on the grounds of freedom of information. Secondly, access to the Internet in public areas does not always allow for a full use of the Internet because users are afraid of potential control and do note dare to use some services openly.

Support of universal access to information services by encouraging the use of the Internet in private homes through direct or indirect subsidies. For example, in France, the city of Parthenay can rent computers at low price and has signed agreements with France Télécom to offer discount rates to the Internet. In Italy, the city of Bologna has become the Internet access provider and city residents do not have to subscribe to a commercial IAP.

In addition to providing free access, public authorities can support training programmes which give people the basic skills to use information services and tools. Schools seem a natural place to achieve this goal, although the benefits of online learning are often overestimated, notably because the debate on the Internet in schools is narrowed down to the means rather than the objectives (Selwyn, 1999). For those people who are out of the educational system, public authorities can provide training and assistance in creating dedicated centres which help citizens using services, entering community networks or even creating their own Web pages or services. Of paramount interest here are the experiments launched by cities such as Manchester or Bologna. They aim at establishing community access centres, also known as telecentres or Electronic Village Halls, through which people, including minority groups, benefit from facilities, training, advice and support to use information services. These experiments have an economic goal. It is expected that greater access to the Internet will result in enhanced telematic applications (for example teleworking, electronic trade, etc.) directly stimulating the local economy. They have also political objectives: they want to overcome the current domination of cyberspace by the corporate sector and young, technically skilled white males (Carter, 1997) by networking social forces, encouraging initiatives from below and empowering citizens to participate in active policy making.

In order to fully develop digital democracy, universal access to networks and ability to use information services are not enough. The notion of freedom of information implies not only the possibility of getting access to various sources of information but also the capability of providing information. This second component is often neglected by public policies which view citizens as passive receivers but rarely as active content providers. The issue is especially crucial, as the rampant commercialization of the Internet may not necessarily lead to the greatest desirable diversity of content. It is likely that commercial providers will not meet all needs and tastes but primarily those of users ready to pay for services. Social organizations – which are necessary to make the civil society rich and lively – do not have always the required resources to become information providers. As a consequence, public actions are required to encourage citizens and social groups to express their concerns, statements and points of view through the Internet. This can be achieved by providing free space on computers, software and technical assistance for citizens or associations to create their own sites or home-pages, as in the case of the policy implemented by the French city of Parthenay.

Public action in this domain can also consist of subsidies granted to specific associations which meet peculiar demands, fulfil important social missions or contribute to the achievement of governmental goals and general interest. For example, in France and in Quebec, governments have given financial support to some non-profit service providers who contribute to the development of service in French or with local content. Insofar as public authorities of some countries subsidize theatres and a variety of cultural associations to dynamize creation, there is no reason why they should not do the same for culturally-oriented services on the Web.

Public Authorities as Catalyzer

Digital democracy can be seen either as an objective or as a process. In the latter case, the political conditions under which the move toward the information society takes place are of concern, as well as the way information society will operate on an accountable and democratic basis. Such an orientation implies new policy styles in which public authorities stimulate social debates, encourage citizen participation and help to aggregate interests.

One of the roles of government in information superhighway plans has been a catalytic role. Public authorities served as a propagandist (Catinat, 1998); they launched promotional actions to demonstrate the desirability of the information society (Vedel, 1997b) and raise awareness among corporations and citizens about their vision of the future. Much of the public effort so far has been directed to business and stressed the economic dimension of the information society more than the social one. While public authorities should continue to stimulate a social debate on the information society, they should do so in ways which take into account democratic values rather than only market values and which mobilize all citizens and not primarily economic actors.

Such a shift is apparent in recent efforts undertaken by the European Union. In 1997, the High Level Group of Experts on the Information Society issued a report in which it called for a change in the agenda for the information society.[23] While European policy for the information society focused on technological development in the 1980s, and on the economical context of technical innovation in the 1990s, in a third phase more attention has to be paid to social issues (such as access, users needs, quality of contents). The European Council adopted a 5-year programme (1998 to 2002) to stimulate the establishment of the information society in Europe (PROMISE), and more particularly people's motivation and ability to participate in the change towards the information society. The programme includes measures for gathering information on citizens' and users' needs, increasing visibility and transparency of on-going policies, and promoting electronic literacy in the educational systems.[24] The European Union has also established an Information Society Forum regrouping all components of society: industry, academia, trade unions, politicians, consumer and user groups in order to advise the Commission on the challenges to be overcome and highlight potentialities of the information society.

By contrast in the USA, the NII initiative did not pay special attention to such societal concerns. In a certain way, the broad social acceptance of new technologies by the American society does not require any awareness campaign or effort to demonstrate the opportunities.

A democratic design of technical systems has basically two goals: associate all social forces to the design of new technical systems; design systems so that their compatibility with democracy is guaranteed.[25] A larger number and more diverse range of participants increase the chance of creative insights and provide enhanced opportunities for cross-fertilization of ideas. Social needs, concerns and experiences can be reflected in the design process, which eventually increases the acceptance of new systems. Adoption costs are reduced as it allows the anticipation of potential problems, obstacles or resistance that would be more difficult and costly to solve or overcome *ex post*.

It is important that democratic values are embodied in technical systems at the design stage. If the Internet is often seen as a democratic system, it is in part due to the decentralized architecture and communication protocols which were established openly and early in its evolution. For instance, the adoption of data packet transmission makes censorship and content control more intricate (although not impossible). Thus information superhighways can be technically designed so as to maximize democratic values and minimize non-democratic uses.[26] In this prospect, public authorities can for instance encourage research on privacy enhancing technologies, while barring attempts to establish control devices (such as built-in identifying chips in computers).

In operational terms, democratic design of technical systems can take several forms. Inventories of technologies and of their possible applications help users imagining their usage and opportunities for improvement. Such an inventory has been decided by the G7 Ministerial meeting in Brussels in 1995 in order to diffuse best practices world-wide.

Social trials and local experiments can also be undertaken to allow a first assessment of consequences and impacts of ICT, reorient further developments and help the design of regulatory procedures. For instance, a lot can be drawn from early experiences of cities, like Santa Monica in California, which have set up public forums and conference services on their Web sites. They have shown the necessity of moderators and clear rules of conduct, the interest of involving targeted users to create a positive dynamics, but also the difficulty in maintaining lively discussions, and the long-term trend to de-emphasize interactive applications against information applications (Docter and Dutton, 1998).

For those people who regard the NII as a tool for revitalizing democracy, it is necessary to adopt a strategy integrating NII implementation with local organizational developments and grassroots creativity. This bottom-up strategy would push top-down and market-driven NII policies into democratic directions. As Steven Miller (1996) pointed out, rooting cyberspace in the social realities of neighbourhood organizations increases the odds that the needs and priorities of potential 'have-not' areas will be effectively aggregated and expressed. Grassroots organizations – labour unions, housing associations, ethnic groups, social clubs, etc. – know how to bring people together for mutual exchange and are able to reach people of all age groups, income levels, ethnic background and educational attainment. According to Miller, community networks in which grassroots organizations have been involved are a national treasury of experimental data on the public interest for the information society and demonstrates that people when properly trained and supported are able to use ICT for activities that meet their needs and capture their interest.

In modern societies, politics is evolving more and more into a sort of broker style in which governments play an organizing and catalyzing role. The model of the state as being at the top of the political system and in command of every aspect of social life is being replaced by a more horizontal vision of politics.

> Vertical bureaucratic relations of command and control are substituted increasingly by horizontal relations of compromising and organizing consensus on a non-hierarchical basis. Regulation as the archetype of governmental steering is replaced by contracting in and out, by co-production arrangements, by consensus seeking configurations, by negotiation, by wheeling and dealing.
>
> (Frissen, 1997: 119)

In a context in which policies are designed and implemented in a more fragmented way, an important and new role for public authorities is to ensure social cohesion by helping the co-ordination of individual actions, framing options for the future and stating the basic principles and values which define any society.

Conclusion

The way towards the information society and digital democracy will be a fully interactive process where all actors, be they governments, citizens, companies, institutions or media, will channel change through their acceptance, refusal and reactions to new applications, services or systems. Although there are thousands of pages describing the evolution and hundreds of visions by experts, nobody knows what will be the shape and the functioning of the future digital democracy.

In this context, the role of public authorities is of paramount importance as guardian of fundamental rights of citizens.

This chapter has to be read as a strong plea in support of the government role: not to oppose market forces, but to accompany them and compensate for market failures; not to impose binding regulations, but regulations striking the right balance between conflicting interests and protecting public interest. It has striven to identify the principal challenges, to highlight the basic principles for public action and to describe the governmental policies which are being – or could be – implemented in the European Union and in the USA with their respective characteristics, strengths and weaknesses.

Serious threats exist on the way forward. Amongst them, the risk that technology supersedes the law and emerges surreptitiously. The influence of proponents for a technology-driven society cannot be ignored. Their arguments are however simplistic: the increasing complexity of society and rapidity of evolution make any regulation out of date before being enacted and unable to integrate all the dimensions of emerging problems. Only technology can deal with complexity and be flexible enough to adapt to continuous change. This view fails to acknowledge that any society as a collectivity of individuals needs rules defining the border between duties and rights, and between individual freedom and collective obligation. Such an equilibrium requires regulation and representatives who are democratically elected and mandated to protect the collective interest, be the guardian of universal rights and guide the legislators to design laws. In this scheme, technology is a driving force but has to be channelled through precise regulatory frameworks and sometimes bridles when inconsistent with ethical, human or philosophical objectives.

Notes

This chapter reflects the views of the authors and does not commit the European Commission.

1 The argument for free communication in a democracy is usually contributed to Meiklejohn, 1960.

2 The notion of freedom of communication encompasses different components:

- the freedom of speech means the right for every individual to hold his/her own opinions, to speak freely about these opinions without fearing the consequences of doing so;
- the freedom of information means the right to know and relies on the principle of open access to information especially about governments and by extension the necessity of informing people;
- the freedom of information flows relates to the necessity of a free circulation of ideas so as to make them known as widely as possible.

See Trudel et al., 1997 for a general discussion of the notion of freedom of communication and how it can be adapted to cyberspace.

3 For example, services which deny the privacy right of people.

4 Including inequality; information commercialization and abuse; risks for privacy; community disintegration; instantaneous plebiscite and democracy dissolution; tyranny of gatekeepers; and decline of public service and social responsibility values (Brown, 1994).

5   Various UNESCO studies have shown that the illiteracy rate is still high in many countries. Even in industrialized countries a significant proportion of the population is not able to fully understand written documents.

6   For instance, first users could design electronic democracy applications in a way which meets their requirements and their visions of the world.

7   An anonymizer is a system which conceals the identity of Internet users. It is provided by a number of specialized Web sites.

8   Report to Congress, 10 April 1998.

9   Five conditions were imposed by the Ministers to the full liberalization of telecommunication markets in the European Union: provision and financing of universal service, the establishment of interconnection rules, the setting up of licensing procedure conditions, comparable and effective market access including in third countries, and fair competition.

10   The so-called Regional Bell Operating Companies (RBOC) created from the dismantling of AT&T in 1984.

11   Of course, most European operators simultaneously provide national and international voice services as well as network services and their respective number cannot be estimated. The increase in telecom operators is nevertheless extremely high.

12   Directive 95/46/EC of 24 October 1995 on the protection of individuals with regard to the processing of personal data and on the free movement of such data.

13   For the current situation in each European Union member state regarding legislation on access to public sector information see http://www2.echo.lu/info2000/en/publicsector/gp-annex.html

14   As the case of France, where a form of state entrepreneurship termed as high tech colbertism predominated for decades, illustrates (Vedel, 1997a).

15   In accordance with the 1986 Uniform Freedom of Information Act Fee Schedule and Guidelines issued by the Office of Management and Budget, pricing principles consist of charging for search, duplication and review costs when providing public data. The principles allow to pay the taxpayers back, but prevent the administrations from any profit making.

16   Refer to the Information Technology Management Reform Act of 1996 for further details.

17   For a detailed analysis of national legislation in the EU, see the Green Paper on public information in the information society released by the European Commission at the beginning of 1999.

18   Article 255 of the Treaty of the European Community.

19   This project was decided as a result of the G7 Ministerial Conference in Brussels in February 1995, jointly with ten other pilot projects aiming at stimulating new global applications.

20   In effect, most European public broadcasters have opened Web sites. Yet, it is not clear whether these sites meet broadcasters' public service requirements.

21   In the usual carrier model, infrastructure operators indifferently serve the public without editorial control or interference on transmitted information. See Pool, 1983.

22   On this initiative and similar ones in other countries, see Selwyn, 1999.

23   As stated in the title of the report: 'Building the European Information Society for us all'. Available on http://www.ispo.cec.be/hleg/building.html

24   However, it must be noted that this programme represents a small amount of money (Euro 25 million) and that many other measures are aimed at optimizing the economic benefits of the information society, especially with regard to small and medium enterprises (SMEs).

25   See Sclove, 1995, which provides a state of the literature on the topic and documented case studies, and suggests a strategy for democratizing technology.

26   It should be made clear that we do not subscribe here to the deterministic view that some technologies necessarily drive democratic uses. However, technologies define opportunities and constraints that, in a given economic context, might facilitate democratic uses and hamper non-democratic uses.

References

Barber, B. (1984) *Strong Democracy. Participatory Politics for a New Age*. Berkeley: University of California Press.

Bardoel, J. and Frissen, V. (1999) 'Policing participation: new forms of participation and citizenship and their implications for a social communication policy', *Communications & Strategies*, 34(2): 203–27.

Brown, L. (1994) 'The seven deadly sins of the digital age', *Intermedia*, July: 32–7.

Catinat, M. (1998) 'The National Information Infrastructure Initiative in the United States – policy or non-policy', *Computer and Telecommunication Law Review*, 3, April: 68–86; 4, May: 134–49.

Docter, S. and Dutton, W.H. (1998) 'The First Amendment online. Santa Monica's Public Electronic Network', in R. Tsagarousianou, D. Tambini and C. Bryan, *Cyberdemocracy. Technology, Cities and Civic Networks*. London: Routledge. pp. 125–51.

Frissen, P. (1997) 'The virtual state. Postmodernisation, information and public administration', in B.D. Loader (ed.), *The Governance of Cyberspace*. London: Routledge. pp. 111–25.

Gandy, O.H. Jr. (1993) *The Panoptic Sort*. Boulder, CO: Westview Press.

Gasparinetti, M. (1999) 'Personal data and Directive 95/46/EC: "The great wall of Europe", or too much ado about nothing?', *Telecommunications and Broadcasting Networks under EC Law*.

Lyon, D. (1994) *The Electronic Eye. The Rise of Surveillance Society*. Cambridge: Polity Press.

Meiklejohn, A. (1960) *Political Freedom: The Constitutional Powers of People*. New York: Harper.

Miller, S.E. (1996) *Civilizing the Cyberspace: Policy, Power and the Information Superhighway*. Reading: Addison Wesley.

Pool, I. de Sola (1983) *Technologies of Freedom; On Free Speech in an Electronic Age*. Cambridge: Belknap/Harvard University Press.

Raab, C.D. (1997) 'Privacy, democracy, information', in Brian Loader (ed.), *The Governance of Cyberspace*. London: Routledge. pp. 155–74.

Reingold, H. (1993) *The Virtual Community: Homesteading on the Electronic Frontier*. Reading, MA: Addison Wesley.

Robins, K. and Webster, K. (1988) 'Cybernetic capitalism: information, technology, every day life', in V. Mosco and J. Wasko, *The Political Economy of Information*. Madison, WI: The University of Wisconsin Press.

Sclove, R.E. (1995) *Democracy and Technology*. New York: The Guilford Press.

Selwyn, N. (1999) 'Schooling the information society? The place of the information superhighway in education', *Information, Communication & Society*, 2(2): 156–73.

Trudel, P. et al. (1997) *Droit du cyberspace*. Montréal: Editions Thémis.

van Dijk, J. (1997) 'Universal service from the perspective of consumers and citizens'. Report to the Information Society Forum. (Available at: www://ispo.cec.be/inforum/documents/ann-rep-97.htm)

Vedel, T. (1997a) 'Information superhighway policy in France: the end of high-tech Colbertism?', in B. Kahin and E. Wilson (eds), *National Information Infrastructure Initiatives. Vision and Policy Design*. Cambridge, MA: The MIT Press. pp. 307–48.

Vedel, T. (1997b) 'The ecology of games shaping information superhighway policies', *Trends in Communications*, 3: 35–51.

12

Summary

Jan van Dijk and Kenneth L. Hacker

In this chapter the main findings of the authors of this book are summarized and put in a wider perspective. We intend to compare the preliminary practical results of digital democracy with the many promises made in its wake. Some of these promises were contained in the 18 questions in the Introduction (see p. 5). The conclusions are set out in three parts: theory, practice and issues of further research.

Theory

A View on Technology

Tom Friedman, author of *The Lexus and the Olive Tree* says that we live in an age in which everything is true along with its opposite. Long ago, Charles Dickens said it was the best of times and the worst of times. Marx repeated what others said about the rich getting richer and the poor getting poorer in a society of surplus and political consultant Dick Morris says the smart get smarter and the dumb get dumber in this age of information. There is a simple reason why these paradoxes exist. As the French philosopher of technology Jacques Ellul noted, all technologies bring both good and bad consequences. Such is the case with digital technology.

It is impossible to evaluate digital democracy without an implicit or explicit conception of technology, democracy and communication. Most contributors of this book have a view on technology as a duality of enabling and defining capacities combining opportunities and risks, good and bad potential consequences. This duality serves to avoid mistakes often made with regard to the causes and effects of technology. According to John Street (1997) there are three mistaken claims about technology: that it is neutral, that it is autonomous and that it can be selected freely.

Proponents of digital democracy appear to be most vulnerable to the claim of neutral technology. Many of them suppose the problems of democracy are primarily practical and to be solved by the application of technology as a neutral instrument. For them ICT and CMC provide a *technical fix* to limits of time, place, information and access in the daily practices of democracy. As digital technology enables people to break particular limits of time, place and size of people able to communicate simultaneously, and because this technology offers an abundance of information and terminal access to networks, they suppose it can cure ills of modern democracy. Opposed to this, the contributors of this book have stressed that the problems of contemporary democracy go much deeper. No technology is able to 'fix' a lack of political motivation, lack of time, effort and skills required for full participation in democratic activities. No technology can dissolve the social and material inequalities that appear to be so strongly related to differences of participation.

Moreover, digital democracy is not only a potential cure of democracy in general, it might just as well harm it. In Chapter 3 it was claimed that ICT amplifies the tendencies of a spread and concentration of politics. The locus of control in social and political systems is turning away from the most important democratic entity in the last centuries, the nation state. It is handed over to transnational corporations and all kinds of (in)formal networks with no tradition of democracy and accountability. The other tendency, a concentration of politics in the registration, control and surveillance by states, corporations and societies at large would not be an advance of democracy either. There are no easy solutions to such structural problems of democracy.

The second mistaken view on technology is that it leaves no choice because it develops autonomously. Some advocates of digital democracy claim that the state and other hierarchies will inevitably wither away to make room for all kinds of networks, markets and virtual communities. In the optimistic version of this technological determinist position networks just have to result in 'horizontal' types of communication and 'flat' organizations. Contrary to this, the authors here have emphasized the choices political actors have in shaping digital democracy from its numerous, extremely diverging applications. In general, horizontal and 'flat' communication are not the only options. Networks have centres as well and they offer all kinds of opportunities for new complex hierarchies intelligently combining centralization and decentralization. In particular, this book has described diverging views on democracy leading to different designs and applications of the same technology.

However, digital technology is no collection of tools enabling altogether free selections and completely open political choices. Digital technology has particular characteristics defining what is possible or likely to be done and what is not. For instance, it is known for its speed, big geographical reach, large storage potential, accuracy of registration and interactivity. These characteristics will define future politics in one way or another. For example, inevitably there will be some speed-up of political processes following the application of digital technology. For example, there will be more daily telepolling, continuous government registration and instant political news on the Internet and interactive broadcasting. Inevitably, they will put heavy pressure on the representative system that actually needs time for thinking, consultation and deliberation. However, the degrees of freedom in bending technological characteristics are large for every political system and culture as Hagen has demonstrated in Chapter 4. Even individuals are able to influence the course of technology at decisive moments as Rogers and Malhotra have shown describing the early history of the Internet. While computers were invented as number-crunching devices, they were transformed into communication media by particular groups of users.

We may agree with John Street's conclusion (1997: 34): 'Technology is not something that exists as a simple object for our use. It acts to structure our choices and preferences, but not in a wholly determinist way. The relationship is in constant flux: political processes shape technology; and it then shapes politics.' This means that we have to move forward with empirical research exactly determining how political activity changes the development and design of technology and how technology shapes politics on particular occasions (see below).

The Need for Conceptual and Historical Analysis

In this book the authors have tried to demonstrate that not only a concept of technology but also concepts of democracy and communication are required for an understanding of the real chances and results of digitalization in politics. Recently, a host of books has appeared about 'cyberdemocracy', 'cyberpolitics', 'electronic democracy', 'teledemocracy' and the like. They remain remarkably silent when it comes to defining democracy or explaining what concepts like access, interactivity, horizontal communication and public debate really mean in the context of digital technology. Therefore, in this book much effort was made to unfold these concepts. It appears that the ideals of digital democracy are not easily put into practice. Splendid opportunities of better access to, responsiveness of and interactivity with political institutions result in much more sober practices.

Moreover, solid theory and historical analysis are urgently required. In the twentieth century one new communication medium after another was hailed for its democratic potential. Radio, television, cable, satellite, micro-wave transmission, VCR and video camera, they were all projected to be creators or saviours of democracy. Within one or two decades disillusion reigned. It appears as a long series of confirmations of Winston's 'law of the suppression of radical potential' following the arrival of new communication technologies (Winston, 1998).

However, pessimism is not called for either. Who could have predicted that a safety system for communication built by the American defence and state hierarchy would turn into a world-wide network of more or less free communication among millions of civilian users? Rogers and Malhotra have described this transformation. They have shown how the first applications of this network entered local political community building in the US within a decade.

The question of what democracy is, whether digital or traditional, was the central issue in van Dijk's Chapter 3. He argued that at least six views or models of democracy hide behind all promises and practices of the new media in the political system at large. The advocates of four of these six models, pluralist, plebiscitary, participatory and libertarian democracy, are trying to use the new media to spread politics into society and across the borders removing it from the centres of institutional politics (governments, public administrations and parties). They prefer civic networking, public debates, community building, independent political information supply and televoting or telepolling. Proponents of the other two models, legalist and competitive democracy, are using the new media to reinforce or reinvigorate institutional politics. They are applying the new media to public information supply, registration by governments and public administrations and powerful election campaign techniques. These opposite movements can be extended to future directions of digital democracy. The movement of spreading politics into society will prefer an Internet model of designing the future information superhighway. The movement to concentrate politics tends to develop so-called Marketing and Infocratic models of the same highway (as van Dijk has called them). The actors concerned will primarily adapt traditional political and media practices into formats of interactive broadcasting, e-commerce and political marketing and polling.

The actual road of future development largely depends on the context of the political systems and cultures concerned. In Chapter 4, Hagen shows that the same digital technology is able to acquire completely different shapes and types of application in particular political systems and cultures. The differences in the nascent digital democracies of the US, the UK and Germany are striking. In the US one looks for electronically supported direct types of political activity and local community building. Increasingly, direct communication links between citizens, representatives, governments and media are the most important option. However, Hagen argues that there is a bad historical experience of direct democratic relationships in Germany. Germans think close political relationships might be good for purposes of communication but not for decision making. Digital technology is scarcely used for local community building either. Instead, it is adopted to reinforce institutional politics for the benefit of a more efficient state and party system. In the UK the use of digital technology in politics is also output-oriented and top-down. There is a strong public service orientation addressing citizens as consumers who need better information to decide in civilian and political affairs.

There are other requirements for an appropriate context of digital democracy, such as economic, social and educational conditions and favourable properties of media design and media markets (see below). All these conditions taken together explain how irresponsible it is to talk about the opportunities of digital democracy in the abstract. To rehearse John Street's expression: digital democracy is not neutral, it is not autonomous and it cannot be selected freely.

Public Spheres and Media

Traditionally, democracy – in every view on it – has a close relationship to public life and the mass media as the infrastructures of society. However, things are changing fast in contemporary society. According to Keane (Chapter 5) the old hegemony of state-structured and territorially bound public life mediated by radio, television and newspapers is being rapidly eroded. The conventional ideal of a unified public sphere and its corresponding vision of a republic of citizens living up to some 'public good' are obsolete. Instead, we get a complex mosaic of differently sized, overlapping and interconnected public spheres. This mosaic is a combination of micro-spheres (interpersonal communication), meso-spheres (local/national media) and macro-spheres (international media). Of course, the Internet is an appropriate medium to link these spheres, that is, to overlap and interconnect them.

However, a common impression of Internet communication among social and communication scientists is that it produces fragmentation as well as unification. One refers to the numerous separate newsgroups, discussion lists, virtual communities and interest groups on the Net. Contrary to this common perception, Sassi (Chapter 6) claims that the publics may be fragmenting, while the issues are uniting. All kinds of combinations of issues and publics, local and global, become possible on the Net. The overlaps, the interconnections and the hyperlinks are conspicuous features of the Internet both internally and externally (links to other media).

In this restructuring of public spheres on the Net, many of its early adopters have seen an opportunity to remove the old mass media as 'distorting' mediators in processes of political communication and decision making. These media were rejected as being biased by vested commercial and political interests in close co-operation. Television in particular was increasingly accused of being a medium more reducing than supporting the political knowledge, motivation, activity and community building of citizens (e.g. Hart, 1994). Instead, the Internet would make redundant the intermediary role of journalists, politicians and even representatives. Henceforward they could be bypassed. Citizens would get the opportunity to search, select and interpret political information all by themselves and communicate opinions among each other, and by doing so create a new kind of politics. However, if there is any mistake among the early adopters of the Internet, it is this one. 'The Internet is no neutral zone of citizen activity or a realm of freedom' was Sassi's reply in Chapter 6. In a short period of time, this network of networks has been transformed from a primarily public medium with open discussion into a medium of e-commerce and entertainment. Internet sites are rated and filtered, attempts at censorship are made and increasingly information is offered in pay-per-view formats. Of course, opportunities of public and free communication or information supply remain and even grow. However, the relative part of it in total Internet communication is shrinking. In a growing number of ways, the Internet is becoming a 'normal' mass medium.

The idea that intermediaries have become superfluous in using the Internet is a grave error. It has only benefited those who have come to meet the real needs of average users with professional commercial services, among them services of political information. Ironically, a medium that is touted for its radical disintermediation has spawned an entire industry of mediation companies to sort out and catalogue Internet content. The enormous information overload and the difficulty of using services on the Internet necessitate more, not less intermediaries as compared to traditional media. Web portals, search engines, electronic papers, magazines, information services, voter guides and broadcasting channels are already dominating the political information supply on the Net. They are developing their own kinds of political power which are not inferior to the power of traditional media in politics. Non-commercial intermediaries have a role to play as well. In Chapters 7, 8 and 9 of this book the importance of political information sites like the White House CMC system, voting guides like the Democracy Network and organized public debating lists for the democratic participation of the average citizen were explained.

Practice

The Claims and the Results of Digital Democracy
Now it is time to strike a preliminary balance sheet of 10 to 15 years of experiments with digital democracy after the first beginnings as described in, for instance, Arterton (1987) and Abrahamson et al. (1988). The claims made by the strong advocates of digital democracy as listed in Bryan et al. (1998) among others can be summarized under three headings (cf. Tsagarousianou, 1999):

1 Digital democracy improves political information retrieval and exchange between governments, public administrations, representatives, political and community organizations and individual citizens.
2 Digital democracy supports public debate, deliberation and community formation.
3 Digital democracy enhances participation in political decision making by citizens.

Now, with all the caution required for such a short period of time, it can be defensibly argued that digital democracy has contributed in reaching the first claim. The second claim appears to be only partially justified. However, the third and strongest claim cannot be maintained at this moment. We will explain these conclusions as we summarize some of the most important results of this book.

The greatest achievement of digital democracy at the time of writing is the offer of better opportunities for information retrieval and exchange. An enormous stock of politically relevant information is available to citizens having access to the new media. When they have the skills required they can freely select from this body of knowledge themselves, instead of being dependent on traditional preprogrammed mass media supply. Of course, journalists and all kinds of information brokers have benefited most from these opportunities. However, sufficiently educated and experienced net users are also able to do this with the aid of some tools. Hacker's study of the White House CMC system shows that this system has produced more and easier citizen access to government documents, greater connectivity between government agencies and citizens and, in return, more channels for citizen input by sending questions, complaints, opinions and electronic petitions. Elberse, Hall and Dutton (Chapter 8) have studied the Democracy Network in California and found that it is an innovative electronic voter guide designed to better inform voters about the full range of issues and candidates. In this way the

DNet contributed to a broader and more in-depth discussion of the issues than available over the mass media. Moreover, candidates outside the mainstream, with limited means to reach the public in expensive mass media campaigns, were equally included in the guide and the issues of debate it contained.

While these are only case study examples, the general impression among observers of digital democracy is that more and better information access and exchange are among its most important accomplishments. However, the interpretation of its value for democracy is quite another affair. Accessible, reliable and valid information is a necessary condition of democracy. But is it a sufficient condition for democratization? We think it is not. There are numerous steps between retrieving information and having any impact on decision making. First, information has to be selected and processed from an abundance of sources of data. The result of these mental steps is unpredictable and it strongly depends on individual skills and preferences. Then there is the question of what one actually does with information. Is it transformed into political action? Finally, the effects of potential action on actual decision making in a democracy crucially depend on relationships of power in the political system and in the media. Even when the stage of decision making is reached, it does not follow that more information enhances democracy. According to John Street (1997: 31) 'decisions are not necessarily improved by the simple expedient of acquiring more data. All decisions are ultimately matters of judgement, and the art of judgement may, in fact be hampered by an excess of information (Vickers, 1965; Dennett, 1986).' Psychologists know that people reach decisions with few factors and pieces of factual information simultaneously processed in their mind and also relying on needs, emotions, norms and values.

Perhaps more and better collective debate about information, the second main claim attached to digital democracy, offers better chances of being transformed into action and effects on decision making. This claim is based upon the capacities of interaction in (the use of) digital technology. However, interactivity is one of the vaguest and most misused concepts in political science and communication science. In this book, several authors have tried to dissect and operationalize this concept.

Hacker attempts to work out the concept in general kinds and levels of interactivity and a particular model of political interactivity between citizens and government (Chapter 7). First, there is the elementary level of simple feedback launching a two-way process. Then there is interactivity in a more narrow sense: a chain of action and reactions implying message interdependence (Rafaeli, 1988). Finally we have reciprocity as an exchange and mutual understanding of interacting partners and the relevant social contexts. Van Dijk (Chapter 3) has tried to summarize these concepts in four levels of interactivity as a broad or general concept close to Williams et al. (1988) and Hanssen et al. (1996).

Hacker's model of political interactivity (Figure 7.1) is intended to be a concrete, empirically verifiable elaboration of five stages in the exchange of information between citizens and government. Citizens send questions, complaints, opinions or pieces of information to governments (phase 1) and governments reply, most often automatically or by staff. This means feedback mechanisms on information sites and more or less standard responses to an e-mail message (phase 2). Citizens will evaluate this feedback and they might respond on their turn (phase 3). However, frequently the process of interaction already stops here: government feedback is either satisfactory or disappointing. When the citizen does respond and urges the government to take action (phase 4) the government will either do this or explain to the citizen why no action is taken (phase 5). The experience of the White House CMC system, at least, shows that the last phases are not reached very often. With regard to the first two phases, it must be recalled that a number of buffers are inserted between citizens and governments. Of course, the responsible politicians rarely respond personally: a staff is engaged with partly or wholly standardized responses. In practice, this response sometimes transforms into information campaigning by the government and messages received are used for opinion research.

So, the use of these direct channels between governments and citizens might mean that government becomes easier and faster to approach. But does it also mean that citizens acquire real access, in the sense of getting through and having an impact? The use of the WHCMC system is a case of vertical communication between levels in the political system (see Figure 12.1 below). However, Jankowski and van Selm (Chapter 9) have shown that horizontal communication of equals (in principle) in Internet debates is also lacking in interactivity (also see Rojo and Ragsdale, 1997). In the debates analysed by them there were no extensive exchanges between contributors. Most people appeared to simply read the contributions of others and not contribute themselves. When they did, the favourite people addressed were political representatives. Frequently, the debate is dominated by a few persons. Finally there is not much pressure to come to a conclusion, let alone reach consensus in electronic debates as compared to face-to-face discussions. They are only weak attempts to resolve a collectively perceived problem.

However, this does not mean that all claims of electronic debates are untenable. Following Schneider's criteria (described in Chapter 9) the quality and equality of these debates pose serious problems. However, the diversity and the (limited) reciprocity of contributors of electronic debates are promising. Otherwise, one would not be able to explain their enormous popularity as there are tens of thousands of discussion lists and newsgroups on the Internet. Approximately 20 per cent of Internet users discussed political issues online in 1997 (GVU Center, 1998, see Figure 3.3). The exchange of opinions must have influence on the consciousness of the participants and hence on their online and offline political activities. Undoubtedly, electronic debates will cover large parts of all future public spheres and community building.

The big problem, however, is that there is no perceivable effect on decision making of institutional politics at this moment. Here we touch on the third claim of digital democracy: assumed impact on decision making. Horizontal communication on the Internet circulates in one or more public spheres contributing to civil society. This is their achievement. However, neither private nor (semi)-official Internet debates (like the Dutch 'Besliswijzer' described in Chapter 9) seem to have any impact on political decision making at the time of writing. The Internet as a medium still has to connect to traditional mass media to reach a

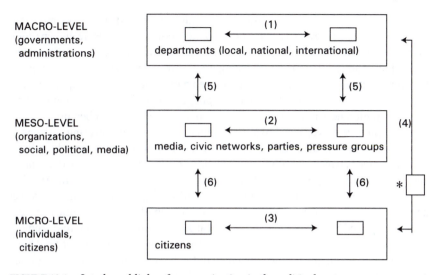

FIGURE 12.1 *Levels and links of communication in the political system*
*Hacker's model of political interactivity, Chapter 7

larger audience and to have influence according to Sassi (Chapter 6). The only exceptions are news and rumours about disasters, wars and political scandals in the US as they are first distributed on the Internet.

The observation that large-scale Internet activity is able to flourish without any impact on governments and public administrations is easy to explain when we look at the model of levels and links of communication in Figure 12.1. Keane and Sassi have shown that the Internet has the capacity to connect, and disconnect (!) macro-, meso- and micro-levels of communication in several kinds of public spheres. At the macro-level the departments of the government, the public administration and international bodies exchange enormous amounts of data and information internally and between each other (arrow 1). Almost all ICT investment of these institutions is allocated for these purposes. The meso- and micro-levels of horizontal communications between and within media and other organizations or between individuals on the Internet are completely separate communication domains to start with. Here we find the activities of civic networks, newsgroups and discussion lists or intranets of organizations (arrow 2). At the bottom of the model there is the interpersonal exchange of political information by individuals. The GVU data presented in Chapter 3 indicate that this was done by 15 per cent of Internet users in 1997.

Presently, the horizontal communication on the three levels mentioned is much more effective than the vertical communication between them. The link between individual citizens and governments (arrow 4) is still a problematic one. It is buffered and it lacks higher levels and phases of interactivity according to Hacker's model of interactivity summarized earlier. The link between the media or other organizations, public and private, and governments or public administrations, is extremely important in this age of media politics, pressure groups and electoral funding (arrow 5). However, it is still completely dominated by the old mass media. The impact of the Internet is marginal, except on some occasions (see earlier). The link between individual citizens and media or other public and private organizations (arrow 6) is very important as well from a political point of view. Here citizens communicate with Web sites predominately. This is the area of electoral campaigning, telepolling, public relations and e-commerce. In these exchanges a citizen easily transforms into a consumer. In this case citizen participation takes the appearance of consumer choice on information and shopping channels. The registration of questions and preferences replaces civic education, discussion and deliberation.

The difficulty of vertical links of communication in empowering citizens is clearly related to the difficulties of direct democracy. This is also based on direct vertical links between governments, citizens and intermediaries (media, voting and polling agencies). Lawrence Grossman and others argue that the Internet has brought a new age of direct democracy. Unfortunately, the claims of direct democracy, digital or otherwise, oversimplify the complexity of a political system such as depicted in Figures 3.1 and 12.1. Citizens can now have more document access than ever before. But we have seen that this does not mean that they have any more impact on governance than they did in the days of the telegraph. Voters have easier access to campaigns if they use Web sites. Still, this does not mean that they can communicate with candidates, nor does it mean they can influence the candidates more than they did with telephone or letter.

Evidently the future of digital democracy will be much more complex. Presumably it will be some combination of direct and representative modes of democracy, combinations varying across political systems and cultures, as they are today (Chapter 4).

Conditions of Digital Democracy

One of the reasons why we have not called this book virtual democracy is the popular assumption that so-called virtual politics (see earlier) are able to replace what we have called organic politics. Instead we think that virtual politics will add to organic politics. Digital networks and other new media keep resting on the material environment of social, physical, biological and mental conditions. So-called cyberspace is no freely floating communication space. (Internet guru John Perry Barlow once ridiculed himself in the eyes of a part of the audience in a debate with William Buckley responding 'I come to you from Cyberspace', as if he was from another planet.) Instead, the Internet is designed in a particular way by specific interests, it is used by people of flesh and blood for particular purposes, and it can not exist without definite resources in technology, economy, society and individual human minds and bodies (Mantovani, 1996; van Dijk, 1991/1997, 1999).

All this goes for politics as well. The future relies on the interaction of virtual and organic politics. Hopefully, digital technology will shape conditions for a fruitful interplay between virtual and organic, online and offline political activities. Best chances for such an interplay are at the local community and organizational level. Here it is easy to combine all kinds of online and offline activities. Unfortunately, local civic networking, digital cities and other local media have not acquired much attention in the section practice of this book. For these media we can refer to the book *Cyberdemocracy, Technology, Cities and Civic Networks* by Tsagarousianou et al., 1998.

At a lower level of abstraction one can pay attention to the concrete economic, social and educational conditions of access to the new media. In Chapter 10 van Dijk explicated the multi-faced concept of access. A number of mental, material, social and cultural hurdles have to be crossed to fully benefit from the opportunities of digital democracy. Otherwise participation in digital democracy will not be bigger, but smaller as compared to existing organic democracy. Earlier in this chapter, it was stressed that digital democracy has improved the conditions of information retrieval and exchange. However, this goes for people with sufficient digital skills. For people lacking these skills conditions get worse. Even in developed Western countries this threatens to be the case for at least one third of the population.

Most political activities on the Internet require relatively high levels of intellectual or technical skill and much motivation and effort. However, the ability, training, energy, motivation and desire to engage in these activities are very unequally divided among populations. Van Dijk warns that these unequal divisions might lead to a usage gap. This means that some will in fact be excluded from political participation by means of digital technology while others will participate differently to an increasing degree. Among the last ones some will adopt the relatively simple usage opportunities of telepolling and televoting or signing electronic petitions, while others will benefit from the advanced great opportunities of the Internet: information retrieval, electronic debates and decision support systems.

Fortunately, this division is no matter of natural necessity. Social, economic, cultural and educational policies of governments, public organizations and corporations are able to prevent, or at least mitigate the rise of such information inequality (see Chapter 10). Other important conditions are the infrastructures, the components and the regulations of the information superhighway under construction. In the course of the 1970s and 1980s a historic decision was reached by Western governments. Following the increasingly dominant policies of liberalization and privatization the construction of the information superhighway was left to business enterprise. This decision will have a lasting impact on the nature, the opportunities and the actual use of this highway in the twenty-first century. Among these characteristics are the conditions of digital democracy. Governments will only be able to marginally correct undesirable consequences and promote socially relevant uses of the new infrastructure. Still, government policies do matter and they will have an impact on the conditions of digital democracy. As Catinat and Vedel explained in Chapter 11, government policies in the US and the EU try to stimulate and to correct the design of the information superhighway in respects which are all related to conditions of digital democracy. Universal and public access to digital technology is regulated and partly put into practice by American and European governments. Information and communication freedom on the Internet is under national jurisdictions, although international escape options are widely available. The relationship between intellectual property rights and fair use rights of individual citizens is established by new copyright acts. Privacy and personal autonomy in digital communication, political and other, are partly safeguarded by privacy regulation. Finally, the most important present job of governments is to fund R and D activities and to care for public education. Education is the crucial factor for equal access of citizens to digital technology as was amply explained in this book. Catinat and Vedel did not only distinguish similarities but also differences between American and European government on the issues mentioned and others. This means that there still is room for government policies.

Issues of Further Research

In the past few years, digital democracy research has been dominated by ideological discourse. Strong advocates of digital democracy, teledemocracy, cyberdemocracy and the like hailed the blessings of the new technology and welcomed it as a technology of freedom. On the other side traditionalists, sceptics and technophobes have emphasized the risks and the losses of relying on (digital) technology in politics and communication. Some of them feared a political system of total registration, surveillance and control. Now it is time to get over this stage of global oppositions and enter a phase of empirical research and conceptual elaboration. Evidently, digital technology engenders both good and bad potential consequences. The authors in this book want to adopt balanced positions and statements. They are neither strong advocates nor strong opponents of digital democracy. They have attempted to be both critical and realistic. In the current phase of discussion this often means debunking illusions and untenable assumptions.

The first thing the authors have attempted is conceptual clarification. This has to be continued. Concepts like interactivity, public sphere, debate and deliberation, virtual politics and virtual community, universal and public access, information and communication freedom, all of them crucial to digital democracy, have to be clarified and operationalized to make them suitable for empirical research. Of course, theoretical discourse is indispensable too in this age of difficult to grasp structural transformations. However, eventually speculations have to be supplanted by testable statements. The concrete applications of digital democracy will be spotlighted in the years to come. This requires reliable and valid evaluation research. However, evaluation research of digital democracy has been frustrated by a lack of explicit goals and detailed means to accomplish them among designers and adopters of particular applications. Therefore, the substantial views on democracy behind the applications of digital democracy were stressed in this book. Potential actors have to be explicit in the results and performances expected. Then scientific evaluation research becomes possible and has a chance of replacing the current practices of trial and error which lack sufficiently explicit learning practices.

The next issue of further research is the testing of basic assumptions. Such an assumption is the central idea behind the *Cyberdemocracy* book (Tsagarousianou et al., 1998). Their premise is that the existing infrastructure for the support and encouragement of public debate and political action has been eroded and undermined (1998: 5). Their assumption is 'that by altering the form of communication the content can be changed and more participation encouraged' (1998: 5). We have doubts about this. Are the new forms of communication offered by digital democracy, like so-called interactivity and virtual debate, really leading to substantial changes in political communication? Are they encouraging more participation? We have seen how crucial the problems of access to and actual usage of the new technologies are in political participation. Therefore, the elaboration, operationalization and empirical investigation of concepts of communication, levels of interactivity and quality of public debates will become crucial issues on the research agenda.

Other issues include the consequences of the structural transformation of the modern public sphere. When we get a complex mosaic of different public spheres, both connected and disconnected, the question becomes how the media, old and new, are able to link these spheres in the new fabric of societies. We will get all kinds of media mixing relationships in political communication and public debate. For instance, the concrete links between the Internet, broadcasting and the press will be crucial for any future political communication.

Related issues have to deal with the relationship between virtual and organic politics or communication. We made a plea for fruitful interplays between them. But which links between online and offline political activities are fruitful, and for what purposes? How can a combination of face-to-face and Internet political meetings, pressure groups, petitions, debates and information exchanges be organized? What are the problems of scale and proximity (local, (inter)national)? An association of virtual and organic activities should benefit from the detailed comparative research of electronic and non-electronic channels of (organizational) communication conducted by social psychologists and communication scientists in the last three decades.

The concrete applications of digital democracy must be prepared for evaluation research concerning their most detailed characteristics. How can political Web sites be improved to satisfy users? What kind of moderation is suitable for electronic debates in particular situations? How can televotes and telepolls be made more representative in this age of non-response? How can group and individual decision support systems be designed to result in appropriate decisions for anyone engaged? To mention just a few questions.

Dealing with these questions we have to make distinctions between the different types and levels of digital democracy. Large-scale national systems such as the White House CMC system will differ from local systems such as the Santa Monica Public Information Network (PEN) system. Secondly, successes and failures should be recognized at the levels at which they occur. Ed Schwartz (1996), an Internet political activist, correctly argues that an inherent characteristic of politics is collective action and that political conversations can be used to create new forms of political organization. Yet, Schwartz acknowledges that CMC is not a total substitute for face-to-face political organizing. Schwartz (1996) sees profound changes in government and democracy taking place because of digital communication. He lists a number of indications for his vision: Chinese students using e-mail to protest the Tiananmen Square massacre, the Santa Monica PEN system accomplishing the acquisition of showers and lockers for homeless people, successful Christian Coalition efforts against the National Endowment for the Humanities, EnviroLink providing environmentalist information to over a million users per month, increased public exposure gained by the Children's Defense Fund and other examples. He argues that this involves gaining power and that people at more local levels can also gain political power by using CMC to organize within their communities in order to influence their representatives. Schwartz never proves any revolution in American politics due to CMC; he simply argues that CMC adds more means for activists to gain attention, to organize themselves and to force leaders to respond more to grassroots demands. We must recognize that empowerment results from activism, not from the technical characteristics of the new channels.

To argue that the technical sides of the Internet do not determine their effects does not mean that the technical aspects of technologies must be neglected. For example, as computer scientist Jacques Vallee noted long ago, computer scientists have the power to obfuscate what goes on in software programming. Those who maintain control over the directions of software, browsers, search engines, protocols, etc. do have an interesting, yet nearly unnoticed, handle on power. A report by NUA Surveys (22 March 1999) indicates that there is a problem with the perpetual claim that individuals are empowered by being able to design and post Web pages enabling them to be their own reporter, publisher, pundit, etc. The NUA report notes that information such as Web pages, have little value and effect if not found and not read. In other words, for any significant topic, a search engine is likely to find millions of documents. Those listed first will have met the criteria of advertising, offering other site hyperlinks and practising search engine promotions techniques. The report concludes, 'It may be that as the Internet grows, it relinquishes the publishing process to the political agenda of the very agents employed to make structure from chaos, the search engines' (NUA Internet Surveys, 1999).

Digital democracy research must become more finely tuned into layers of effects, some of which are good, some of which are bad, and some of which are simply unknown, simultaneously. We believe that digital democracy research must be both empirical and theoretical to determine exactly who is benefiting how, when, and why from the new technical options. We need more research such as that reported in *Cyberpolitics* by Hill and Hughes (1998) wherein they report numerous statistical tests done on user data gathered by the Pew Research Center along with their own content analyses of newsgroups. These researchers correlate these data with measures of democracy in various nations. Furthermore, they make theoretical analyses and formulate propositions that can be tested as hypotheses.

In this book the contexts and conditions of digital democracy were emphasized. So, finally, further research for necessary and sufficient conditions of digital democracy and fertile or sterile contexts is required. Which policies of universal and public access, public information supply and civic education are realistic options in our differentiating and increasingly divided societies?

References

Abrahamson, J.B., Arterton, F. and Orren, G. (1988) *The Electronic Commonwealth. The Impact of New Technologies upon Democratic Politics*. New York: Basic Books.

Arterton, C.F. (1987) *Teledemocracy, Can Technology Protect Democracy?*, Newbury Park/Beverly Hills/London/New Delhi: Sage.

Bryan, C., Tsagarousianou, R. and Tambini, D. (1998) 'Electronic democracy and the civic networking movement in context', in R. Tsagarousianou, D. Tambini and C. Bryan, *Cyberdemocracy, Technology, Cities and Civic Networks*. London/New York: Routledge.

Dennett, D. (1986) 'Information, technology, and the virtues of ignorance', *Deadalus*, 115(3): 135–53.

GVU Centre, Georgia University (1998) GVU's 7th WWW user survey. Georgia University, http://www.gvu.gatech.ed/user_surveys/

Hanssen, L., Jankowski, N. and Etienne, R. (1996) 'Interactivity from the perspective of communication studies', in N. Jankowski and L. Hanssen (eds), *Contours of Multimedia*. Luton: University of Luton Press, John Libbey Media.

Hart, R.P. (1994) *Seducing America: How Television Charms the Modern Voter*. New York/Oxford: Oxford University Press.

Hill, K.A. and Hughes, J.E. (1998) *Cyberpolitics: Citizen Activism in the Age of the Internet*. New York: Rowman & Littlefield Publishers.

Mantovani, G. (1996) *New Communication Environments: From Everyday to Virtual*. London/Bristol, PA: Taylor & Francis.

NUA Internet Surveys (1999) 4(11), 22 March. NUA Limited.

Rafaeli, S. (1988) 'Interactivity: from new media to communication', in R.P. Hawkins, J. Wiemann and S. Pingree (eds) *Advancing Communication Science*. Newbury Park, CA: Sage.

Rojo, A. and Ragsdale, R. (1997) 'Participation in electronic forums', *Telematics and Informatics*, 13(1): 83–96.

Schwartz, E. (1996) *Net Activism: How Citizens Use the Internet*. Sebastapol, CA: Songline.

Street, J. (1997) 'Remote control? Politics, technology and "electronic democracy"', *European Journal of Communication*, 12: 27–42.

Tsagarousianou, R. (1999) 'Electronic democracy: rhetoric and reality', *Communications; The European Journal of Communication Research*, 24(2): 189–208.

Tsagarousianou, R., Tambini, D. and Bryan, C. (1998) *Cyberdemocracy, Technology, Cities and Civic Networks*. London/New York: Routledge.

van Dijk, J. (1991/1994/1997) *De Netwerkmaatschappij, Sociale aspecten van nieuwe media*. Houten/Zaventem: Bohn Stafleu van Loghum.

van Dijk, J. (1999) *The Network Society, Social Aspects of New Media*. London/Thousand Oaks/New Delhi: Sage.

Vickers, G. (1965) *The Art of Judgement*. London: Chapman and Hall.

Williams, F., Rice, R.E. and Rogers, E. (1988) *Research Methods and the New Media*. New York: Free Press.

Winston, B. (1998) *Media, Technology and Society, A History: From the Telegraph to the Internet*. London/New York: Routledge.

Index